THE MILITARY IN GREEK POLITICS
The 1909 Coup d'État

THE MILITARY IN GREEK POLITICS
THE 1909 COUP D'ÉTAT

S. VICTOR PAPACOSMA

The Kent State University Press

Library of Congress Cataloging in Publication Data
Papacosma, S   Victor, 1942-
  The military in Greek politics.

  Bibliography: p.
  Includes index.
  1. Greece, Modern—History—George I, 1863-1913.
I. Title.
DF831.P36   949.5'07   77-22391
ISBN 0-87338-208-0

Στή μνήμη τῆσ Μητέρασ μου

ERRATUM

The Dedication on page v should read:

Στή μνήμη τῆς Μητέρας μου

Contents

PREFACE

The complexities of Greece's ancient and Byzantine periods have been studied seriously and carefully for centuries, but only a few scholars have ventured to analyze Greece's strife-ridden politics during this century. The reasons for the dearth of scholarship are many, and include a traditional deemphasis of social and recent political history in the Greek educational system at all levels and an accompanying wariness of treating—for political reasons—sensitive issues in a detached, objective manner. The foreign researcher who comes to Greece, in turn, confronts multifarious difficulties in tracking down appropriate primary source material, much of which has been lost, destroyed or closed to investigation. Consequently, the study of Greece's intricate internal politics has suffered.

The 1909 military revolt is one topic to which Greeks allude almost uniformly in favorable terms. Conservatives stress that the Military League's intervention in politics prepared Greece for her Balkan War victories in 1912-13, while liberals emphasize important social and economic consequences that followed the coming of Eleftherios Venizelos and his party into prominence. To underscore the positive connotations of the army's action, this interlude is generally referred to as a "revolution." Thus, the 1909 revolt joins the victories in the Balkan Wars and against the Italians in 1940-41 in receiving the unqualified reverence of most Greeks. And because of the many fratricidal conflicts plaguing Greek society since World War I, these few moments of glory attract undue attention—with the achievements at times assuming legendary proportions. Greek journalistic and popularized accounts, which embellish these events, abound. It becomes the task of the historian to distinguish between the myth and the reality of the Greek experience—similar to the challenge confronting scholars of other nations whose peoples have witnessed repeated tragedies and national frustrations.

A basic purpose of this study is to counter imprecise generalizations with a detailed representation of events and issues during these crucial pre-World War I years. Since the 1909 sedition proved to be the first in a series of military revolts this century, this intervention into politics must be distinguished from the others and placed in an appropriate historical perspective. To accomplish these objectives it was necessary to go beyond available Greek sources. Investigation of relevant materials in the diplomatic archives of Great Britain, Germany and Austria produced valuable information not only on the problems of the Greek Royal Family and foreign policy, but also on some of the more confusing aspects of the Greek economy and politics.

The first stage of research for this book was conducted in Greece on a Fulbright-Hays Graduate Fellowship, and its results appeared in an Indiana University doctoral dissertation. Subsequently, a Kent State University Summer Research Appointment and a six-month grant from the American Council of Learned Societies permitted further investigations in Greece and England. Dean Alan Coogan and the Research Office of Kent State University provided other much-needed financial support for the completion of this book.

Limited space permits me to express my gratitude to only a small number of individuals who assisted me in the preparation of this book. Dr. Domna Dontas, Director of the Historical Archives in the Greek foreign ministry, served as a valuable source of professional help and friendship during my work in Greece. Dr. Eleftherios Prevelakis of the Academy of Athens, Eugenia Chazidaki of the Benaki Museum and the late Basil Laourdas of the Institute for Balkan Studies also generously gave their help. Dr. Francis Walton, Director of the Gennadius Library in Athens, and his efficient staff consistently extended their services. Philippos Dragoumis graciously allowed me to inspect some of his father's private papers, which are housed in the Gennadius Library.

Still other individuals have to be thanked for assistance which is not, in all cases, entirely professional. Professor Ernst

Helmreich of Bowdoin College urged me in my undergraduate years to pursue my budding interest in Greece and the Balkans. Professors Charles and Barbara Jelavich of Indiana University guided, aided, supported and encouraged me during all phases of my graduate school career—I am extremely grateful to them. Professor John Petropulos of Amherst College read earlier versions of this manuscript and offered important criticisms. Professor J. Garry Clifford of the University of Connecticut, a historian of America by training and a friend of Greece by feeling, supplied valuable stylistic suggestions; he is the rare person ready to extend help automatically on request. John Kampouris, my late uncle, provided companionship and hours of enlightening conversation about Greece during my first two visits to Athens. Staff and colleagues at Kent State University who aided me are Barbara Hostetler and Professors Maury Baker, Coburn Graves, John T. Hubbell, Lawrence Kaplan, and Henry Whitney. Michael DiBattista of The Kent State University Press regularly provided professional guidance, even before the manuscript reached him.

It is to my parents, though, that I owe my greatest debt of gratitude. My father early introduced me to the fascinating world of Greece, the Balkans and the Ottoman Empire as he recounted the trials and tribulations of his eventful youth. But it was my mother who consistently provided irreplaceable love, inspiration and selfless concern for my welfare, education and professional advancement—even during her last illness. The intensity and breadth of her love and giving nature can never be forgotten. This book is in memory of her.

S. V. P.
Kent, Ohio
March 1977

1830-1897
INTRODUCTION

Few countries in twentieth-century Europe can match the political tumult and frequent institutional changes of Greece. For example, kings have been forced to abandon their thrones or leave Greece on four occasions (1917, 1922, 1923, 1967) and republics have been established twice (1924 to 1935 and since 1973). One constitution, that of 1864, was revised in 1911 and 1951, while three other national charters were promulgated in 1927, 1968 (revised in 1973) and 1975. In all these instances the armed forces contributed directly or indirectly to the outcome of events. The activist military has, in fact, revolted nine times since 1909 and exerted its political influence in numerous other ways. The foundations of this political function, however, appeared in the preceding century and initially as an outgrowth of unresolved conflicts stemming from the War of Independence.

The Greeks rebelled against their Turkish overlords of nearly four centuries during the early spring of 1821. Capturing the sympathy of European public opinion, this struggle nonetheless threatened the carefully written settlements of the Congress of Vienna, which aimed at curbing revolutionary uprisings. Eventually the pressures of the Philhellenic movement and mutual suspicions among the English, French and Russian governments, not necessarily a sincere desire for Greek independence, drew the three great powers into this Balkan war which had failed to burn itself out. To avoid strife among themselves, the powers drafted compromises approximating as closely as possible the previous status quo. By the time the fighting against the Turks ended in 1829, the three powers, although battlefield allies of the Greeks, ignored the

1

appeals of their leaders for a new nation with expanded frontiers. Under the terms of the London Protocol (3 February 1830) independent Greece emerged with restricted borders and fell under the strict tutelage of Great Britain, France and Russia, the guaranteeing powers.

On 6 February 1833, Othon, the seventeen-year old son of Bavaria's King Ludwig and the choice of the powers, disembarked from an English frigate at Nauplion as king of Greece. Although popular assemblies during the War of Independence indicated a definite preference for representative government with a democratic constitution, the Greeks could not unite because of disputes among various regions, social groups and leaders. In the Ottoman system the Greeks had been granted extensive privileges in governing themselves at the local level, but inherent sectionalism and jealousies prevented them from transferring this experience to the national level. The young Othon and his advisers, therefore, justified an absolutist regime on the grounds that the Greeks required strong centralized rule.

The subsequent political concerns of the Greek state focused on the *Megale Idea* ("Great Idea"). The new country's population of barely 800,000 comprised only about one-fourth the total number of Greeks residing in the Eastern Mediterranean under the rule of the Turks or on the British-controlled Ionian Islands. Ultimately, this *Megale Idea* sought to liberate these Greeks from foreign domination and to incorporate them into a nation-state with Constantinople, the former imperial Byzantine city, as the capital. This expansionist policy dominated the conduct of national politics well into the next century, arousing the opposition of the great powers and Greece's neighbors. The preoccupation with irredentist ventures also came at the expense of social and economic reforms.

Othon had thus accepted the throne of a nation with inherited problems, great aspirations, and a troubled future.[1] His regime faltered from the start by failing to maintain the support of important elements of the population. The king pursued a policy of personal government with a highly centralized and inflexible administration that had Bavarians occupying many high bureaucratic posts and monopolizing key positions in the army. Several thousand German volunteers arrived in Greece by 1835, while only a handful of Greeks joined the regular army. Inevitable friction arose between the disbanded revolutionary armies not on the national payroll and the well-paid Bavarian administrators and mercenaries.

The persistence of Bavarian absolutism intensified the desire for power and political change in various Greek circles. Financially, the nation floundered in large debts incurred during the struggle for independence, the peasants suffered from heavy taxation, and brigandage abounded in the country-side. In 1833 the government decreed the establishment of a national Orthodox Church independent of the Patriarchate of Constantinople, a separation which, with Othon's Roman Catholicism, troubled many Greeks.

During and after the Revolution Greek political groups tended to associate their policies with the individual guarantee-ing powers—hence, parties were identified as "English," "French," and "Russian." In this period of disenchantment with Othon's rule, leaders of the "Russian" and "English" parties joined in a scheme to overthrow the king's autocracy. The English and their protégé party sought specific limitations on the monarch's powers and the formation of constitutional government. Although Othon could attract little support for his policies within Greece, his opponents proved unable to generate a mass uprising against him.[2]

At this juncture the military played a decisive role. In 1838 the last German troops departed from Greece, but Othon retained the services of a small group of Bavarian officers. The latter's high ranks, good salaries, and commanding positions antagonized Greeks within the armed forces, who thus shared grievances with the politicians against Othon's rule. Colonel Demetrios Kallerges, the Cretan commander of the infantry, conspired with Colonel John Makrygiannis, a hero of the 1821 Revolution, to demonstrate opposition to the existing system.[3]

News of several plots reached the court, but Othon failed to take appropriate countermeasures. To allay the suspicion of the king's forces on the evening of 14 September 1843, Kallerges attended a performance of *Lucretia Borgia*. Shortly after midnight he made his way through the deserted streets of Athens to the infantry barracks which he commanded. Upon entering he murmured several unintelligible sentences but then roared: "Long live the constitution!" Aroused from their slumbering state, the troops responded enthusiastically to this

3

cry. With military music, some musket shots, and much shouting, the soldiers marched, accompanied at this point by some civilians, to the new palace which Othon had moved into only several months earlier. Hearing this commotion, the king appeared at the window, whereupon Kallerges confronted him with the demand for a constitution. After initial hesitation and extensive consultation with his advisers, Othon acknowledged that he had no backing for his position and agreed to the convening of a National Assembly of 225 members to draft a constitution. In addition he promised to dismiss all foreigners except the old Philhellenes from his service. By mid-afternoon the troops returned from the palace to their quarters with cries of "Long live the constitutional King Othon!"—a title the beleaguered ruler reluctantly assumed.[4]

The National Assembly conducted its opening session on 30 November 1843. For the first time in over a decade representatives of the Greek people were in a position to determine the governmental system of their young nation. Still, the Bavarian ruler insured a continued strong voice for himself in future policy making. In the Royal decree convoking the National Assembly he stipulated that the assembly would collaborate with him in the drafting of the constitution. The final document, promulgated on 30 March 1844, was the product of negotiations between monarch and deputies rather than of deliberations exclusively among representatives of the Greek people. The 1844 Constitution called for a "limited monarchy" and assured the maintenance of considerable royal prerogatives. A bicameral legislature consisted of a lower house elected on a wide franchise and a Senate with members nominated by the Crown. Othon, however, shared the legislative power with Parliament while also retaining the right to veto measures he disapproved. Ministers exercised executive powers, but Othon held the important prerogative of appointing or dismissing them without Parliament's approval.

Historians and popular writers of history in Greece have labeled the events of 15 September 1843 a "revolution." There was, it is true, general disenchantment with Othon's absolutist rule, but an organized nationwide revolutionary movement did not exist. Disaffected politicians, representing the ruling elites of the War of Independence, comprised the politically articulate opposition, and by itself this oligarchy could have accomplished little. It therefore sought and attracted the aid of high-

4

ranking military officers in Athens. The vulnerable position of Othon permitted several hundred soldiers and their officers to push through the liberalizing principle of constitutional government in a virtually bloodless demonstration of force. A minute percentage of the population, ostensibly reflecting the interests of the large majority of Greeks, executed this revolt, the entire course of which took place in Athens; therefore, this sequence of events must be classified, at most, as a coup d'état. Within the framework of the 1844 Constitution, Othon retained the major part of his former authority. The most permanent legacy of this interlude in Greek history proved to be that of military intervention to introduce political change. The officers of 1843 withdrew into the political background, but they had established a precedent for future action.

Although the new constitutional structure bore many conscious similarities to that of France's July Monarchy, the Greeks placed their own stamp on the conduct of politics under this imported system. A political figure did not win and maintain position merely on the merits of his programs, and once in office the successful politician became the master of patronage. He organized an apparatus to insure continued power and depended upon a highly centralized hierarchy of prefects, subprefects, judges, tax collectors, mayors, and gendarmes. Bribes, violence and promises aided in the recruitment and disciplining of political dependents. Street riots were utilized to demonstrate opposition to an adversary's policies; brigandage coerced and intimidated whole villages in rural areas. The lure of government positions or favors kept large numbers of people relying on promises even though very few were actually carried out.[6] Some Western European observers might have criticized such conduct, but the Greeks generally accepted these methods as a way of life.

Othon's staunch espousal of Greece's *Megale Idea* during the Crimean War in the face of British and French opposition raised his popularity to its highest point. Yet after 1844, as before, there remained an underlying dissatisfaction with his rule. Othon studied closely the corrupt maneuvers of some of his politicians, but he proved a less successful tactician; and his authoritarian administration chafed at the democratic inclinations and ambitions of many of his subjects. With the outbreak of the Austro-Italian War of 1859 the limited backing for Othon's policies declined further. As expected, the Greeks championed the Italian struggle for independence, but their Bavarian-born ruler displayed his Germanic lineage and expressed openly his Austrophile sentiments.

The negative attitude of the powers compounded Othon's plight. The British wished to contain any forces that could disrupt the territorial status quo in the Eastern Mediterranean and therefore opposed his ambitious irredentist policies and autocratic tendencies. Moreover, the line of succession remained in doubt because Othon and his wife, Amalia, had no children. The constitution stipulated that any heir to the throne must be Orthodox or convert to Orthodoxy, a step Othon's Roman Catholic brothers did not wish to take. Russia naturally eyed with disfavor a Roman Catholic dynasty with no prospect of an Orthodox succession.[7]

A new generation of politicians, headed by Epaminondas Delegeorges, added an ideological base to anti-dynastic sentiments and general feelings of discontent. Sparked by the spirit of the 1848 French Revolution, these critics insisted that a popularly elected, truly democratic government, unhampered by royal interventionism, would create a political, economic and social climate commensurate with the visions of the Greek people. But the omission of any provision for amendment in the constitution shackled these reformists. Blocked by the nation's inflexible constitution and monarch, the advocates of political change resorted to extralegal measures.

In contrast to 1843 there were indications that a rebellious spirit ran deeper through Greek society. Military forces once again played a fundamental role in political events, with junior officers and noncommissioned officers assuming the initiative this time. The government discovered a plot in the army during May 1861 and transferred the conspirators to Nauplion which soon became the headquarters of the rebellious movement. On 18 September 1861, several students failed in an attempt to assassinate Queen Amalia while her husband traveled abroad. The garrison in Nauplion, the town which enthusiastically welcomed Othon to Greece twenty-nine years earlier, revolted on 13 February 1862, and demanded the convocation of a National Constituent Assembly. Simultaneously, smaller uprisings erupted in several sections of Greece, but without coordination these mutinous efforts made little headway against pro-royalist forces.[8]

6

Rebellious elements persevered nonetheless. During the following months Othon's measures to curb further outbreaks miscarried as the spirit of protest, momentarily frustrated by failure, gained strength. When the king sailed to Kalamata in mid-October 1862 in an effort to ingratiate himself with the people of the provinces, Theodore Grivas, one of the few still living heroes from the 1821 Revolution, led the Vonitsa garrison in revolt. Mesolongi, Patras and other centers followed. Informed of these uprisings in Kalamata, Othon ordered the royal yacht, *Amalia,* back to Piraeus. But before the anxious monarch could return, the Athenian garrison followed the example of provincial regiments and raised the standard of revolt on the evening of 22 October. Shortly afterward, Demetrios Voulgaris formed a provisional government, demanded the immediate abdication of Othon and summoned a National Assembly to draft a constitution and to select a new monarch. With no prospect of assistance internally or from the powers, the tall, thin monarch sadly transferred his possessions from the yacht to the British frigate *Scylla.* Some local citizens, exulting in their triumph, boarded small craft in the Piraeus harbor, sailed alongside the *Scylla,* and jeered the ill-fated ruler. The heartbroken Othon retreated to Bavaria where in 1867 he died in obscurity, still wearing the *foustanella,* the national dress of Greece, and professing his affection for the country.[9]

Allied in their opposition to the Wittelsbach ruler, Greek rebel leaders failed to cooperate upon victory. The politicians blamed Othon for the sad condition of the nation, but characteristically drifted into factionalism and anarchy. Each leader sought to place himself in an influential position on the arrival of a new king. Military unity broke down with individual detachments providing aid for the several rival groups. Eventually pressure from the powers and fatigue among the combatants after several months of intermittent civil war contributed to the restoration of order in the early summer of 1863.

Concurrently, the National Assembly had convened on 22 December 1862. By virtue of inherent jealousies among Greek leaders, its members knew quite well that a native ruler could not reign in the fashion of Alexander Cuza in Rumania or Michael Obrenovich in Serbia. After lengthy debate Greece's guaranteeing powers agreed on William Ferdinand Adolphus

George, second son of Prince Christian of Schleswig-Holstein (the future Christian IX of Denmark). As an inducement for the Greeks to accept this candidate, Great Britain offered to cede the Ionian Islands to Greece and stated that the king's heirs should belong to the Greek Orthodox Church. The eighteen-year-old member of the Glücksburg dynasty arrived in Greece on 30 October 1863 as "George I, King of the Hellenes."[10]

Although Greece suffered still another period of internal dissension and violence, the work of the nation's representatives indicated a serious attempt to establish conditions necessary for political stability. The Greeks approved the powers' choice of George in their National Assembly, and the constitution, instituted in 1864, reflected liberal doctrines of the period. Legislators tried to prevent any recurrence of the centralized absolutism they dreaded. Article 21 of the 1864 Constitution stated: "All powers are derived from the nation and exercised in the manner prescribed by the Constitution." Generally defined as a "crowned democracy," the new system vested the monarch with executive powers exercised by responsible ministers appointed by him. In a significant departure from customary practice for that era, the Greeks decided upon a unicameral legislature elected by universal male suffrage. The Chamber of Deputies (*Boule*), chosen for a four-year term, shared legislative power with the king.[11]

This affair, as that of 1843, should be classified as a coup d'état. Existing institutions had not responded to the demands for change, and for a second time elements of the military aligned with the political opposition to employ extralegal measures for the overthrow of the regime. Each coup liberalized the system which had preceded it. The drafters of the new constitution designed it to launch the nation on a course of progress and reform. The framework for the practice of politics had been transformed, but it remained to be seen if the spirit and values of the Greek people would shift enough to allow the new political machinery to operate in the desired fashion. If the new system could not cope with national problems satisfactorily, the armed forces had established a standard for enacting change through extraparliamentary procedures.

The years after 1864 revealed that politics, with few departures, continued to be conducted in the traditional style. The 1821 Revolution and Othonian period displayed some characteristics of the Greeks and their politicians which diverged little in succeeding decades: their high degree of individualism, their cooperation only in the face of a common enemy, and the extensive usage of *rousfeti,* or political favors, for advancement. The earlier linkage between Greek parties and the three guaranteeing powers disintegrated in the post-Crimean War period. Patron-client relationships persisted, however, as party members clustered around a leader (*archegos*) rather than a clearly defined political ideology. As a result, a party was classified by the name of the leader instead of the customary "conservative," "liberal," or "radical," the general practice in most areas of Europe.

The period of Ottoman domination had encouraged regionalism and decentralized authority by which Greek notables held prestigious positions among the local population. In the post-independence era this predominance of local notables and military chieftains was grafted onto a society still largely uneducated and with no appreciable middle class. With the exception of the *Megale Idea,* politics had few long-range goals and tended to stress private or regional interests. People voted for local magnates who promised them the most personal rewards upon victory. For the Greek, the candidate was not so much the exponent of specific political views as the man to appeal to for help in time of need. And many of these influential leaders, in order to solidify ties with families in their districts, became *koumbaroi,* or godfathers, for hundreds of children. This was a costly process, so the candidate sought in turn guarantees of personal reward from his party leader. Since party loyalty often hinged upon material gains rather than adherence to political concepts, defections by politicians from one party to another were commonplace. Party discipline required skillful manipulation of the Greek version of the spoils system. With each party's formation of a new government came a change of personnel in the civil service, sometimes all the way down to the level of the elementary school teacher and *Boule* attendant.[12]

Five parties vied for office during the 1864-1881 period, which witnessed nine elections and seventeen governments. Politicians like Demetrios Voulgaris and Epaminondas Delegeorges, both in the vanguard of the 1862 rebellion, found it difficult once in office to convert their democratic notions into

9

practice; and they indulged in patronage just as much as the politicians they criticized in earlier stages of their careers.[13]

Some semblance of a two-party system emerged after 1881. Charilaos Trikoupis and Theodore Delegiannis took over the reins of politics from the old leaders who all died within a relatively short period. A new era evolved with the administrations of Trikoupis, a former foreign minister and envoy to Great Britain. He was the son of Spyridon Trikoupis, the famous historian of the Greek Revolution. Although both Delegiannis and Trikoupis actively pursued the traditional game of patronage with vigor, the latter's politics revealed a heretofore unknown dedication to domestic reform and progress. Among all nineteenth-century Greek leaders, Trikoupis with his programs came the closest to being a "liberal" in the Western European connotation.[14]

As political rivals Trikoupis and Delegiannis offered two different approaches for the realization of the *Megale Idea.* Trikoupis stressed that Greece should strengthen her economy and armed forces before embarking upon a bold foreign policy. His program of economic expansion and administrative reorganization required heavy borrowing, and between 1879 and 1893 Athens contracted loans totalling 640 million gold francs. To Greece's disadvantage these funds were issued well below par with only seventy-five percent of the amount reaching Greek hands. Large sums spent abroad on armaments, for Greece's expanding indebtedness and for covering budgetary deficits, left relatively little for internal improvements. To augment state revenues, Trikoupis increased taxes on such popular items as tobacco and matches, much to the dismay of the population. In spite of a limited treasury and inherent mismanagement, the Trikoupis era provided Greece with the superficial trappings of a developing state. The ambitious prime minister from Mesolongi reorganized the police and the army and increased the strength of the navy. He instituted the framework for a neutral judiciary and raised requirements for civil-service positions. His extensive program of road, railroad, and harbor construction broke down the old barriers to transportation and communication within the nation, while his protective tariff policy encouraged the growth of infant industries.[15]

Yet Trikoupis's heavy taxes and his long-range objectives did not make him popular. Delegiannis, appealing more to the active chauvinist emotions of the Greeks, automatically challenged the immediate situation, often with little thought to possible consequences. Using the grievances of the population as his platform for victory, this consummate orator repealed, among other laws, Trikoupis's tax legislation and measures for electoral reform. Delegiannis's opportunistic politics also led to great difficulties in foreign policy. His mobilization of the army in 1886 during the Eastern Rumelia crisis and the resulting blockade of the Greek coast by the powers created a large budgetary deficit. Returning to office, Trikoupis found his economic programs curtailed. More seriously, the disastrous drop in the price of currants, Greece's main export, forced Trikoupis to announce in December 1893 that the nation was bankrupt. Compelled to lower interest payments on international loans, the prime minister met with the hostility of the powers, formerly his supporters. He retired from politics after an electoral loss in 1895 and died a disheartened man the following year. Although Trikoupis rightly recognized that impulse and desire were insufficient armament for military and diplomatic victories, large segments of the population responded enthusiastically to the jingoistic outbursts of Delegiannis, whose artful demagoguery attracted votes. Such short-sighted tactics in actuality retarded the advance of the *Megale Idea.*

For decades the great powers consistently had checked Greek attempts at unauthorized expansionism. Thus during the Crimean War, Britain and France blockaded Greece in order to prevent her from supporting the Russians against the Turks. British threats to blockade thwarted Greek attempts to extend her borders at Turkey's expense during the Russo-Turkish War of 1877-78. And more recently, there had been the aforementioned blockade of the country during the spring of 1886. Irredentist fervor persevered and in the 1890s the contest for Macedonia increasingly caught the attention of the Greeks who, along with the Bulgarians and Serbs, vied for power and influence in this polyglot area still controlled by Turkey. Popular pressure forced the government in Athens to support Greeks in this region with arms and money.

There was also Crete. In their inimitable manner the persistent Greeks of Crete had revolted once more during the 1875-78 Near Eastern crisis and again in 1889. When in February 1896 Moslem-Christian relations deteriorated to the point of war, the Delegiannis government hardly ignored the

11

cries of the people for *enosis,* or union, in Crete and Greece. Lack of unity among the powers and the exuberance of the Greeks drove the militarily unprepared nation into a foolhardy war with Turkey in the spring of 1897. With its army recently reorganized by the Germans, Constantinople found the Greeks a weak enemy. Within four weeks the Turks soundly defeated an ill-prepared Greek army without allies in Thessaly, and on 20 May 1897 an armistice was signed.

The Greeks, oddly enough, though totally defeated on the battlefield, did gain a mixed victory at the negotiating tables. On 4 December 1897 a treaty was concluded whereby Greece yielded small bits of territory on the Thessalian border to the Turks while also paying a heavy indemnity of 100 million francs to the victors. In the future the normally chaotic Greek economy was to be subjected to the review of a newly instituted International Finance Commission located in Athens. The powers, which had landed occupation forces on Crete in 1897, convinced the Turks to grant an autonomous regime to the island. Britain, France, Russia and Italy arranged to keep detachments on Crete to insure peace; Austria-Hungary and Germany withdrew their units, not wishing to alienate the sultan's government. In 1898 it was agreed to name Prince George, second son of the Greek king, the High Commissioner of Crete. Union eluded the Greeks on Crete, but they now had the opportunity to govern themselves.

As Greece approached the close of the nineteenth century, it found itself confronted with problems similar to those which had faced the young Othon in his first days as king. The nation remained economically poor and overwhelmingly agrarian with few advances in farming techniques, industry and transportation. That Greece still had no direct links with the main railway routes of Europe was one indicator of the nation's limited economic development. The acquisition of the Ionian Islands from the British in 1864 and of Thessaly and the Arta district of Epirus from the Ottoman Empire in 1881 hardly satiated expansionist appetites; thousands of Greeks still lived under Ottoman rule in Epirus, Macedonia, Thrace, Constantinople, the Aegean Islands, and Asia Minor. Concerned about the course of the Eastern Question, the great powers continued to exert, sometimes forcefully, a constraining influence upon the irredentist program of the Greeks, who also found themselves rivaled by the Serbs and Bulgars.

No leader emerged capable of formulating durable policies to divert Greek energies from patronage-clientage and unrealistic chauvinist aspirations. The electorate, in turn, failed to criticize effectively the politicians for *rousfeti* practices, primarily because most people willingly participated in the process. And since no politician could ever fulfill all his promises, it was difficult for one party to consolidate itself in power for a lengthy period—hence the frequent shifts in national leadership. The stress on personal relationships between politician and voter distracted attention from national to regional and individual concerns, hindered economic development on the nationwide level, and posed an obstacle to the formation of political parties distinguished more by ideology and less by personalities.

Greeks in acknowledging these faults generally attributed their existence to the heritage of nearly four centuries of Ottoman overlordship. Although their culture and political practices in many ways resembled those of their Turkish neighbors, the Greeks had established political institutions similar to those found in Western European constitutional monarchies. Instead of complementing each other, the "eastern" cultural and "western" institutional characteristics found themselves in irreconcilable conflict. Significant political change during the century occurred less in practices and more in institutions, and only then as the result of coups d'état in 1843 and 1862 in which civilians aligned with like-minded interests in the military. Officers had performed a positive function in liberalizing the format of politics, but the inability of political leaders to reform their methods and to reorient their mission contributed to economic complications, not to mention the disaster of 1897 and the accompanying disgrace to the nation and its armed forces.

I
1898-1907
TROUBLED DECADE

Defeat at the hands of the Turks in 1897 cast a dark shadow over Greek politics for more than a decade. Still foremost in Greek minds stood the achievement of the *Megale Idea,* a goal made increasingly difficult by the aggressive competition for territory from the other Balkan states. Obviously, a successful irredentist policy required an intensive military and economic buildup. To facilitate such a program a revamping of the political process seemed mandatory since the old machinery and practices had proved both inefficient and ineffective. Yet despite these ambitious foreign policy objectives and domestic challenges, national leaders provided few reforms to ameliorate conditions in the years immediately following the 1897 war.

Political Trends

In the confused postwar period public opinion portrayed King George and his eldest son, Crown Prince Constantine, as largely responsible for the military disaster. Constantine, the young commander of two divisions in Thessaly, was criticized for his poor military generalship, while his brother-princes were accused of never having reached the front lines. George, originally against the war, was blamed for negligence in failing to employ the fleet when needed. Photographs of the monarch disappeared from customary niches in many stores and homes to be replaced by those of Colonel Constantine Smolenskis, the one high-ranking army officer who displayed admirable courage and leadership during the short conflict. The dynasty's popularity declined to the point where George seriously considered abdication. The troubled ruler recovered some lost prestige in late February 1898 after he demonstrated personal bravery during an assassin's attempt on his life. Greeks also came to realize that the final treaty would have been much harsher without the backing of George's interests by his relatives among the European courts.[1]

Except for this temporary outburst of anti-dynastic sentiment, the political scene essentially maintained its pre-1897 forms. Two parties dominated, while two smaller political groupings exerted influential roles. George Theotokis, member of a distinguished Corfiote family, assumed leadership of the Trikoupis party. Contrary to previous experience, this party survived its leader's death, although Theotokis failed to provide the inspired, forceful guidance of his predecessor. Theodore Delegiannis, soon recovered from the stigma of the 1897 debacle, led the other major party until June 1905 when a professional card player, irked by Delegiannis's measures to curb gambling, ended the octogenarian's career by plunging a dagger into his chest. Kyriakoulis Mavromichalis, a high-ranking member of Delegiannis's party, and Demetrios Rallis, the leader of a smaller party, thereafter divided the prime minister's followers with the majority following the former. Alexander Zaïmis, head of a small but active fourth party, had the opportunity to form two governments which attracted the temporary backing of deputies from the larger parties.[2]

Talk of national reform intensified after 1897. King George on a tour of the Peloponnese in May 1898 met with calls for improvements in the defective systems of central and provincial government. The monarch, in turn, stressed that the people should assist in breaking normal patterns by voting only for those candidates pledged to institute the most essential reforms. The king revealed in confidence to Sir Edwin Egerton, Britain's minister in Athens, that a coup d'état under his leadership would be acclaimed but that he did not wish to violate the constitution; he also probably recognized that his popularity, only recently restored, would be ephemeral in such a situation. George then resolved to induce Zaïmis, prime minister since the preceding October, to sponsor a vital reform program.[3]

Zaïmis in late November 1898 drafted a well-publicized "Memorandum to His Majesty the King." Ambitious in its goals but vaguely expressed, the long list of proposed measures sought to improve the ecclesiastical and judicial systems, the consular service, police and civil service. The army and navy required considerable reorganization with increased budgetary allocations, and only through financial and tax reforms could this process be facilitated. Other proposals called for completion of the Piraeus-Larissa railroad, draining of marshes, supplying of Athens with water, improvements in mining laws, legislation for the currant trade and changes in the civil code and prisons.[4] As a mouthpiece for the king and a minority leader, Zaïmis could at best hope that his proposals might be accepted in part by either Theotokis or Delegiannis, leaders of the two largest parties.

Elections held on 19 February 1899 produced a majority for the Theotokis party, and in his speech convening the new Chamber of Deputies on 16 March the king reiterated the need for national reform. He also suggested greater decentralization of government in the provinces and establishment of a ministry of agriculture, commerce and industry. Notwithstanding the favorable climate for change, few real accomplishments occurred in the two years after defeat. Moreover, traditional Greek politics made the prospect of future reforms uncertain. Even with a parliamentary majority Theotokis still experienced difficulties creating a government until 14 April 1899 because of the fierce rivalries among his supporters for ministerial posts.[5]

It became apparent that Greek politicos would transfer many customary tactics of the nineteenth century into the twentieth, frequently sacrificing reforms and ideological platforms in the struggles for political power. Party propaganda, extravagant promises, bribery and patronage flourished. Since party discipline was virtually nonexistent and individualism rampant, deputies continued to shift parties for politically selfish reasons. Parliamentary obstructionism remained standard practice with politicians, generally adept in oratory, often filibustering up to three days to block legislation. At other times sizeable groups of deputies absented themselves from the *Boule* so that quorum requirements necessary for business could not be met.[6] In a December 1902 report, Vincent E. H. Corbett, the British representative on the International Finance Commission, summarized a view shared by other Western European observers critical of Greek politics: ". . . no difference of principle divides one party from the other; some of the smaller groups have a faintly perceptible anti-dynastic tinge, but otherwise the difference is of men, not measures—the sweets of office versus the cold shades of opposition."[7]

The intense competition between parties occasionally aggravated and politicized peripheral issues, resulting in street demonstrations and distracting attention from more crucial problems. For example, in November 1901 the translation of the Gospels into Modern Greek became a highly volatile subject as several large groups in the capital voiced their opposition. Spurred on by the supporters of Delegiannis, Athenian students organized large demonstrations which on 21 November, amidst great confusion, resulted in the killing of eight people and the wounding of twenty-nine. Public criticism blamed the Theotokis government for authorizing armed troops and police to fire on the crowds. Clear-cut evidence to condemn the Theotokis ministry for this bloodshed never emerged, but with the Delegiannists exploiting the negative publicity, the prime minister submitted his resignation on 25 November. To the dismay of Delegiannis and his followers, King George turned to Alexander Zaïmis who, with the support of the Theotokists, formed a new government. Delegiannis condemned the king's action as unconstitutional since the new prime minister had a sparse following in the Chamber of Deputies. When the elections of 30 November 1902 provided no majority for either of the two major parties, the king indicated that Zaïmis would be maintained as prime minister. Delegiannis exhorted the Athenian mobs who launched a series of demonstrations over five days in support of the aged politician. Referred to as the *sanidika* for the planks torn from kiosks and wielded by protesters, these riots forced the king to empower Delegiannis with the formation of a ministry on 7 December.[8]

Military Developments

Nationalist aspirations still ran high, but the decisive and humiliating defeat of 1897 sobered most Greeks to the harsh realities of careless adventure. That conflict, Greece's first foreign war since her struggle for independence, had glaringly revealed the backward condition of the nation's fighting forces. In the nearly seven decades since the arrival of Othon,

17

Greek governments had provided few substantive programs to develop the nation's military.

The crisis in the Balkans and the resulting Russo-Turkish War of 1877-78 prodded Greek leaders to institute a uniform program of military conscription. Among the last European states to enact such legislation, Greece with a population of 1,700,000, could muster a peacetime army of only 12,000 men; recruited by lots, the soldiers owed three years' service in the ranks and three in the reserves. A November 1878 law substituted an army raised by universal conscription. Foreseeing exemptions of about 16 percent, officials estimated that each class would provide an average of 11,000 men. The new law, which came into effect in January 1880, facilitated the mobilization of the nation's forces later that year in order to coerce Turkey into ceding Thessaly and Epirus. An estimated 82,000 men joined the colors by late spring 1881.[9] With its acquisition of Thessaly and the Arta district of Epirus under the terms of the Convention of Constantinople (24 May 1881), Athens moved its forces into these regions in the latter part of 1881. Nonetheless, the newly raised and enlarged army demonstrated many weaknesses in these maneuvers. One report concluded: "The only effect this Greek military demonstration had on foreign military critics was to convince them that the Greek Army if called upon to act could have done nothing. . . . Everything showed that the leaders were profoundly incapable and ignorant, the Officers useless, and the soldiers a mere collection of men with arms."[10]

During 1882 a series of laws sought to cope with the related problems of recruitment, training, exemptions and finances. In a revision of the 1878 law for universal conscription, every Greek male was now subject to nineteen years of military duty: one year of active duty in the infantry or two years in the cavalry, artillery, and engineers were to be followed by ten or nine years, respectively, in the reserve and then nine years in the militia. An important law in 1884 established a School for Noncommissioned Officers from which selected noncommissioned officers could graduate with a commission to the infantry or cavalry. Traditionally, few officers in these branches received extensive education or training; of the 303 graduates of the Evelpidon Officers Candidate School in fifty years, only thirty served in the infantry.[11]

In still another attempt to improve the armed forces, the Trikoupis government hired a French military mission headed by General Victor Vosseur which arrived in November 1884 and remained until December 1887. A critical report by the General in July 1885 condemned the sham nature of the nation's peacetime strength on the grounds that only half the proposed number actually served under the colors. The Bulgarian activities in Eastern Rumelia in the autumn of 1885 and growing tensions in the Near East prevented temporarily any effective reorganization when the Delegiannis regime mobilized the army. For eight months the 86,000 man army served no effective purpose except to increase substantially the budgetary deficit and to provoke Great Britain and France into blockading the Greek coast in May 1886. Moreover, during the midpoint of mobilization in January 1886, General Vosseur declared that the Greeks could not attempt any operation for at least two months without utter disregard of military prudence. None of the required steps preparatory to launching a campaign had been taken. Before his mission's departure in late 1887, however, Vosseur did see the enactment of several recommendations, particularly the regrouping of the infantry and artillery from battalions into larger regiments and the reorganization of the recruiting system into larger districts.[12]

Since 1878, largely under the direction of Charilaos Trikoupis, the Greek army had undergone a series of modernizing reforms which, though impressive on paper, effected few actual advances in the nation's battlefield capabilities. An evaluation by British officers in 1886 records:

> If we except the Rifles, who are a corps of mountain-bred Albanians enlisted for military service, and kept scattered in detachments in wild and mountainous districts free from the demoralizing effect of the coffeehouse politics in Athens and the larger towns, we may conclude that the Greek army is thoroughly worthless.... In all the reports and accounts that have been written of the Greek Army since 1881, when it wished to frighten Europe, there is not anywhere to be found a single word of praise, or a single mention of any military virtue.[13]

With little legislation or reform in the subsequent decade, foreign observers uttered similar appraisals during and after the fault-ridden campaign of 1897. Despite the reorganization

19

undertaken by Germany's General Colmer von der Goltz, the Turkish military machine would have experienced greater difficulties before a stronger army. Only superior discipline, organization, mobility and weaponry—all lacking—could have compensated for Greek numerical inferiority on the battlefield. Thus, ineffective political guidance, reduced military budgets due to the national bankruptcy of 1893, and an inadequate battle plan contributed to confusion and last minute attempts at organization. One British analyst commented: "The disorder which reigned from the very beginning can only be compared to that which preluded the French disaster of 1870, and was quite sufficient by itself to make it an absolute impossibility that the Greek army should have the initial advantage of assuming the offensive."[14]

Other than the general weaknesses already cited, additional problems must be mentioned. The peacetime strength of the army remained small, and in 1900 official statistics placed its level at 25,180 men. In line with past practices, however, a significant percentage of this force was devoted to nonmilitary activities such as police duties in the cities and countryside, forestry service, and customs inspection. Designed to save money in other areas of the national budget, this policy limited the training of recruits and hurt the professionalism of officers, many of whom found much spare time to indulge in coffeehouse politics. Although many officers, especially those in the infantry, rose out of the ranks to receive their commissions, very often with limited education, graduates of the Evelpidon Officers Candidate School were not much better trained in the practical problems of combat. The courses at Evelpidon stressed mathematics and the theoretical aspects of war with minimal attention directed to applied exercises in tactics and weaponry. Moreover, no war college or system of advanced education existed to provide training and study for career officers. And only a handful of officers received specialized training in foreign countries.[15]

Simple logic emphasized that any effective pursuit of the *Megale Idea* in the post-1897 period required widespread changes in the leadership, organization, training and equipment of the armed forces—a challenging assignment for any nation, but particularly difficult for a state with unstable politics and poor economic resources. Only when these latter aspects are considered can one comprehend the slow pace of reform in the armed forces in the years immediately following 1897.

The first significant step to revamp the nation's armed forces came with George Theotokis's controversial plan for the establishment of a General Command for the army. In November 1899 King George encouraged his prime minister to introduce a bill appointing Crown Prince Constantine as commander-in-chief and granting him full independence of action in matters of army personnel, discipline and reorganization. It was argued that with an apolitical Constantine at its head, the army's administration would be purged of any political considerations; too frequently, war ministers, upon assuming power, concerned themselves more with the promotion of their partisans in the officer corps than with the problems of creating a better army.[16] Theotokis presented this bill before the *Boule* in February 1900 and immediately stirred a storm of opposition. Demetrios Rallis claimed that the appointment of the crown prince was incompatible with the institutions of the country and warned his colleagues: "By proclaiming such a responsibility on the heir apparent to the throne you are preparing a revolution."[17] Theodore Delegiannis and Alexander Zaïmis labeled the bill unconstitutional, while Stephen Dragoumis prophesied that the country would divide along "royalist" and "constitutionalist" lines. The opposition maintained that since the crown prince was to be responsible to no one in his new position, any minister of war in disagreement with him would have to resign. Consequently, the scope of these powers overshadowed the prerogatives of the king, who could do nothing without his ministers, and of the cabinet, which required the assent of the king. Despite the outspoken resistance, Theotokis utilized his parliamentary majority to pass the bill in late March 1900. The new law did not contain the details of reorganization which were to be drafted by the new hierarchy of the army. But the former separate commands disappeared and the army's direction centered in the senior general, the crown prince, and his appointed staff.[18]

The designation of Constantine obviously stemmed from his prestigious position as heir to the throne rather than from proven experience or mettle. Although in his youth Constantine wore the uniform of the Evelpidon cadet, he had not attended the school but instead received private lessons prior to commissioning from Major Constantine Sapountzakis. In 1888 the young crown prince visited Germany and involved himself with military studies for several months but did not graduate from the *Kriegsakademie* as many Greeks later came to believe. During his sojourn he did, however, become engaged to Sophie, the sister of Wilhelm, the new Kaiser. Constantine commanded the divisions fighting in Thessaly during the inglorious 1897 war and, notwithstanding the consequences of certain strategic decisions, he could not, in all fairness, be blamed for the overall lack of preparedness and dismal performance of his soldiers. Then at the relatively tender age of 32, with limited experience, a tarnished reputation from 1897 and amidst political furor, he assumed the major responsibility for the strengthening of the army, a decision which from its first stages augured a controversial career for the future monarch.

Prior to the above legislation the Theotokis government in July 1899 passed a law that allocated 90,000 drachmas for the summoning of foreign military and naval advisers. Most observers speculated the German government would supply the army officers, and the following spring Constantine, preparing himself for his new responsibilities, visited his brother-in-law, Kaiser Wilhelm. But largely on the protestations of the Turkish sultan, Abdul Hamid, who claimed that Constantinople's cordial ties with Germany, developed through the latter's military missions, would be endangered, the Kaiser turned down the proposal of his Greek relative. By 1902 budgetary problems and new considerations made the 1899 law a dead issue.[19]

Criticism of the crown prince's augmented powers persisted with Delegiannis, Rallis and Dragoumis all stressing the unconstitutional prerogatives of the army's leader. Delegiannis repeatedly stated that if he came into power, he would repeal the law. Invariably, Greek politicians voiced opinions with greater conviction when out of power, harping on the faults of the ruling party and its policies. Thus when Delegiannis formed a government with a slim majority after the elections of 30 November 1902 he acted with less certainty. Upon assuming his position Delegiannis apparently promised King George not to raise army issues unless he first consulted Constantine. Delegiannis's minister of war, Colonel Theodore Lymbritis, insisted on introducing a bill in late February 1903 which included among its articles the elimination of the crown prince from his position of authority. Never fond of the aged politician, George reacted vociferously to news of the pending legislation that threatened his son's command. The king then informed the ministers of foreign affairs and justice that there were limits to his endurance and that he would rather leave the country than submit to this insult to himself and his son. In a meeting with George, Delegiannis reportedly "shed floods of tears" over the poor judgment of his minister of war, with whom he had to disagree. By late March the crisis passed as Lymbritis resigned over his prime minister's failure to support the proposed legislation.[20]

With the fall of Delegiannis's ministry on 27 June 1903, Theotokis formed a short-lived cabinet. Demonstrations in the provinces by peasants opposing tax laws affecting their crops convinced Theotokis to relinquish power on 11 July rather than to use force to quell the revolt; within two years Theotokis had resigned twice under the pressure of rioters encouraged by Delegiannis. Rallis, among the leading critics of the crown prince, succeeded Theotokis and quickly arranged a compromise bill with Constantine, an amended version of an earlier proposal by Delegiannis but never brought before the *Boule*. On 18 July the Chamber of Deputies passed the new army command bill which left to the crown prince the entire authority over the regular army and the promotion of its officers. The minister of war held jurisdiction over the gendarmerie and noncombatants. This timely compromise temporarily calmed the furor surrounding Constantine's leadership.[21]

It was not until February 1904, nearly seven years after the defeat by Turkey, that a Theotokis cabinet in conjunction with Constantine's staff introduced before the Chamber of Deputies an elaborate plan of army organization; and by the summer several important proposals became law. For the purposes of administration the nation was partitioned into three military districts with headquarters at Athens, Larissa and Mesolongi, each with an army division to be augmented during mobilization by forces from the reserve. The effort to organize the army by large districts attempted to curb the longstanding problem of many undersized detachments scattered throughout the countryside. This practice resulted from the political pressure placed on deputies by local constituencies which, in poor

23

economic condition, required the monetary injections of small army units stationed in the area. A new conscription law provided for increasing the number of men trained annually from 7,000 to 13,000. By shortening the conscript's tour of duty from twenty-four to eighteen months, the valuable sums saved could be diverted for the training of additional men. If effectively pursued this program would create a mobilized army of 120,000 soldiers, but not before at least a decade had passed. The *Boule* also approved the formation of general staff during peacetime to aid the commander-in-chief in the administration and training of the army.[22]

To facilitate expansion of the armed forces Theotokis proposed and had established a National Defense Fund in 1904. Special taxes and gifts by individuals would provide the assets for this new treasury which, in turn, would cover the interest and eventual liquidation of a large internal loan. This extra money beyond normal budgetary allocations was directed exclusively for the purchase of new war materiel and for the construction and repair of military buildings. The opposition led by Delegiannis unsuccessfully fought the new taxes and advocated instead economies in the civil service.[23]

Although impressive on paper, the important reorganization laws of 1904 quickly encountered difficulties upon implementation. A larger, modernized army required new weapons, ammunition, supplies, barracks, machinery, transport animals, and all these items were lacking. In November 1905 the Rallis government signed an important contract with the Steyr Arms Factory of Austria for the purchase of 60,000 Mannlicher-Schönauer rifles of the 1903 pattern to replace Greece's outmoded weapons. The following spring the Theotokis cabinet modified the contract and commissioned the Austrian factory to supply 40,000 additional rifles by the end of 1907. But Theotokis on regaining office in late December 1905 publicly acknowledged that the regular budget and the coffers of the National Defense Fund could not subsidize adequately the ambitious buildup within the timetable of the 1904 laws. Rather than strive too quickly for a large, poorly instructed, ill-equipped army, Greece should temporarily emphasize a small, effectively trained force with modern weapons. In the meantime the government could buy the appropriate arms, artillery, animals, and clothing and construct

24

adequate barracks and buildings for training. The funds acquired through economies and the decreased number of men instructed annually (10,000 instead of 13,000) would then be shifted to the National Defense Fund for the new purchases.[24]

Only mild criticism confronted Theotokis when he presented these new policies in February 1906. Simultaneously, however, the prime minister proposed legislation to discount for consideration in promotion calculations the time served by army and naval officers in the Chamber of Deputies. Such legislation, it was hoped, would discourage officers from running for political office. As twenty-seven of the 177 deputies actually served in the armed forces, shouts of opposition disturbed debates. Basing his decision on resistance to this bill, Theotokis called for the dissolution of the *Boule* and summoned new elections. The prime minister perhaps overemphasized this controversy deliberately and, if so, he gambled successfully since new elections on 8 April provided him with a large majority. Before the Chamber completed its labors for the summer the members passed twelve army bills to effect the principles of the Theotokis plans forwarded in February, including the bill regarding promotions for officers serving as deputies and another measure eliminating army officers from police duties. These legislative efforts thereby postponed the complete enactment of the 1904 proposals for at least five years. The revised program concentrated on a mobilized force of 60,000 men adequately equipped with new Austrian rifles and supported by new French Schneider-Canet field artillery. To help train the reserve, Crown Prince Constantine scheduled war games in 1907 and 1908 for several classes. Necessary funds for the new equipment and construction would come from an internal loan of twenty million drachmas.[25]

Land forces were not the only subject of strategic review. The crucial maritime location of Greece demanded a strong naval force to defend her shores and to support her army. Destroyers and three small, aging cruisers acquired during the Trikoupis era could not supply the appropriate power for a successful fighting navy. To help collect revenue for the strengthening of the fleet, the Theotokis ministry in 1900 established the National Fleet Fund, very similar in principle to the National Defense Fund founded four years later. Special taxes, personal contributions, and later a lottery gathered vital income for the specific purpose of acquiring new vessels. Drawing exclusively on this fund Greece ordered eight torpedo-boat destroyers in 1906, which were delivered in 1907 and 1908.[26]

During this period considerable debate centered around whether to renovate and rearm the existing cruisers or to buy new, large cruisers to support the destroyers. Revised proposals aroused considerable public interest in the summer of 1907 after retired Vice Admiral Francois Fournier of the French Naval Reserve recommended a reorganization of the Greek fleet. Requested by King George and Theotokis to comment on Greek naval plans, Fournier stressed that Greece should depart from conventional strategy, which relied on large naval ships. Essentially, the French admiral's plan assigned an important role to the Greek fleet in the seas of the Levant but as an auxiliary to the navies of Western European powers. Moreover, the Greek fleet was to consist almost entirely of torpedo boats, destroyers and submarines. The newly created general staff of the navy and the overwhelming majority of naval officers, supported by the exhortations of the Athenian press, heatedly opposed Fournier's project for smaller warships. Theotokis in 1908 finally had to dismiss the proposals, and naval planners resolved to order at least one large battleship and to refit the three old cruisers.[27]

Notwithstanding the series of reform laws and acquisition of modern equipment from abroad, "Greece as a military factor [counted] far below the other Balkan states."[28] Comparative statistics for the Balkan nations reveal that Greece's peacetime force, although well equipped by the end of 1907, fell behind in total numbers to the armies of Serbia and Bulgaria; and this difference increased with mobilization.[29] Nevertheless, if Greek leaders maintained or quickened their efforts, the nation could in several years possess a small army with important capabilities in a limited war or in support of a larger ally.

There was, however, a growing reaction among civilians and army officers to the supreme command of the crown prince and his brother-princes who held influential positions in the several arms of the military. A clique of favorites inevitably formed around Constantine and his handpicked general staff. To the dismay of officers in the army's largest branch, the infantry, the future monarch favored more technically oriented personnel for higher positions, in particular artillery officers and engineers for their supposedly superior education. Postponement of several laws perpetuated old evils such as police work for the military, and thin forces were still dispersed throughout the countryside. The public nurtured grand irredentist ambitions but was constantly reminded by newspaper editorials and diatribes in the *Boule* of the unhealthy situation. Visionary national officers, especially those involved in the Cretan and Macedonian campaigns, found their anxieties intensified with the passing of time.[30]

Economic Conditions

This unfortunate status of the armed forces stemmed not entirely from failings in leadership. The sad state of Greece's economy restricted any major national undertaking, and all politicians recognized the monetary shackles placed on any zealous undertakings. Indeed, very few bright spots existed in a generally dark economic picture. The consequences of the 1893 national bankruptcy and the 1897 war convinced the powers that they should subject the Greek economy to the constant scrutiny of an International Finance Commission (IFC). With representatives from Great Britain, France, Italy, Germany, Austria-Hungary and Russia, this group supervised the payment of the Indemnity and Economic Loans of 1898, of the six loans contracted from 1881 to 1893, and of three new loans in 1902, 1905 and 1906 for railway construction. Revenues were supplied from the six government monopolies of salt, petroleum, matches, playing cards, cigarette paper and Naxos emery, from stamp and tobacco taxes, and from import duties collected at Piraeus. Greek regimes carefully drafted their annual budgets, constantly attempting to show a surplus as a means of demonstrating to foreign investors the renewed vigor of national finances. Although Greek governments could raise loans without the consent of the IFC, the powers had provided certain obstacles to insure that receipts guaranteed to foreign bondholders would not be threatened.[31] Greek leaders reluctantly viewed the prospect of imposing new taxes on an already heavily burdened population and from which, in those instances where revenue collecting on the IFC-controlled duties increased beyond the mandatory level, Greece received only forty percent of the resulting advantage. Britain and its colleagues on the commission discouraged unrestricted loans to Athens, which would in all likelihood be directed towards military preparations, the cause of many economic difficulties in the recent past. Greek regimes held back on several important programs, but the state of the nation's public debt, the payment of which accounted for approximately twenty-five to thirty-five percent of every national budget, did not improve in the decade following the war. A net increase of 28 million francs in indebtedness over the ten-year span more than swallowed up the debt paid back. These extra funds went for railroad construction, re-equipment and rearmament of the armed forces, and for the costly settlement of 25,000 refugees who fled terrorist activities in Macedonia and Eastern Rumelia.[32]

The agricultural economy of Greece did not allow her to overcome a perennial balance of payments deficit in which exports usually averaged only sixty percent of the value of imports. Heavy taxation provided an ever present hardship for the poor peasants and workers, and it was estimated in 1904 that taxes consumed twenty-three percent of the general population's income. Much of this revenue for the government came from indirect taxes on everyday consumer items, thereby hitting the thin wallet of the peasant and worker more severely than that of their richer countrymen. High interest rates in this capital-starved nation made the plight of the poor even more treacherous. Their concerns ignored by the state, the peasants rarely observed or appreciated the returns on this heavy taxation, usually relegated to improvements in far off Athens and other urban areas.[33]

An overpopulated countryside, primitive agricultural methods, a low standard of living, high taxes, unresponsive governments and recurring financial crises—all contributed to the aggrieved state of the Greek peasants. Despite these unfavorable conditions no organized agrarian movement existed to consolidate the potential political strength of the peasantry and there were only a few isolated cases of open rebellion against the government during this period. Many citizens evidently conceded the inherent poverty of the nation and took solace in a brighter future with the realization of the *Megale Idea*. Still others sought relief through emigration. For centuries Greeks had emigrated throughout the Mediterranean basin, Russia, Eastern and even Western Europe, but nothing compared to the mass exodus of Greeks to the United States which began in huge numbers after the 1897 war. Between 1900 and 1921, 383,993 Greeks streamed to America, most of them uneducated and disenchanted peasants seeking a better life. This outflow of humanity aided Greece by eliminating some of the problems of rural overpopulation, and by raising the value of the drachma and the standard of living of many families through millions of dollars in remittances sent home. But on the negative side, their departure from Greece created labor shortages in certain areas and a loss of energetic individuals since the overwhelming majority of the emigrants were male (ninety-five percent from 1901 to 1910) and aged 15 to 45, prime years for labor productivity. In the age bracket from 15 to 29 a definite decline in numbers occurred from 1900 to 1912, and had not the Balkan War conquests and later events intervened, Greece would have suffered a serious population decrease with continuation of this high level of emigration. Of more immediate concern, the loss of such large numbers of young men posed still another obstacle for the government's program to develop a well-trained, mobilized army of 120,000.[34]

In 1907 with nearly two-thirds of her population involved in agricultural activities, Greece retained her predominantly agrarian character, but on closer inspection signs of budding urbanization, a slowly shifting economy and a growing middle class began to make their appearance. Statistics indicate that by 1907, 12.8 percent of the population concerned itself with industry and light or handicraft manufactures. Yet the laborers fared no better than the peasants, as they worked under unfavorable conditions with virtually no protection or support from laws. With minor exceptions, no legislation existed dealing with labor in general, employers' liability, workmens' compensation, hours of work or restrictions in the employment of women and children in factories. Strike activity increased during the first decade of the new century, but labor organizations remained primitive and bore little resemblance to unions in Western Europe.[35]

Political Ferment

Although in terms of relative growth her industry surpassed that of her Balkan neighbors, Greece was the only Balkan state not to have an organized socialist party. Steps toward the establishment of a formal socialist movement

29

lagged behind similar efforts in Serbia, Bulgaria and Rumania. Several factors account for this phenomenon. Greek factory workers comprised a small minority of the total population, and in the absence of large industry any labor movement would have had difficulty maturing. Because of her southernmost position in the Balkans and her non-Slavic background, Greece did not have geographical proximity or cultural relations with Russia, whose activist intellectuals influenced thinkers in Bulgaria, Serbia and even Rumania. While the most advanced socialist thought in Europe came from German circles, the small amount of socialist literature available in Greek was mostly translated from the French, since Greece's cultural ties with France predominated until the turn of the century. Moreover, it was difficult to disseminate propaganda among largely illiterate workers. Many individuals disgusted with economic conditions found the avenue to relief through emigration rather than political agitation; the numbers leaving Greece far outstripped those departing from other Balkan lands. Of equivalent importance, the *Megale Idea* retarded the growth of socialism by captivating the emotions of Greeks and dominating national actions and internal politics; socialist principles never penetrated the liberation movement of the Greeks. It might be added that the persistence of personality parties and *rousfeti* practices also stunted maturation of a movement with an ideological base.[36]

There were several unsuccessful attempts at organizing Greek workers during the last two decades of the nineteenth century. The few socialist-inspired journals failed to capture a noticeable following until Platon Drakoulis, English-educated and influenced by the Labor movement, published *Arden* from 1885 to 1887. He, Stavros Kallerges, and several others failed to coordinate a viable program to organize workers. Later Marxists defined the early Greek socialists as utopians whose ideas were more clearly related to a type of Christianity with its philanthropic, democratic views than to any scientific socialism.[37]

After 1900 the spread of socialist ideas slowly increased. Drakoulis in 1901 founded *Erevna (Inquiry),* a monthly journal in Greek published in England, which included a greater range of socialist-based articles. A series of socialist newspapers appeared in Athens, Patras, and Volos, encouraging the formation of labor and trade organizations. George Skleros, a Greek doctor living in Germany, educated in Russia, and influenced by George Plekhanov, drafted the first Marxist interpretation of Greek history in 1907. In addition, a small group of young men, most of whom were educated in Germany, formed the Sociological Society in 1907. Its leaders, Alexander Papanastasiou, Constantine Triantaphyllopoulos, Alexander Mylonas, and Panagiotis Aravantinos, were influenced by the views of the revisionist socialists. Their journal, *Epitheoresis ton Koinonikon kai Nomikon Epistemon (Review of Social and Legal Sciences),* presented their outline for social reform in a scholarly format.[38]

A small radical movement did emerge in the latter part of the nineteenth century under the leadership of George Philaretos. This active lawyer and parliamentary deputy headed a small coalition of politicians who advocated the establishment of a republic in Greece. Even with periodic outbursts of antidynastic sentiment in the populace, this small clique never made much headway towards ousting the monarchy. Their platform borrowed lightly from socialist principles but did little to push through constructive legislation. In February 1908 Philaretos began publishing the weekly *Rizospastis (Radical)* to air his program for a new Greece. His proposals proved less extreme than his earlier stance in the *Boule* now that he tried to create a formal "radical" movement. Tolerating the monarchy, but only as long as it remained impartial to the conduct of party politics, Philaretos advocated a national assembly for the revision of the constitution, war against the old politics, improvements in the educational system, and increased benefits for workers. Philaretos's activities failed to generate a large following, but his many outspoken articles against longstanding political evils caught the attention of the reformist-minded.[39]

During this period the daily press played an important function in the development of critical public opinion. The Greeks were avid newspaper readers and in Athens alone the average number of dailies hovered around ten from 1890 to 1910. The plethora of newspapers, however, allowed only a few to surpass a circulation figure of more than 10,000 issues daily. Several of the journals acted as official organs of the individual parties while the others shifted in their allegiances. In the

1905-08 period some of the most prominent dailies—*Astrapis, Athenai, Esperini, Chronos, Akropolis*—spoke out against the old parties and called for a new spirit to transform the conduct of politics. Of this group, *Akropolis*, edited by Vlases Gavrielides, consistently produced the most effective, critical editorials. From the standpoint of literary polish and political objectivity, *Nea Hemera*, published weekly in distant Trieste, reigned supreme and remained immune to the infectious subjective nature of Greek politics.[40]

Outside the Chamber of Deputies, criticism of existing political practices increased in tempo annually. Within the Chamber itself the deputies continued their traditional ways seemingly aloof to the outside furor. In the autumn of 1906, however, a small but energetic opposition emerged in the *Boule* to challenge the Theotokis government and all members of the "old" parties. Led by Stephen Dragoumis, other members of this group included Demetrios Gounaris, Petros Protopapadakis, Emmanuel Repoulis, Charalambos Vozekis, and Apostolos Alexandris. Ideologically they were neither socialist nor left-oriented, but demanded efficiency and high-principled methods in politics and public administration. Their pleas for reform, supported by several newspapers, aroused considerable publicity among the masses. Gavrielides of the *Akropolis* dubbed them the "Japan" party, paralleling their lofty goals to those of the dynamic leaders of Japan who transformed a formerly backward nation into the world power that defeated the Russians in 1905. The Japan party's highly touted reputation, however, far exceeded its actual achievements. A constant thorn in Theotokis's side, this party's existence motivated the prime minister to offer the position of minister of finance to Gounaris, its most ambitious and vigorous member, during the reshuffling of the government in July 1908. Gounaris accepted, considering a ministerial post the ideal platform from which to voice his views and influence legislation. He not only failed to push through reform bills, but the Japan party disintegrated after his departure.[41]

Diplomatic Developments

Despite the poor economy and the divisive nature of politics, Greeks united in their collective desire to achieve the *Megale Idea*. Pursuit of this irredentist program had dominated national policy-making for decades and continued to do so after 1897—albeit in a subdued manner which gave greater consideration to Greece's weakened potential to extend her borders. Nevertheless, the conflict between a realistic foreign policy and a more popular and aggressive brand of diplomacy never disappeared.

Crete, although autonomous, refused to accept this halfway status and the ultimate objective of the Greeks continued to be *enosis* with the mainland. The quirks of power politics provided Crete with a unique international position. She appeared to be more independent than Bulgaria, since the latter area was in theory tributary to the sultan while Crete was not. Moreover, the Bulgarian prince's election required the sultan's approval, whereas the king of Greece appointed the Cretan High Commissioner. The Porte controlled no domain of public life and could not veto nominations of officials or legislation. The right to fly one Turkish flag at Suda Bay stood as the only reminder of the nearly three centuries of Ottoman domination.[42]

Cretan frustration at being so close to union with the motherland, the sultan's insistence on holding his symbolic measure of control, and the powers' obsession with maintaining the status quo kept the Cretan pot boiling. The rule of Prince George complicated the situation by bringing Greek into conflict with Greek. Many of the more liberally inclined elements on the troubled island challenged the efforts of the high commissioner to consolidate his authority and claimed the prince's methods delayed the island's eventual union with Greece. At the head of this opposition group stood Eleftherios Venizelos.

Born in 1864 Venizelos, whose first name means "liberator," received his law degree from the University of Athens in 1887. Returning to Crete he quickly became involved in politics and associated himself with the island's progressive elements. A staunch nationalist and "unredeemed Greek," Venizelos participated actively in the 1889 and 1897 uprisings. After the latter revolt he collaborated in the drafting of Crete's constitution, became a member of the island's assembly and rose to the position of minister of justice. Venizelos's influence and followers on Crete mushroomed, especially after he resigned his cabinet post in protest over Prince George's policies. Events reached a climax in the early spring of 1905, when Venizelos led a band of insurgents in revolt against the prince's rule, also proclaiming Crete's union with Greece. The powers used their forces against the revolutionaries to preserve the fragile status quo in that part of the Mediterranean, and the uprising ended unsuccessfully in November 1905.[43]

This short action nonetheless had significant conclusions. Venizelos's forces lost the campaign but Prince George, acknowledging his unpopularity, left the island in September 1906. Much to the satisfaction of the islanders, King George selected Alexander Zaïmis, the former prime minister, as the new high commissioner. In another maneuver which inched Crete closer to complete independence from the Porte, the powers in the summer of 1906 authorized its government to enlist Greek officers and noncommissioned officers for the Cretan militia with no restriction on number. Perhaps most significant of all, Venizelos emerged from this "revolt of Therisso" (so named after the area of combat) as a hero of national proportions: the entire Greek world became familiar with his name.

The Greeks recognized the inevitability of Crete's union with the mainland; only the date remained uncertain. But the Turks controlled still other regions of irredentist concern: Aegean islands, Thrace, Epirus, and Macedonia. In the last area Greece faced the aggressive interests of her Balkan neighbors, Bulgaria and Serbia, with all three nations investing large sums to establish schools and spread propaganda. Guerrilla bands (*komitadji*) and regular army officers sent by Athens, Belgrade and Sofia terrorized the countryside, aiming to curb the influence of rival ethnic groups; the Turks frequently sat back, playing one side against the other. Anarchy and bloodshed reached their highest levels during an uprising in 1903, which the Turks squashed with brutality. The powers intervened, proposing the Mürzteg reform program in the autumn of 1903, but the hoped for pacification of the area never evolved and guerrilla bands continued their campaigns of terror.[44]

In only one sense did Athens's diplomatic position prove to be favorable during this period: Greece did not have to fear unprovoked foreign aggression, owing to the treaty obligations incurred by its guaranteeing powers, Great Britain, France and Russia, at the time they helped establish Greek independence. Bearing in mind irredentist goals, Greeks could not satisfy themselves with this apparent security of national frontiers. Greek leaders, witnessing the division of Europe into alliances, sought to bolster the nation's potential to expand through diplomatic initiatives with other states. Yet a nation with chronic financial problems, a weak army and navy, and belligerent intentions offered little to attract stronger alliance partners. Since Bulgaria, with her activities in Macedonia, loomed as the most serious threat, Athens investigated the possibilities of finding allies to thwart the advances of this Slavic enemy. Some Greek strategists in early 1907 even contemplated cooperation with Turkey against Sofia, but the Porte was not attracted by the proposal.[45]

Fearing the penalties of diplomatic isolation, Prime Minister Theotokis and King George agreed that Athens should initiate discussions in June 1907 with French officials on a possible alliance between the two nations. Theotokis maintained in his discussions with La Boulienière, the French minister in Athens, that Greece, cherishing her long-standing ties with France, would be an effective addition to the Mediterranean coalition rumored developing among France, Great Britain, Spain, Portugal and Italy. French material support could help strengthen the army and navy of Greece, creating an effective counterweight to the eventual drift of Bulgaria and Turkey into the orbit of Austria-Hungary and Germany. It was also during these weeks that Vice Admiral Francois Fournier expressed his preliminary suggestions for Greece's naval reorganization. La Boulienière attempted to develop an agreement whereby Athens, in accepting Fournier's scheme and a French program for the army, would buy its equipment and ships from France, which would also supply the necessary loan. In return, France, which supported the status quo in Macedonia, would, in case the conditions in that region became disturbed, back Greek interests. Considerable debate ensued among France's diplomats on the value of such a pact. As stated above, however, the French admiral's recommendations for naval reorganization became public knowledge and the subject of great controversy. With the foundering of Fournier's plan on the shoals of internal politics, the Franco-Greek negotiations for an alliance ended.[46]

Initial Greek contacts with the British in July 1907 for a similar alliance provoked a chilly response from the Foreign Office. Theotokis professed that Greece desired "both from inclination and from policy, to gravitate . . . [towards] the Western Powers, yet just now she was receiving nothing but knocks from them, and especially from England . . . ." London by its actions appeared to be more partial to the advances of Bulgaria in Macedonia. Theotokis hoped that when the Ottoman Empire broke up ("it might be in two years or it might be in fifty"), Greece's allies would see that it obtained satisfaction of its irredentist aspirations. The reply of Sir Edward Grey stressed that London appreciated this expression of good-will by Athens, but British policy precluded secret agreements. Furthermore, London sought to maintain the status quo in Macedonia while doing everything possible to improve the conditions of government under which the Christian races lived. The Foreign Office by no means tried to favor one nationality over another in Macedonia, and if there had been frequent protests to Athens, they were designed to bring Greece's attention to the reports of British consular offices on the renewed activities of Greek bands in the area.[47]

Grey and his subordinates obviously appraised Greece's value as an ally in low terms. In a November 1907 conversation with Paul Cambon, France's ambassador to London, the foreign secretary stated that the French plan to strengthen Greece with a loan and a naval reorganization was desirable from the political point of view. But Grey also added that he believed the Greek army to be "perfectly useless" and that he "very much doubted the capacity of the Greeks, even if they had the money, to create an efficient naval force."[48]

The calamitous 1897 war with the Ottoman Empire dramatically symbolized the failures in political leadership. But even with this hard lesson Greek politicians continued to employ methods which did not further the country's interests. Limited or no progress in coping with outstanding problems characterized the decade following the war. The economy made few advances, although the nation's finances regained some respectability under the stern guidance of the International Finance Commission. Thousands of young Greeks sought relief from their poverty-stricken status through emigration to the United States. Despite its new equipment the army remained small with questionable potential for successful battlefield operations. The prime focus of national energies, the *Megale Idea,* stalled.

Urbanization, slow development in the nonagrarian sector of the economy, and a growing middle class indicated a gradual process of modernization. Concurrently, certain observable changes loomed on the political horizon. Although Greece had no traditional aristocracy, its politics since 1821 had been dominated first by famous names of the 1821 Revolution and later by their descendants, large landholders and regional magnates. An uneducated and politically inarticulate populace, unable to voice grievances effectively, facilitated this oligarchy's continued success at the polls. But by the end of the nineteenth century the sway of the old leaders started to wane and new groups began their ascendancy. It must be stressed, however, that their influence was not immediately felt nor were their political positions clearly defined. The first years of the twentieth century exposed an agitation among rising elements which was eventually to add greater ideological pigment to Greek politics. These groups were neither sufficiently large nor adequately consolidated to overthrow the established parties, yet the undertow of dissent began to make itself felt. Except for the short-lived Japan party, the formal governmental apparatus failed to generate the drive from within to produce necessary reform. It remained to be seen if the established parties could continue to control the political destiny of the nation or if extraparliamentary forces would assume the initiative for change.

II
January 1908—August 1909
THE MILITARY'S DECISION
TO INTERVENE

Although the Greek people possessed a constantly agitated and critical political conscience, their political parties manifested a lack of direction and strength to handle outstanding problems in the decade following 1897. The first six months of 1908 produced no startling changes in national politics. This failure of the government to deal effectively with old issues was unfortunate, but, more seriously, it forewarned of an inability to cope with any new crises. The period extending from early summer 1908 into the following summer provided challenges with which the Theotokis administration and its short-lived successor could not deal effectively. In the meantime, nonpolitical groups expressed their opposition to the sequence of events. Amid these crumbling conditions, certain elements of the armed forces deemed it necessary to demonstrate their concern for national affairs. And as had so often been the case, foreign policy matters launched the domestic crisis.

The Young Turk Revolt
The autocratic rule of Sultan Abdul Hamid had stimulated criticism from elements both inside and outside the Ottoman Empire. Nationalist uprisings in Crete, Macedonia and Armenia defied the Porte's authority, and Turkish forces feared the sultan's inept rule would lead to the complete disintegration of the once-mighty realm. Finally, Salonika-based conspirators, who held the support of a large section of the army and who became known as the Young Turks, sent an ultimatum to Constantinople threatening to march upon the capital and to depose the sultan unless the 1876 Constitution

38

was restored. Recognizing that large military units now openly opposed him, Abdul Hamid, after some hesitation, proclaimed the long dormant constitution in force again on 24 July 1908.

Enthusiasm for this revolutionary action did not limit itself to the Turks. Christian nationalities in the Empire welcomed the prospect of improved political conditions. Enver Pasha, a Young Turk leader, proclaimed: "There are no longer Bulgars, Greeks, Rumans, Jews, Mussulmans. We are all brothers beneath the same blue sky. We are all equal, we glory in being Ottoman."[1] The Young Turks asserted that the various minorities had more to gain by solidarity with the Empire than by seeking its breakup. Within Greece public demonstrations of support for the Young Turks reversed traditional feelings of animosity. Many Greeks voiced their backing for a Greco-Turkish pact against Slavdom, the common enemy. The Greek press, which for years covered its pages with acrid anti-Turk articles, now printed Turcophile statements. The front page of the 6 August issue of *Patris,* a leading Athenian daily, displayed large portraits of King George and Sultan Abdul Hamid above Greek and Turkish flags. Below the two banners stood the expressions: "Freedom, Equality, and Brotherhood" and "The Two Masters of the Levant."[2] Even in Macedonian areas of guerrilla band activity, "political crime ceased as if by magic." Deaths due to violence dropped markedly in the three month period following the revolt.[3]

The euphoric reaction to the Young Turk Revolt did not last long. The separatist instincts of the Balkan nationalists dulled the initial optimism enunciated in Enver Pasha's declaration. More significantly, the Young Turks themselves divided into ideological camps. The Liberal Union led by Prince Sabaheddin supported some measure of decentralization with autonomous rights for the religious and national minorities. The Committee of Union and Progress came out more clearly for central authority and Turkish domination. Eventually, this latter group controlled the formulation of Constantinople's policies, and what little voice the minorities had gained slowly disappeared.

International politics also influenced the course of Ottoman policy. Alexander Izvolski and Count Alois Aehrenthal, the Russian and Austrian foreign ministers, respectively, seeking to exploit unsettled conditions in Constantinople, appear to have agreed upon a mutually advantageous alteration of the status quo in Southeastern Europe. But due to what has been classified as a misunderstanding of their oral Buchlau Agreement, Russia suffered a humiliating setback. Bulgaria, apparently encouraged by Vienna, violated the Treaty of Berlin by proclaiming her independence on 5 October 1908. On the following day Aehrenthal declared Austria's annexation of Bosnia-Herzegovina. Izvolski, caught unprepared, could not successfully pursue his plan to open the Straits to Russian warships.

Then acting on their own initiative, the Cretans startled an already disturbed European community by proclaiming the union of Crete with Greece on 8 October. In the absence of the high commissioner, Alexander Zaïmis, the Cretan government seconded this popular outburst, declared for union, and summoned an extraordinary session of the Chamber which confirmed the Proclamation of Union and appointed an Executive Committee, representing all parties, to carry on provisionally the island's government in the name of King George. The Cretans adopted the Greek constitution, headed their official notepaper with "Kingdom of Greece," printed stamps with the word "Hellas," and had all civil servants take an oath to King George.[4]

The prospects for union seemed good if Athens acted immediately. In the past Greece had responded to Cretan cries of *enosis* with even slimmer prospects for success. Theotokis, perhaps influenced by King George and fearful of another fiasco à la 1897 or of heavy pressure from the powers, pursued a cautious policy which worked against the country's ambitions. The wary prime minister did not speak out directly for or against the proclamation. Instead, he claimed that Crete's fate rested with the powers and their position toward Turkey. The powers replied with a note on 28 October which acknowledged their jurisdiction over the fate of the turbulent island and stated that they would discuss the issue with Constantinople if order were maintained on Crete and if the security of the Moslem population were assured.[5]

The impact of Theotokis's cautious maneuvering was not immediately felt. Public criticism within Greece remained temperate, while the Young Turks occupied themselves with other diplomatic problems. The Bulgarian and Austrian usurpations, however, induced Constantinople to consider a Greco-Turkish alliance. Theotokis expressed a readiness to conclude a joint treaty against Bulgaria if agreement could be reached on the annexation of Crete. But with the subsequent improvement of Turkish-Bulgarian relations, the attraction of such an alliance faded for the Porte and discussions ended.[6] In any case, the Turks sought to maintain the status quo in the Near East and could reap only limited gains from any pact with the Greeks. The latter held perpetual designs on Turkish territory, and the military potential of the Greek army in such an alliance was questionable.

Declining Domestic Conditions

The Greek economy failed to improve in 1908 and in several categories worsened. A superabundant crop of currants with a resulting reduction in price together with a diminishing demand among European buyers and in the newly-developed market in the United States contributed to a worsening crisis in the currant-growing centers. The Greek wine industry suffered from overproduction and declining domestic sales. The olive crop did not approach expected yields, and weather conditions severely damaged the wheat harvest; tobacco production was also inferior compared to previous years. Remittances from emigrants in America fell off because of the economic slowdown in that country, while a financial crisis in Egypt sharply affected Athenian bank investments there. Besides the many individuals directly influenced by this succession of economic setbacks, the Greek government bore a budgetary deficit due to decreased revenues from taxes on agricultural and consumer goods, the heavy cost of maintaining refugees from Bulgarian provinces, and large advances by the state to local communities in aid of primary education—advances never repaid. The International Finance Commission complained of decreased income from the several government monopolies and the Piraeus Customhouse.[7]

The Greek press amplified the general dissatisfaction. These journals frequently substituted passion and sensationalism for objectivity; nevertheless, many leveled sound attacks against what they considered the sources of Greece's ailments. A rapid survey of the highminded *Akropolis* editorials of Vlases Gavrielides reveals some of the main currents of criticism during this period. As a rule this prolific editor preferred to assail verbally not individuals but groups and the "corrupt system." He also came out against the extravagances of the Royal Family and King George's inclination to remain aloof from parliamentary politics. Gavrielides claimed the king should tactfully intervene at times, thereby giving proper direction to national politics. Primarily at fault, however, were the politicians and their continued corrupt practices ("The wolves are the parties, the lamb is the monarchy"). Internal failures, not external enemies, plagued Greece. The nation demanded a Greek version of the Young Turk Revolt, since neither the king nor the old parties responded positively to the challenges. Ideally, pressure from the people should oust the old politicians from their comfortable positions.[8] From mid-1907 Gavrielides constantly preached the need for a "peaceful revolution" (*eirenike epanastasis*), one that would remove Greece's internal weaknesses and transform her into a strong Balkan power. He did not define in clear-cut fashion the methods and goals of such a "peaceful revolution." Instead, this active journalist referred to various public protests and outspoken statements by social critics as signs of the coming revolution.[9]

The opportunities for Gavrielides and other critics to focus on discontent increased. The new session of the *Boule* convened on 12 November 1908 with few substantive accomplishments in the succeeding meetings. Demetrios Gounaris, the former Japan party member installed as minister of finance during the early summer, aroused a storm of controversy over his national budget. Gounaris's proposals included several well-intentioned reforms in the tax collection system and, in particular, important readjustments in indirect taxation. He outlined a program that would reduce the duty on sugar and other selected imports while raising taxes on alcohol for drinking and heating purposes. The budget featured an excise tax on wine manufacturers and a tax on dividends granted to directors of public companies. These proposals created many enemies among powerful groups associated with the production of alcohol. In an unprecedented demonstration of unity, the presidents of twenty-eight trade guilds in Athens on 16 December signed a petition addressed to the cabinet and *Boule*. The document protested any new taxes and decried the poor economic situation.[10] The public, recoiling at the mention of added levies during this economically difficult period, failed to appreciate that sterner measures for wealthier sections of the population were also being proposed.

The lethargic parliamentary session adjourned for the Christmas holidays on 2 January 1909 (new-style) without a decision on the Gounaris budget.[11] The only measure of significance which passed concerned the formation of a parliamentary committee to investigate and reform the navy. Since the Lenten season followed closely upon the Christmas recess, the Chamber did not reconvene until after the traditional Greek carnival celebrations in late January. The budget reform continued as the prime subject of debate until Gounaris, assessing the forces mounting against him, submitted his resignation on 15 February 1909. His fellow cabinet members resolved to stand by him in spite of considerable opposition and possible defeat, but Gounaris, not convinced of complete support from Theotokis, adhered to his decision and resigned. Led by inexperience to attempt too much at once, Gounaris with his proposed reforms had confronted an antagonistic bloc of influential parliamentary and economic groups.[12]

In the first months of 1909 unrest manifested itself in political protest and requests for reform which departed from the framework of traditional party politics.[13] Constantine Esslin, head of the Athenian Lawyers' Association, declared that a National Assembly should convene to revise the inefficient Constitution. George Philaretos had previously publicized this same view on the pages of his weekly paper, *Rizospastis*.[14] An article in an Athenian journal with small circulation, *Le Monde Hellénique,* in late February stirred up a commotion in both Greek and diplomatic circles. The column referred to the existence of a clandestine party working for the abdication of King George and the succession of Crown Prince Constantine. These statements did not provide the first expression of anti-dynastic statements, but speculation centered on who composed this group and if, perhaps, this note of warning had been sounded by the court itself.[15] Shortly afterwards, on 5 March, printed leaflets addressed "to the Greek people and the national press" under the heading of the *Panhellenios Ethnike Organosis* (Panhellenic National Organization) circulated throughout Athens. In an incoherent and confused manner the contents spoke of the need to drive out the vile elements causing corruption and to turn power over to sound members of the community. The organization professed to deprecate revolution but alluded to secret means of obtaining the desired ends.[16]

Stagnation of trade, unemployment, lack of money, over-taxation, and disapproval of King George's apparent apathy all contributed to general dissatisfaction. In local coffeehouses the people of Athens and Piraeus openly discussed these issues and the possibility of George's forced abdication. On 3 March there occurred a public demonstration in two distinct phases. One small group led by seven trade-guild presidents worked its way toward the palace and received an audience with King George. The monarch cordially accepted their memorandum listing grievances of the working classes. The articles request-ed that the king place pressure on the unresponsive govern-ment to relieve the sluggish economy and to lessen heavy taxes.[17] George agreed to forward the memorandum with a plea for action, but he also remarked to the trade-guild leaders that because the people elected their parliamentary represen-tatives, they were indirectly responsible for the government and its performance in the *Boule*. A much larger group of 500-800 people gathered noisily that same day in one of the main squares of Athens to listen to several speakers. One of them, John Rallis, the son of the main opposition leader, Demetrios Rallis, exclaimed: "The people have waited in vain for the interference of the one person who ought to put the government in its place, but the irresponsible monarch prefers to remain indifferent." The crowd then proceeded to the *Boule* where some violence erupted. Stones and revolver shots shattered several panes of glass in the Chamber and about twenty people were injured, mostly police.[18]

Later that same month another controversy arose when the association of shopkeepers and merchants of Athens-Piraeus requested the dismissal of the director of Piraeus Customs because of the latter's stringent policies toward them. The Theotokis government conceded this point but went through the formality of asking the International Finance Commis-sion, under whose authority the director worked, for permis-sion to act. The IFC, expressing confidence in this official, suggested a joint inquiry. Meantime, the shopkeepers organized a demonstration on 31 March in which about "2000 orderly and respectably dressed individuals" headed for the palace to hand another petition to King George. Military and police guarded the approaches to the structure and, in a sudden action, forcibly prevented the demonstration from proceeding and roughly handled members of the delegation to the king. Hearing of this unexpected outbreak, George ordered the police not to use force and to allow the delegates to see him.[19]

The Theotokis government had not answered the IFC about the joint inquiry and submitted its resignation after the street fighting, an apparently unnecessary maneuver that surprised both king and public. Theotokis maintained, however, that the king's action in countermanding the original orders to the police implied a want of confidence in his government. When George asked the departing prime minister what position his party would assume in the *Boule* toward another government, Theotokis replied that his party would not support it. The monarch next sent for the leader of the largest minority party, Demetrios Rallis, who asked for a promise to dissolve the Chamber if he became prime minister. He also requested a twenty-hour delay before announcing his final decision; this period was later extended another twenty-four hours.[20]

At a meeting with his followers Theotokis explained that the position of his government had become precarious in both internal and diplomatic matters, and obstructionism within the Chamber had become too great for effective leadership. He added that trade guilds and shopkeepers sought and partially succeeded in gaining the sympathy of the king, with whom the government had to work. In fact, the public excuses for resignation were flimsy—a quickly constructed facade to mask the unhealthy condition of his party's rule. Despite a majority in the *Boule,* the Theotokis party demonstrated increased impotency in dealing with domestic problems. Some industries, such as wine, suffering from overproduction, obtained from the government remedial measures at the expense of other industries which, in turn, protested vociferously, causing abandonment of these new laws. Such examples of the malleability of Theotokis's administration worked against political stability. While parliamentary obstructionism did exist to some degree in internal questions, the opposition had practiced marked self-restraint in the always sensitive foreign policy issues. Hence, the prime minister evidently engineered his own downfall to elude an ever worsening situation.[21]

Rumors of an impending dissolution of the *Boule* created great excitement in Crete where it was decided to hold elections simultaneously with those in Greece. The elected deputies would sail for Athens to take seats in the Chamber. Since the Cretans intended this act to signify *enosis,* the government in Athens would be hard pressed to deny admission to the island's deputies; at the same time such an event would naturally create difficulties with both the Porte and the powers. Rallis, assessing the situation, repeated to King George on 3 April that he could take over the reins of government only after the dissolution of the Chamber. But because such action might involve disastrous complications, the minority leader suggested the king summon Theotokis again. In order to facilitate the restoration of the former prime minister, the ministry of interior published a letter revealing that the chief of police had disregarded explicit instructions during the demonstration of the shopkeepers. This tactic settled the dispute over the king's confidence in Theotokis which had led to his resignation. The majority leader now consented to resume the prime ministership on condition that the opposition not block the budget. Rallis agreed to this arrangement. Shortly afterwards, the controversial director of Piraeus Customs voluntarily requested a transfer to another post.[22] The Chamber dutifully passed the budget before it adjourned for the Easter holidays on 7 April.

The Greek parliamentary system was stumbling in its effort to deal with a series of critical problems. The economy and finances sputtered downward. Diplomatic forces and Greece's military weaknesses limited any bold foreign policy initiatives for the advancement of irredentist programs. Even the calling of new elections and a smooth transition to a new ministry became highly difficult because of the Cretan issue. Although the maladministration of the Theotokis government was probably no worse than its predecessors, prolonged tenure called greater attention to its failures. Out of frustration people began to express their disenchantment independently of traditional party politics through street demonstrations, petitions, journalistic criticism and appeals to the king.[23] This political disenchantment surfaced in urban and rural areas, among the educated middle class, shopkeepers, workers and peasants. There was, as yet, no common goal and defined program around which these agitated groups could coordinate their activities. It was also uncertain whether any individual elements held sufficient power or could offer inspirational leadership to provide the political drive necessary for correcting problematic conditions. King George aptly observed that the people elected their deputies to represent them; and increasingly many sections of the population viewed established values and the spirit of traditional politics as inappropriate for the problems at hand.

Formation of the Military League

Elements within the armed forces were the next group to display dissatisfaction with the Theotokis regime. In early May the government with the backing of the general staff submitted a bill to the *Boule* for the creation of a permanent cadre of noncommissioned officers. The proposal intended to terminate the process whereby a noncommissioned officer could acquire a commission after study in the Noncommissioned Officers School.[24] Modeled on the policy employed in Germany, the bill sought to provide homogeneity in the officer corps and to pave the way towards a reformed and expanded Evelpidon Officers Candidate School which graduated commissioned officers. Whatever the merits of the plan, it attracted little enthusiasm from noncommissioned officers suddenly thwarted from achieving officer status and limited to acquiring the rank of sergeant-major as the highest possible grade. A strong reaction set in also among the many officers who had received their commissions from the Noncommissioned Officers School. The majority of Evelpidon's small number of graduates came from the more privileged classes and usually assumed slots within the army's technical branches. The Noncommissioned Officers School, in contrast, served largely to advance professionally—and usually in the infantry and cavalry—those soldiers from the petite bourgeoisie and lower classes.[25]

On 11 May some two hundred noncommissioned officers gathered noisily in front of the *Boule* and submitted a petition against the proposal to the president of the Chamber, Constantine Koumoundouros. Two days later, Koumoundouros received notice of another planned demonstration before the Chamber which, however, did not materialize. Hoping to set a harsh example, Theotokis, who also held the portfolio of minister of war, set up military court trials which convicted twenty-four noncommissioned officers for insubordination; the prisoners lost rank and were dismissed from the army. Crown Prince Constantine, as commander-in-chief, granted clemency to seventeen of the convicted men, reportedly because the ceremony granting a first commission to his eldest son, Prince George, had emotionally moved him. On 31 May, however, military authorities punished nearly two hundred officers, with sergeant-majors receiving one month imprisonments and sergeants twenty-day sentences. Only forty noncommissioned officers from the Athens garrison escaped punishment by providing alibis which proved their absence from the demonstration. Concurrently, the Chamber ended its sessions in the last week of May without reaching a final decision on the disputed bill.[26]

The populace followed the controversy closely, with the Athenian press generally considering the noncommissioned officers' punishments too harsh. The matter of discipline in all forms was hard to understand among a people who did not as a rule respect or practice submission to authority.[27] The disciplinary problem appeared particularly ominous to the military hierarchy under Crown Prince Constantine and to the dynasty against whom potential revolutionary movements might be directed. The guards responsible for the king's safety now took extra precautions in protecting the palace at night, and Constantine made the rounds of the barracks haranguing officers and men on the vital necessity of preserving discipline as part of their national duty.[28]

This most recent protest added to the general discontent of military circles towards the crown prince. The commander-in-chief tended to keep favorites on the general staff and promoted those close to him. Concentrated in the capital, this select group usually avoided the unpleasant task of provincial garrison duty. Meanwhile, it was not uncommon for many years to pass between promotions for other officers. The prince's quick temper and crude language in reprimanding subordinates aroused disrespect for his position. Constantine also refrained from close personal touch with individual military units, an aloofness not appreciated by many officers. Increasingly numerous members of the military critically reviewed the limited achievements of Constantine's general staff and of the Theotokis ministry.[29]

Concern for the leadership and condition of the military reached the stage where secret groups formed to assess the situation. Most existing evidence indicates that serious clandestine activities began in the late spring of 1909. Theodore Pangalos in his memoirs, however, traces the first meetings back to October 1908. Then a first lieutenant, Pangalos summoned several colleagues to his house for a discussion of the deplorable condition of Greek military and political affairs. This small gathering concluded that a nonparty government supported by the army and with dictatorial prerogatives could best push forward a program to strengthen the nation's land and naval forces. Shortly afterwards, this same group, consisting of eight lieutenants, held a second session during which it drafted a first protocol. The most significant article of this document, when viewed in historical perspective, called for the summoning of Eleftherios Venizelos from Crete to head the protest movement. The junior officers saw in Venizelos a revolutionary with political sagacity and the potential for successful leadership, but Pangalos does not reveal if his fellow conspirators made any formal attempt to contact the Cretan politician. The main focus of these officers for the moment became an expansion in membership, and by January 1909 twenty-three lieutenants and two captains joined this secret clique which violated all principles of military discipline.[30]

The success of the Young Turks inspired these reform-minded officers in their behind-the-scenes activities. They were also reacting to the changing policies of Constantinople and to the ineffective diplomatic initiatives of the Theotokis regime. In addition, these Greek officers viewed favorably the examples of secret societies which had recently executed forceful changes in the governments of Serbia (1903) and Portugal (1908); and of course they bore in mind the military revolts of 1843 and 1862 within Greece. As conditions worsened during the spring of 1909, the prospects for attracting a greater following increased.

49

Pangalos and several confidants, all lieutenants, assembled to formulate plans in May. Infected with professional ambition and chauvinism these officers shared anti-dynastic views, criticizing King George for his noninterference in domestic problems and for too much influence in the conduct of foreign affairs, the crown prince for his performance as commander-in-chief, and Constantine's brothers for their privileged ranks in the armed forces. Another clique of seventeen captains met separately in early June to discuss political conditions and, of this group, only two advocated expulsion of the dynasty. Epaminondas Zymbrakakis, a cavalry captain originally from Crete, headed these officers, many of whom had served bravely as agents of the Athens government in organizing guerrilla bands in Macedonia and had regularly expressed concern for the growing strength of the Bulgarians and Serbs in this region. In contrast to the lieutenants who spoke of possibly using armed force, the majority of these captains favored more moderate political goals, stressing the sponsorship of laws for strengthening the military. Concurrently, noncommissioned officers, in the aftermath of their conflict with the army's hierarchy, formed a league with George Karaïskakis, an infantry captain, parliamentary deputy, and grandson of the famed revolutionary leader, as president.[31]

These three groups existed independently of each other in the initial stages of their development. By mid-June it has been estimated that the faction dominated by the lieutenants grew to more than one hundred. The captains, on learning of the activities of their juniors, began to fear that the initiative might be wrested from their hands. Captain Constantine Gouvelis discussed with Lieutenant Pangalos the general methods and goals of the two respective factions. Less radical in their program, the captains could not agree with the lieutenants about the potential role of Venizelos or the use of force. The two officers decided to summon a joint meeting of captains and lieutenants at the home of Lieutenant Christos Hatzemichalis at eleven in the evening of 8 July.[32]

For a gathering with rebellious intentions the assemblage was ill-conceived. Some 160 officers attended with no great attempt to maintain security. The division of interests between the captains and the larger group of lieutenants was revealed in the first stage of the meeting. No compromise agreements were reached on the two separate programs nor on a proposal demanding an additional twenty-five million drachmas for the armed forces in the next budget. At this juncture higher military authorities, having learned of the meeting, sent Colonel Nicholas Schinas, Commandant to the Palace, to investigate. Confusion and shouting greeted the colonel who, after the restoration of some semblance of order, attempted to seize the sheet of paper listing the demands of the lieutenants. Prevented from doing this, Schinas threatened disciplinary action and left to report to the crown prince. Before the meeting disbanded well after midnight, the officers, apparently more unified in purpose after the intrusion of Schinas, concurred in holding elections for an administrative committee to coordinate a program of action for their newly baptized Military League (*Stratiotikos Syndesmos*).[33]

Within two days the officers involved in the disrupted meeting voted for a fifteen-man administrative committee composed exclusively of lieutenants and captains. On the evening of 10 July this newly constituted body conferred at the home of gendarmerie Captain Spyridon Spyromelios until 2:00 a.m. The host and Captain Zymbrakakis advocated the immediate summoning of a National Assembly to revise the constitution and to provide for the rapid strengthening of the army and navy. The majority at the meeting maintained that convening a National Assembly would waste valuable time; the nation's armed forces had to be the first priority. It was recommended that a list of strategic suggestions be relayed to the ministers of war and marine which, for success, would require the backing of the government and king; force might be considered by the committee, if necessary, to implement the program.[34]

In an important maneuver, Lieutenant Athanasios Loidorikis, secretary of the administrative committee, visited Kostes Hairopoulos, editor of the Athenian daily, *Chronos*. Hairopoulos, who for many months had written lengthy criticisms of existing conditions, agreed to have his newspaper become the journalistic mouthpiece of the Military League. With rumors flying around the capital about a secret military movement, a first article in *Chronos* on 14 July related the overriding desire of many officers to dissolve the cliques of favorites in the military and for the immediate buildup of the army and navy.

51

In the weeks that followed, Loidorikis contributed unsigned articles almost daily which expressed the position of the military activists under such headings as: "The Need for Sincerity," "Everything in the Light," and "The People Speak for the Army."[35]

To expand the base of their movement the scheming officers next organized comrades outside the capital. Representatives contacted junior officers in provincial garrisons who, in turn, formed sections with a chairman and three-man committees to coordinate activities. Within the navy several officers sympathizing with the army officers joined in the growing conspiracy. In this manner naval Lieutenants Constantine Typaldos and Pericles Argyropoulos persuaded close to fifty colleagues to join the Military League.[36]

Not all of the higher ranking army officers willingly tolerated existing conditions in order to maintain the security of their privileged positions in Constantine's command structure. A few colonels acknowledged the need for change but, moderate in their methods, wished to bring about reform within the existing system. They also recognized the dangers to military discipline and to their own positions if lieutenants and captains seized the initiative in a radical movement. Colonels Panagiotis Danglis and Leonidas Paraskevopoulos arranged a meeting at the latter's house with thirteen other senior officers to draft a program. Danglis composed a memorandum for consideration by the king. Much less extreme but broader in scope than the proposals contemplated by the Military League, this document sought reforms which would affect parliamentary life, the economy and, of course, the army and navy. But before this small movement could gain any momentum, the crown prince learned of it, forcefully intervened and had Colonel Danglis placed under house arrest for one month in early July. This action by the commander-in-chief nipped in the bud any reform movement among field-grade officers.[37]

Although the Danglis group eliminated itself from further conspiratorial activities, the Military League of lieutenants and captains continued to plot despite punitive action threatened by Constantine's staff for the disrupted meeting at Hatzemichalis's home. To aid the development of a common policy and to avoid problems between officer ranks, the lieutenants thought it best to withdraw voluntarily from the

administrative committee. On 17 July a new nine-man committee of seven army captains and two naval lieutenants replaced
the fifteen-man group. This new leadership drew up a protocol
outlining in general terms the goals of the Military League.
The foremost objective was the military and naval preparation
of the country; the League would work to facilitate this process
by recommending guidelines to the government and king and
also through possible direct action. Those men belonging to
the Military League would all work, as honorable officers, for
these objectives.[38]

To promote harmony and to eliminate the possibility of
jealousy within the Military League, members of the administrative committee considered the appointment of an outsider
with a rank higher than captain as an appropriate leader.[39] It
was also thought that if and when the League asserted itself
against the government, the public would more readily accept
the leadership of an individual with long military experience,
someone commanding the confidence that a collection of
captains and lieutenants could not provide. The League spoke
with several colonels before one finally consented to assume
the responsibility. Leonidas Lapathiotis expressed his sympathy with the movement but declined the leadership post,
fearing that he might be deserted in the resulting struggle
with the authorities. Doukas Vakaloglou, former aide-de-camp
to King George, concurred with many of the League's goals,
but did not wish to involve himself in subversive actions;
Constantine Psarodemas responded similarly. The delegation
of Captains Phikioris, Zymbrakakis, and Gouvelis then found
Colonel Nicholas Zorbas willing to accept the key position.[40]

Born in 1844, Zorbas graduated from the Evelpidon Officers
Candidate School and pursued supplementary studies in
France. By nature a nonrevolutionary, he was, nevertheless,
quite critical of existing conditions in Greece and did hold an
outstanding grievance against Crown Prince Constantine.
Zorbas had earned a reputation as a fine and knowledgeable
officer, but from the 1897 war, a conflict infamous for its
scapegoats, he emerged with tarnished credentials. In a matter
never cleared up publicly, Zorbas was accused of losing his
composure and failing to follow orders in a crucial battle
situation. Then a lieutenant colonel, Zorbas was deliberately
passed over for promotion in the period after the war. Only

after eight years of outstanding service (1898-1906) as director of Evelpidon did he attain the rank of colonel. A large number of the officers in the Military League had studied at Evelpidon during his tenure and obviously respected his leadership abilities. As Supervisor of War Materials after 1906 Zorbas regularly criticized the low stocks of arms and munitions, another source of concern to the young officers.[41]

During July the various newspapers all ran bold-faced headlines and articles based only partially on real information about a military movement and an impending revolution. Lieutenant Loidorikis submitted his anonymously-authored articles to *Chronos* on a regular basis, adding to the curiosity of the public. A growing lack of confidence in the government's ability to deal with economic, political and diplomatic ailments of the nation made the people increasingly receptive to talk of revolution. Vlases Gavrielides, wary of the prospect of military rule, did not commit his paper to supporting the movement, unlike the majority of his editor-colleagues.[42] The editor of *Akropolis* continued to stress his hope for the "peaceful revolution" more strongly than ever, citing England's reform program as an example. He published a long scheme of reform in which he sought the support of the trade guilds and called for the creation of a ministry of agriculture, reorganization of the army and navy under foreign advisers, dismissal of incompetent or dishonest examining magistrates, reduction of custom tariffs, and establishment of an income tax. With a view to publicizing national reform, Gavrielides instituted a "plebiscite," asking his readers to write in their grievances and suggestions for improvements in governmental practices. Many readers complied and the editor published these letters, some quite vociferous in their criticism of the prevailing order.[43] On 3 July Kostes Hairopoulos ran in *Chronos* a "Panhellenic Plebiscite for Salvation" in which he called for the encouragement of the people through their letters to summon Eleftherios Venizelos from Crete.[44] Few forces emerged to counter this spreading mood of disaffection and the British minister in Athens had to agree when his consul in the port of Volos remarked: "There is a strong and dangerous current of discontent amongst the lower orders and considerable alarm is really felt by the upper classes."[45]

54

The Cretan Problem

The dismal condition of Greece's irredentist program contributed significantly to the grievances of the people, restricted the options of Greek politicians, threatened the monarchy's prestige and spurred conspiratorial groups to further action. The press, government and even the political opposition tried to tone down the hopelessness of Greece's bargaining power and the inability to assert forcefully its position in diplomatic negotiations; frustration, however, was felt at all levels of the population. A main cause of concern continued to be Crete, for years a complicating factor in the Eastern Question. Since 1897 Athens's initiative in this issue remained limited, while the activities of the Greeks on Crete regularly created the explosive situations. The Turks, under heavy domestic pressure, assumed a stiff stance towards any attempts by the Cretans to sever the island's slim bonds with Constantinople. Concerned with the sensitive balance of international politics, the powers steered an ambivalent course, always attempting to maintain the status quo as closely as possible.

The July 1906 collective note permitting the use of Greek officers to organize the Cretan militia stipulated that detachments of the four protecting powers on Crete would withdraw upon the satisfaction of certain requirements: when the Cretan gendarmerie and militia had been organized and placed under the orders of the high commissioner, when order and tranquillity had been restored, and when the protection of the Moslem minority had been assured. In May 1908 the powers conceded conditions on the island made it appropriate to begin a graduated withdrawal. Approximately 250 soldiers from each nation departed on 24 July 1908, with the remaining forces pledged to leave by that date the following year.[46] In the diplomatic confusion of October 1908, Theotokis might have achieved Crete's union by a simple proclamation. But as the weeks passed, the government in Constantinople recovered from its early autumnal embarrassments while the Greeks quietly conceded that they could not defeat the Turks on the battlefield. Instead, the Theotokis government depended on the good will of the powers, hoping in time to reap rewards through "good behavior."

Whereas the question of annexation had arisen in Greco-Turkish negotiations in late 1908, the Turks began to rule out any such solution after the coming of the new year. The Porte suggested that Crete become a privileged province of the Ottoman Empire on the lines of Lebanon, a retrograde status which the Greeks on Crete would never have accepted. The Turks then recommended that the international troops remain on Crete beyond the proposed July 1909 withdrawal date; the powers declined, not wishing permanently to undertake the maintenance of order there. In April the four powers expressed the hope that a definite decision would be reached for complete evacuation in July. They also suggested that a detachment of *stationnaires* should guard the Turkish and international flags in Suda Bay. When Theotokis near the end of May protested against the proposal to leave a guardship, the powers replied it was meant to prevent any further movement by the Cretans toward union, an act which would undoubtedly provoke an ultimatum from Turkey. Theotokis professed his inability to believe that Greece, after putting itself unreservedly in the hands of the powers, should be placed in such a situation, face-to-face with unprovoked aggression from Turkey. When the Greek people discovered that nothing would be done to satisfy their national ambitions, Theotokis predicted an uprising on Crete and a revolution on the mainland overthrowing the monarchy, since George had placed confidence in the powers and would be held personally responsible. Theotokis also stressed his lack of faith in the army, which was undermined with anti-dynastic ideas. In separate conversations with the French and English ministers in Athens, King George questioned the viability of his position because of the powers' lack of support for Greece's irredentist interests.[47]

The obdurate position of Turkey stemmed from the consequences of the April 1909 counterrevolution. The Young Turks regained control, beat down both the liberal and reactionary factions and became the real masters in Turkey by late April. They then forced Sultan Abdul Hamid to abdicate, replacing him with Mohammed V. Seeking to divert attention from troubles at home, the Young Turks deliberately pressed the dispute with Greece over Crete. The Turkish press in June launched a violent anti-Greek campaign, using threats of war frequently. The Greeks reacted with unprecedented moderation to these verbal barrages since they were determined to avoid

56

even the semblance of provocation. They continued to believe that the protecting powers would not allow them to fall victims to aggression. Theotokis failed, however, in an attempt to start negotiations on a pecuniary indemnity for Crete and on the settlement of all outstanding questions with Turkey.[48]

Greece's difficult bargaining position could not improve without the support of the powers. But such backing did not appear likely, particularly because the British from the time of the Young Turk Revolt sought to demonstrate their sympathy to Constantinople. In October 1908 London had advised the Turks to yield to Austrian and Bulgarian demands and to accept monetary compensation in return. The British government, therefore, was in a sensitive position regarding Crete, and an official report of 2 July 1909 cogently stated:

> It would, however, be reducing our sympathy and good will toward Turkey to a farce if, after the Turks had accepted in these two cases [i.e., Bulgarian independence and the annexation of Bosnia-Herzegovina by Austria-Hungary] our advice, disagreeable though it was, we went on to put pressure upon the Turks to give way to Greece in a manner which they considered humiliating. . . . The Turkish flag still flies there [i.e., Crete], and it would be very humiliating to Turkey for the flag to be hauled down and replaced by that of Greece, a Power not only much weaker than Austria or Bulgaria, but also one which the Turks know quite well they could defeat so easily again as they did in fact [twelve years ago].[49]

The same report affirmed that the Greeks were taking up "a most unreasonable attitude" in view of Theotokis's predictions of revolution if the Cretan question were not settled favorably. English diplomats countered that Greece could afford to be patient and that the island's annexation was not essential to Greek welfare or independence. The Turks, in turn, claimed that the humiliation of relinquishing suzerainty over Crete would inevitably lead to further revolution in Turkey.[50] In short, London, on whom the Greeks depended so heavily, did not wish to jeopardize its diplomatic position at Constantinople over the Cretan issue.

The Rallis Ministry

The nearly four years of rule by George Theotokis bore heavily on dissatisified Greeks. The prime minister, advancing in age and rumored to be ill, felt his control of affairs slipping. In a sudden action he surprised the public as he had done in

April by once again submitting his resignation to King George on 16 July. The announced reason for his departure concerned a public demonstration scheduled for 18 July to protest the treatment of subject races in the Ottoman Empire. Citing the rebellious temper of the army, Theotokis felt he could not be responsible for maintaining order at a public gathering which might easily turn its wrath against the government. In theory the meeting had the support of Rallis, the opposition leader; and there were rumors, later disproved, that armed peasants would be brought into Athens from outlying villages.[51]

Parliamentary stability characterized the Theotokis years, but this condition was attributable primarily to his party's majority in the *Boule*. Otherwise, the prime minister from Corfu proved a lackluster politician, unable to lead Greece effectively in conquering economic poverty and pursuing an ambitious foreign policy. Budgetary limitations regularly inhibited efforts to build up the army and navy because new tax laws could not be passed. Some bolstering of Greece's military arm did occur, but not enough to match her more powerful Bulgarian neighbor. A comparison with Turkey's military potential could not even be attempted.[52] Moreover, Theotokis had faltered in the autumn of 1908, losing the opportunity to achieve union with Crete; and in the succeeding months he anxiously awaited favorable action by the powers in what was essentially a hopeless situation for Greece. His pro-Constantinist tendencies won him the disfavor not only of much of the army but also of the press and public. Critical conditions prevailed and the prospects for improvement appeared dim. There is thus reason to believe that Theotokis, in an act of political sagacity, resigned in the hope of regaining power when his successor failed to cope with the same national problems.

King George summoned Demetrios Rallis, the most likely candidate to form a new government.[53] Rallis expressed his willingness to form a new ministry provided he had a free hand to dissolve the *Boule*. The monarch replied that a dissolution at that time was impossible due to complications resulting from probable joint elections in Crete and the arrival of Cretan deputies in Athens. The wary politician rejoined that it would be impossible for him to accomplish anything positive without the support of the Chamber. The king, in turn, pointed out that Rallis could govern without the Chamber for four months and that there were constitutional means of postponing the opening of the session for six weeks and then dissolving it. The new *Boule* would not meet until March 1910, and the Cretan question would, it was hoped, be resolved by then. Rallis asked for two days to consider the offer, but three days passed and he still had not arrived at a decision.[54]

As an outspoken opposition leader, Rallis had presented a reform program which contested the privileges of the Royal Family. Among his main points he advocated: the abolition of the post of army commander-in-chief held by the crown prince; the retirement of the other princes from the military commands held by them; strict economy in the administration including the abolition of diplomatic posts at the rank of minister; immediate application of Prince Constantine's 1904 program of military reorganization with other necessary measures calculated to boost the army's strength to 180,000; the ministries of war and marine to be in the hands of experts instead of civilians; the direction of foreign affairs to be abandoned by the crown and assumed by the responsible governments. On 20 July, the king and Rallis arrived at a solution which, in light of Rallis's eventual political movements, indicated a retreat from some of his more anti-dynastic statements. George also agreed to allow Rallis to dissolve the *Boule* at any moment when it appeared publicly advantageous.[55]

The new prime minister immediately concerned himself with the Cretan imbroglio, seeking to establish better relations with Constantinople. Rallis assured Naby Bey, the Turkish minister in Athens, that he would pursue a friendly policy toward Turkey, prevent the passage of arms or bands into Ottoman territory, recall Greek army officers employed in Macedonian consulates, and seek an easing of tension over Crete. On 26 July, as they had promised, the four protecting powers withdrew the remainder of their troops from Crete amid general rejoicing by the Greek population. But three days after these detachments departed, the impulsive islanders raised the Greek flag at Suda Bay where the Cretan and Turkish flags had previously flown. Popular demonstrations in Constantinople pushed the Turkish government into war-like preparations. On 6 August, the Porte demanded Rallis put in writing the Greek government's disapproval of Cretan agitation and disavow any future ambitions for annexation. If they did not receive a favorable reply in a reasonable time, the Turks threatened to withdraw their minister from Athens. After consultations with the powers, Rallis submitted a reply on 9 August which emphasized that since Crete was the responsibility of the powers, the Greek government could only conform to their decision. He added that Greece would continue to maintain a correct attitude and that not a single Greek officer remained at that moment on Turkish territory since those in Crete had left the Greek army.[56]

Dissatisfied, the Turks declared a boycott of Greek goods in Turkish ports and prepared to send their fleet toward Crete. They presented another note to the Greeks on 13 August which complained of Greek officers in disguise in Macedonia, although admitting that Greece had little involvement with the Cretan question, which concerned only Turkey and the powers. The Porte still required a more satisfactory answer than the first communication of 9 August. Regarding this message as an ultimatum, the Greek prime minister appealed to the powers to prevent war. In the meantime, the powers sought to persuade the Cretan Executive Committee to lower the Greek flag at Canea. The committee, anticipating the consequences of popular opposition, resigned on 15 August, and was replaced by a new Executive Committee of three distinguished lawyers. Three days later, Rallis, after extensive consultation with the powers, handed the Turkish minister a note reiterating that Greece would conform in all points to the decision of the four powers and would refrain from any encouragement of agitation on Crete. That same day 250 marines, representing the four powers, landed in an orderly atmosphere at Canea and cut down the controversial flagstaff. Twenty-two soldiers, commanded by a French lieutenant, stayed to maintain order until 1 September. In a note, also on the same day, the powers pointed out to Constantinople that it had no right to address itself directly to Athens on the Cretan question; and before any *casus belli* should arise over Macedonia, the six powers must be notified of Turkish grievances. The Turks responded positively and on 27 August accepted the Greek reply.[57] For the first time in weeks, Greco-Turkish tensions eased.

The Cretan problem thus dominated the first weeks of the Rallis administration. The diplomatic haggling among Constantinople, Athens and the powers filled the headlines of the daily press, for the moment pushing aside rumors of military conspiracy. Outside of the diplomatic field, Rallis made no deliberate effort to deal with the nation's internal problems. In the mode of Greek politics, the Rallis party, long out of power, became involved in exploiting the fruits of office and dividing the spoils. Having agitated public opinion with tirades against the crown prince and his brothers in the army, the new prime minister failed to take any action and did not provide a substitute policy.[58] Opposition rhetoric aside, the responsibilities of leadership tempered Rallis's approach. No doubt, he was also affected by his pact with King George on the issues to be dealt with first.

Although the Military League and Rallis concurred on the need to eliminate the princes from the high command, the prime minister made no immediate effort to negotiate with the army officers. Nor did he publicly divert attention toward the conspirators. These officers were, as all Greeks, overly concerned with the outcome of the Cretan issue, and they waited patiently. As fierce patriots, these soldiers endured the diplomatic jousts with Turkey and the powers, but they could not tolerate Rallis's open confession that Greek officers operated clandestinely in Macedonia and that they would all be withdrawn. Such statements humiliated these chauvinists, many of whom had exposed themselves to the dangers and rigors of the Macedonian campaigns.[59]

As July ended, rumors again began to circulate in the Greek capital about activities of the Military League and secret meetings. Conflicting reports in the various newspapers clouded the situation for the average citizen.[60] Anonymously-authored articles in *Chronos,* mouthpiece of the Military League, helped to clarify some of the organization's objectives. Essentially, the officers desired not a change in personnel, but in the system and its moral framework to benefit the nation and armed forces. Parliamentary politics, they believed, should strive for general national reforms and should not be restricted solely to military problems. In the end the people, the army and the navy should teach patriotism and must insist upon reform from their leaders. The princes had every right to serve in the armed forces, but they should not have the automatic privilege of command positions without first having proved

61

their abilities. If the government resisted these proposed attempts at improving Greece, the officers would use more direct methods.[61]

Both the general staff and the government sought to curb the officers' movement before it consolidated power. An examining board was convened to investigate the large meeting held on the evening of 8 July at the home of Lieutenant Hatzemichalis. This board, consisting of officers loyal to the crown prince, resolved to cashier twelve of the most active officers in the Military League. The general staff intended to make an example of these men for their disloyal and antidisciplinary activities. In still another attempt to dismantle the Military League, the general staff authorized the transfer of some active officers to remote areas of Greece.[62]

Characteristic of the Greek political process, Rallis felt no compulsion to honor his earlier reform proposals. Rallis's government, without a parliamentary majority and with no early prospect of elections, already operated from a position of weakness. Even though some of his earlier reform statements coincided with several of the Military League's publicized demands, Rallis apparently did not wish to dilute his influence further by yielding to coercion from an extraparliamentary source. The prime minister instead joined forces with the main object of his earlier criticism, Crown Prince Constantine. Moreover, evidence exists indicating that artillery Captain Gouvelis and naval Lieutenant Constantine Typaldos met with John Rallis, the son of the party leader. The two officers requested the young politician to relay to his father the Military League's concern for building up the armed forces and the desire to recommend certain officers for the ministries of war and marine. The new prime minister replied that he would not involve himself with the conspiratorial plots of military units.[63] Judging, however, from the simplistic measures taken to snuff out the League, Rallis obviously underestimated its potential.

As news of the Military League's objectives spread, backing for its activities came from several quarters. The leadership of the various trade guilds in Athens agreed to align with the officers. The noncommissioned officers, holding many grievances with the army's high command, also threw their support behind the dissidents. George Karaïskakis, as head of the Noncommissioned Officers League, addressed a letter to the Greek people on 20 August. Entitling it "The Judgment Day Has Arrived," Karaïskakis called on the people to respond to radical leadership to rectify years of misery under bad politicians. Several university students and recent graduates, gathering in July to air their views, became the nucleus of the "University Union." This association grew to include over 150 members who spoke out strongly for immediate reform. They published their attitudes in the Athenian press, compared notes with others from the ranks of the discontented, and expressed their explicit support for the Military League.[64]

With stories circulating of further meetings by the officers, the newspapers publicized accounts on 22 and 23 August of King George's intention to abdicate. Reportedly, the king in conversation with members of his personal staff had expressed his displeasure with the chaotic internal situation and with Greece's foreign policy position, especially with respect to Crete. The monarch was highly dissatisfied with demands for the resignation of his sons from their command positions in the army. He also tired of criticism of his noninterference in party politics. By itself the activity of the officers did not push him to abdicate; however, the agitated military in combination with the growing discontent of the trade guilds, merchants and noncommissioned officers indicated considerable popular opposition. Originally, the king had contemplated abdication in favor of his eldest son, Constantine, but with the feeling in the army against the princes, he thought of leaving the country with his entire family. Such a contingency also eliminated Constantine's nineteen-year-old son, Prince George, occasionally mentioned by court critics as a possible successor.[65]

Rallis endeavored to obtain a disavowal of the king's remarks, originally relayed to him by one of George's aides-decamp, but the published denial amounted to no more than that the statements had been made public without authorization. *Chronos* called the comments a deliberate attempt by the court to scare the people into a more disciplined state and also stressed the foolhardiness of any abdication. Greece was obligated by its constitution to maintain a constitutional monarchy under the Glücksburg dynasty. This article, printed in the Military League's official newspaper, sought to assuage

suspicion of the movement's anti-dynastic nature. Most journalistic sources of opinion deprecated the idea of abdication
and cited the immense debt which the country owed to George.
Nonetheless, the tone of the press was not uniformly respectful.
When ships from the British Mediterranean Fleet arrived at
Piraeus on 24 August on one of their regular visits, rumors
circulated that the king had asked for their protection.[66]

The reports of possible abdication and the already acknowledged sterility of party politics directed attention to the
alternatives presented by the Military League. There was,
however, considerable vagueness about what measures the
officers would take. Newspaper accounts penetrated some of
this haziness during the latter part of August. *Chronos* on 20
August mentioned that the Military League wished the immediate summoning of the Chamber of Deputies to act upon a
program it would submit to the Rallis administration. Among
other proposals, the officers would ask for radical reform in all
branches of the army and navy, and the resignation of the
princes from their command positions. A later article emphasized that the reasonableness of the officers' demands would
make it difficult for the government to refuse. If the monarch
responded prudently by accepting the proposed reform program, he would gain, *Chronos* claimed, the wholehearted
support and respect of the nation. Too many officers—an
estimated 1,268 in the army and 132 in the navy—had committed themselves to Greece's rebirth. The time for action seemed
imminent. Some newspapers spoke of a definitive scheme
whereby the officers planned to seize the palace, ministries,
and important public buildings if the government rejected
their demands.[67]

The prime minister, attempting to divert attention from the
would-be military reformers, asserted that he and his ministers
were drafting "radical reforms." In an apparent effort to
secure the support of the provinces, he called for the formation
of a ministry of agriculture to insure increasing prosperity for
peasants. With his government's new policies, he also foresaw
an army of 150,000 men through a greatly revamped training
program. An apprehensive Rallis delivered frequent public
statements minimizing the significance of the officers' movement, claiming that only one-tenth of the officers in Athens
were involved and that the people would not back it. In spite of

his outward calm, the prime minister arranged for the temporary transfer of two hundred gendarmes from the countryside into the capital.[68]

Occasional unsubstantiated statements leaked concerning division within the Military League. Reportedly, most of the higher ranking officers on the administrative committee and Colonel Zorbas advocated more conservative goals and methods, seeking a pacific route for implementation of the League's program. The larger body of younger officers favored more extensive change and more radical tactics, if necessary. This second group, according to rumors, also held the support of the noncommissioned officers.[69]

Rallis, in a maneuver which belied his confident public demeanor, contacted the administrative committee in an attempt to negotiate a settlement of the League's grievances. In setting up guidelines for such discussions, the administrative committee encountered opposition from younger officers who demanded exoneration of the twelve officers cashiered earlier by the Examining Board. The committee preferred to postpone this matter until the more pertinent questions of the League's memorandum were discussed with the government. The more conservative officers did not wish to provoke a reactionary attitude from Rallis and the general staff with extreme demands at the outset.[70]

The prime minister, clumsily attempting to exploit the rifts within the League, succeeded only in bringing the factions together. On 26 August he ordered the arrest of twelve officers, supposedly among the most active within the Military League. The authorities were able to arrest only two from the list, Captains Sarros and Tambakopoulos, while the other ten hid in scattered sanctuaries around Athens. A tense atmosphere loomed over Athens as the pace of events quickened. When Rallis informed the Director of Police that the government might request armed backing against the officers, the director refused to commit his forces. Furious at the director's response, Rallis immediately dismissed him and selected a replacement. To forestall the possible spread of revolutionary ideas, the government ordered the cancellation of "Our Athens," a play which criticized corrupt political practices within the nation. That same evening of 26 August, the Rallis ministry held a meeting, the purpose of which was not disclosed. Afterwards

Rallis notified the League's administrative committee of his willingness to negotiate. The committee answered that this would be difficult considering the government's latest action against the twelve officers.[71]

The officers held extensive meetings during the evening of 26 August, and on the following morning *Chronos* ran the headline: "The officers will probably act today." Rallis attempted to counter a military show of force by acquiring the king's signature on a proclamation to reconvene the Chamber of Deputies on 13 September. The prime minister also informed the Military League that he would welcome a group of officers to discuss its memorandum of demands.[72] Whether Rallis could accomplish anything positive without a majority in parliament was questionable unless the armed forces put its weight behind his administration. Such a relationship was unpalatable for the individualistic prime minister, who had already backed himself into defending the crown prince, his focus of personal criticism for so many years.

The junior officers continued to insist that a prime concern of the administrative committee should be exoneration of the cashiered officers and release of the two captains arrested one day earlier. The extremist elements resolved to arrange an escape of Captains Sarros and Tambakopoulos. Lieutenant Pangalos successfully engineered their flight from the guardhouse during the sweltering siesta period of 27 August. Rallis, outraged over this incident, reverted to recalcitrance. When a three man committee of Captains Gouvelis, Phikioris and Hatzekyriakos arrived at the prime minister's house in the early evening with the memorandum of demands, he refused to see them on the grounds that Hatzekyriakos was one of the ten officers who eluded capture the day before.[73]

This abrupt repudiation by Rallis alienated the generally moderate leadership of the Military League, which now leaned with the younger officers toward more forceful methods. Thus this latter group was not unhappy with Rallis's refusal to negotiate. The administrative committee resolved upon a demonstration of military strength that evening by the Athenian garrison on Goudhi hill, located in a suburb of Athens. The irresolute prime minister, reevaluating his earlier refusal not to speak with the officers, sent a note to Colonel Zorbas, requesting the start of serious deliberations. But members of the Military League, now united, refused to accept this last-minute gesture.[74]

The Military League's Demonstration of Strength at Goudhi

Under a bright moon the garrisons of Athens, summoned by their officers to save the nation, marched toward the outskirts of the city. In the early morning hours of 28 August, officers and troops bivouacked on Goudhi hill, two miles southeast of the city, surrounding themselves with a cordon of sentries which allowed only military supporters and a few select civilians to approach. The armed troops also manned twelve pieces of mountain artillery; they had not been able to carry off the field guns owing to a lack of horses. An estimate of the men participating places the figure at 446 officers of the army and navy, 2,546 soldiers, sailors and noncommissioned officers, 135 civilian supporters and University Union members and 67 gendarmes. The Military League threatened to march on the capital by twelve o'clock if its demands were not met.[75]

The outstanding case of resistance that evening occurred when Lieutenant Colonel Leondros Metaxas attempted to stop his cavalry regiment from Kiphissia in its march toward Goudhi. Having slept in Athens that evening, Metaxas, on hearing of the movements of the military in the Athens area, rushed to meet his regiment. He tried in vain to persuade his men to turn back, then several officers of the League interceded, capturing Metaxas. Men seized for resisting efforts of the rebellious officers included Captains Kalinskis and Roïdes, Lieutenants Demopoulos, K. Vassos, and N. Vassos, and Warrant Officer Stavropoulos. Still other officers and men remained in town and took no part in the activities. A detachment of sailors brought into town by Rallis declared in favor of the movement but on the command of its leaders remained in the city to help insure order. The garrison of Chalkis, forty miles to the northeast, began a march toward the capital but received orders from Colonel Zorbas to return to its quarters.[76]

Rallis found himself with virtually no power left to assert the will of the government.[77] He telephoned the king at Tatoi, the monarch's summer palace fifteen miles outside Athens, and submitted his resignation, which George refused to accept.

In many respects, Rallis, of all Greek political leaders, would have been the ideal person to enact the reformist proposals of the officers. Circumstances, however, had compelled Rallis to shift to political positions in which he could not accept requests for reform, many of which he had originally sponsored. He now refused demands being imposed upon him by an extra-parliamentary force.

In the early daylight hours the prime minister dispatched Spyros Merkouris, mayor of Athens, and Major Papoulas, personnel officer for the ministry of war, as emissaries to Goudhi to establish the grounds on which settlement might be reached. Details of what transpired are not available, yet it appears that Zorbas insisted again on outright acceptance of the League program. Theodore Pangalos later maintained that Rallis would have been willing at this stage to concede the demands in their entirety, but that Merkouris and Papoulas wrongly considered the officers to be in a compromising mood. Encouraged by this false information and hoping to secure his bargaining position, Rallis returned his two messengers to Goudhi with the communication that he approved of only part of the demands; he also added some of his own proposals. Zorbas tersely declined the offer.[78]

During the morning King George arrived in Athens. He conferred with Rallis and, concluding that the Military League controlled the situation, accepted Rallis's resignation. The monarch then decided to summon Kyriakoulis Mavromichalis, Theodore Delegiannis's successor and leader of the third party in the *Boule*. Some rumors held that Mavromichalis was in collusion with the rebellious officers, but the king had no alternative for a new prime minister.[79] Mavromichalis for some time apparently knew of the League's inner workings through his son-in-law, Lieutenant Argyropoulos, who was a member. The officers on Goudhi then agreed to extend the time limit for acceptance of their ultimatum beyond the noon hour. The new appointee quickly forwarded a letter to Colonel Zorbas requesting terms.[80] The League's administrative committee replied with the following demands: (1) a written acknowledgement of receipt and acceptance by the government of the memorandum of reforms; (2) a formal assurance that the Chamber would not be dissolved; (3) amnesty for all those who had taken part in the movement and reinstatement of the noncommissioned officers who were dismissed from service for insubordination three months before; (4) the dismissal from the army of Lieutenant Colonel Metaxas, Captain Kalinskis and the other officers who had actively opposed the movement.[81]

Mavromichalis accepted these conditions and at 9:00 p.m. went to be sworn in with the members of his ministry. The new prime minister assumed this position for the first time, although in the past he had held the portfolios for minister of interior, war and marine.[82] Mavromichalis, also handling the ministry for foreign affairs, was not regarded as a man of great intelligence or strength of character. His name, however, reminded constituents of his family's heroic deeds during the 1821 Revolution and he maintained a large following in the southern Peloponnese. Alexander Romas, his minister of justice and brother-in-law, had been an active member in the Chamber and several times its president, but it was reported that he had lately spent some months in a mental asylum for a nervous disorder. Athanasios Evtaxias, the minister of finance, had studied in Germany, headed the ministry of instruction twice, and was known for some advanced ideas on the administration of finances. Mavromichalis picked Nicholas Triantaphyllakos for minister of interior and Panagiotis Zaïmis, brother of the Cretan high commissioner, for minister of instruction. The prime minister offered the ministry of war to Colonel Zorbas who, despite the urgings of many League members, declined, not wishing to profit personally from rebellion. The Military League submitted nominations for the ministers of war and marine, which Mavromichalis decided on three days later. The final choices, Lieutenant Colonel Leonidas Lapathiotis and Captain John Damianos, were not members of the League but obviously picked by the officers for their sympathetic views.[83]

The Military League, seemingly satisfied with the sequence of events, ordered the troops back to their barracks at 6:00 a.m. on 29 August, approximately twenty-eight hours after they began their occupation of Goudhi. Zorbas in his published memoirs remarked retrospectively that if the government had acted quickly and efficiently, the rebellious gathering on Goudhi might have been suppressed.[84] The government, crown prince and senior officers failed to assert their control over the infantry in Athens, the Kiphissia cavalry regiment, naval detachments and field artillery. Instead, the Military League rapidly assumed the initiative, nullifying any retaliatory action by opposition forces. And when one considers that the government's authority over the army had collapsed in the preceding weeks, it appears unlikely, Zorbas's contention notwithstanding, that the Rallis ministry could have commandeered the loyalty of a seditious military.

By 1909 the Greeks had been governed in a constitutional fashion by politicians for nearly forty-five years, a significant fact for one basic reason: this was the longest single period in modern Greek history in which the military would not actively intervene in politics. Adherence to the parliamentary process did not mean, however, that the Greek people were content with their political leaders. Dissatisfaction increased in the years after the 1897 defeat, but particularly in the months after the Young Turk Revolt of 1908. Civilians and personnel of the armed forces both shared many grievances, and when officers chose to take on a political function under the aegis of the Military League, they confronted a vulnerable regime which had to yield to pressure.

The citizens of Athens witnessed these momentous developments of 28 August 1909 as quiet but interested bystanders. On a superficial level one might comment that the religious feast-day, the Dormition of the Virgin Mary (15 August, old-style), which closed the shops, offices and schools, had distracted the attention of the Athenians. Perhaps more appropriately it can be stated that the people assumed they could only be observers and not participants in these important proceedings.

III
September 1909—December 1909
DIFFICULTIES FOR THE
POLITICIZED MILITARY

In peaceful, bloodless fashion the Military League asserted its will, toppling one government and playing a significant role in the formation of a successor. It effectively employed threats of violence to insure acceptance of reformist demands contained in a carefully prepared memorandum. The Mavromichalis ministry promised to push this program through the Chamber of Deputies, which was to convene on 13 September. There was, of course, no guarantee that real national reform would result from the methods employed by the Military League. Moreover, the function of the officers in future political developments remained undetermined. The officers learned in the succeeding weeks that legislation alone did not result in effective change. Original widespread support for the intervention of the Military League gradually lessened as the public realized that sincere patriotic desire, by itself, could not institute a national rebirth.

The Military League Memorandum
A summary of the memorandum addressed "To the King, the Government, and the Greek People" clarifies much about the scope and nature of the Military League. (The complete text of the memorandum appears in the Appendix.) After a general statement of concern for the sad state of the nation, it offered expressions of personal respect for the king and denied any anti-dynastic intentions. The League, however, voiced the opinion that the princes should hold no responsible employment in the army or navy but might retain their ranks. The ministers of war and marine had to be career officers and nonpolitical. It was proposed that reforms should aim at

71

achieving: respect for religion; honest administration; speedy and impartial justice; education directed at the practical needs of the country and national military requirements; security of life, honor and property; reorganization of finances to provide relief from heavy taxation for the people and for the suppression of waste and jobbery; urgent military measures directed at the immediate buildup of the army and navy. The officers insisted on an immediate convocation of the Chamber "because the dissolution and the holding of new elections demand a considerable time, and the slightest loss of time under present conditions is a wrong to the nation." And if these demands were not seriously considered, the Military League "is firmly determined to recoil before no obstacle, whencesoever it may arise, tending to frustrate the patriotic object aimed at."[1]

Essentially, the memorandum contained little the average Greek could oppose. In fact, much of the document's contents echoed the proposed measures of Alexander Zaïmis in his November 1898 "Memorandum to His Majesty the King." The uninformed observer of events in Greece might then wonder why such extreme measures had been utilized. The parliamentary process, however, had faltered to the point where it did not respond to popular and strategic demands. This situation intensified until the lower-ranking officers strengthened their position sufficiently to intervene in the political process. The Military League labeled itself spokesman for the people, maintaining that the politicians had failed to pursue effectively the aspirations of the populace and the armed forces. The government, unpopular and with minimal support, found that it could not defend its legally constituted position.

The proposals for general reform were couched in moralistic, nonspecific terms—idealistic objectives, hard to achieve in any developing nation, much more so in a society with no tradition of political discipline. The memorandum also emphasized that the League: ". . . judges itself incompetent to enter into details which are outside its special sphere and which the government is competent to define in accord with the parliament of the nation. . . ." Naturally considering itself more qualified to speak out on military issues, the League drafted specific proposals for the rapid strengthening and reorganization of the armed forces and included demands for intensified training programs for more recruits and the retraining of reserves, the acquisition of necessary supplies and a new cruiser of 10,000 tons, plus repairs to the three old battleships. Having demanded the elimination of the crown prince's exalted position in the army, the rebellious officers sought a foreign staff to reorganize the military administration. The language of the memorandum, in general, stressed the sincere conviction of the officers that inefficient parliamentary practices had sapped the strength of Greece, as was reflected in the weakness of the nation's military arm.

Response of the Dynasty

The late August events affected most immediately the monarchy. Although the Military League did not seek "the abolition of the dynasty or the replacement of the King," it did order the elimination of any administrative or command responsibilities in the military for the princes—a direct blow to the dynasty's prestige. The British minister in Athens, Sir Francis Elliot, conducted several long conversations during these troubled days with King George, who revealed his dismay and depression. The monarch criticized Demetrios Rallis for having talked too much and done too little and for failing to understand the gravity of the situation until it was too late. He claimed that the crown prince misread the signs of an oncoming crisis and, had Constantine acted, he could have secured the artillery and munitions in time to ward off the mutineers. The agitated ruler conceded that his son had committed grave errors in attempting to administer the army "with German brutality, and using opprobrious and offensive language when reprimanding officers in public; in showing himself too little in the men's barracks, and having no direct intercourse with them." The crown prince did not mix enough with the officers, limiting his social invitations to a small clique and "jealousy . . . was a prominent trait in the Greek character."[2]

The king harbored strong feelings against the rebellious officers who threatened the dignity of his position. George adamantly refused to be "the puppet of a military junta," and if he were pressed into such a relationship, he was ready to leave the country. As a precaution, the king had put all his papers in a safe place, and made all the preparations to leave

73

at a moment's notice. He offered a hypothetical situation where he could feel compelled to abdicate: if the Chamber declined to pass the measures the Military League insisted upon, and if the officers came to him with a proposal for a decree suspending the constitution and to govern for a term of years by Royal decree, he would refuse to sign. Elliot learned from the king that: "... several times during the past years ... a coup d'état [had] been proposed to him, but he had always answered that he had sworn to defend the Constitution and had never allowed one line of it to be infringed." The disturbed ruler, however, neither disclosed the possibility of abdication to Mavromichalis nor even hinted at it publicly, since he thought the ministry might be frightened into resigning. George foresaw many problems in his future relations with Mavromichalis, whom he regarded as "timid, ignorant, and incapable." In the king's estimation, Nicholas Triantaphyllakos, the minister of interior, was the most worthy member of the cabinet and through him he would seek to obtain the release of Colonel Metaxas and the other officers loyal to him.[3]

Succumbing to pressure and acknowledging the impossibility of associating on old terms with their fellow officers, Crown Prince Constantine and Prince Nicholas applied on 1 September to be placed *en disponibilité,* a status already held by Prince George, the former Cretan High Commissioner. Princes Andrew and Christopher and Prince George of Sparta (Constantine's eldest son) applied for a *congé d'instruction* of three years. It was felt that the young Prince George should leave the country for the time being, in order that he should not be set up as an opposition candidate for the throne of his grandfather or father.[4]

In a rearrangement of the army's hierarchy by the government, General Constantine Smolenskis succeeded Constantine as commander-in-chief until a decision could be reached on whether to abolish the post. Colonel Constantine Sapountzakis retained direction of the general staff. Long a trusted adviser of the crown prince, Sapountzakis was believed to have been the League's choice for minister of war but had declined. Although there was no real evidence, the king suspected the colonel of being the chief organizer of the military movement while professing loyalty to Constantine; the latter supposedly failed to heed earlier warnings about the questionable loyalty of Sapountzakis.[5]

Foreign Reaction

The intervention of the Greek military into politics stimulated a negative response among the various European governments. Typical was the reaction of England's King Edward VII, then vacationing in Austria, who expressed great anxiety. He requested that the ships of the British Mediterranean Fleet moored on a visit off Athens not be withdrawn so that "the King of Greece may rely on them for full moral support." He also wished to dissuade King George from any idea of abdicating, but "in the event of the Greek Royal Family being reduced to a position of danger, he trusts that every assistance that can reasonably be given will be given by the British squadron." George welcomed the offer and asked for an extended stay of the fleet until the *Boule* began its sessions.[6] The German government also showed concern, but not to the degree of the British. Berlin did not feel that the military wished to oust the dynasty, but if the officers should push political matters to the extreme, King George should make a show of yielding, "as his abdication would be nothing less than a disaster both for Greece and all the Powers interested in the Balkan Peninsula." Relaying information received from Sir Edward Grey, the German minister in London wrote his government of an important consideration probably inhibiting George's thoughts of abdication: he would not receive an annual income of 12,000 pounds from Greece's guaranteeing powers, which had been assured him upon assuming the throne in 1863, if he abdicated voluntarily.[7] Vienna recognized that the prevailing confusion made it difficult to predict the future course of events.[8] The *Quai d'Orsay* ordered the French minister in Athens to exercise all possible influence on the Greek cabinet and politicians not to push King George into a situation where he might abdicate.[9] The European press, in general, was critical, reporting the military rebellion as reactionary, calling it a poor imitation of the Young Turk Revolt with no hope for success, and emphasizing that an abdication by King George would prove disastrous not only for Greece but for all of Europe.[10]

The heavily chauvinistic overtones of the Military League's program naturally worried Constantinople. The Turks expressed apprehension over the sections of the memorandum dealing with the rapid buildup of the armed forces and with the League's menacingly worded appeal: " . . . that some measures of military concentration, capable of coping with the situation, be taken immediately, of inevitable necessity." King George explicitly ordered Mavromichalis to declare to the representatives of the foreign powers, Turkey included, that his government would disregard the offensive passages of the memorandum and that no change would be made in the foreign policy of Greece. Privately, Mavromichalis assured Naby Bey, the Turkish minister, that no one could expect all points of the memorandum would be enacted and that the Chamber would have to decide upon them individually. In the meantime Mavromichalis would adhere to the Greco-Turkish agreements on Macedonia and Crete arrived at by his predecessors. Naby Bey stressed that Ottoman authorities would not tolerate any revival of Greek propaganda in Macedonia. The prime minister repeated his pledge for no change in foreign policy during his first reception for all diplomatic representatives on September 2.[11]

The First Weeks

After its initial success the Military League worked at consolidating its position. Most provincial garrisons telegraphed messages of support to the capital.[12] A few higher ranking officers who saw their underlings wrest control of the armed forces applied for the retired lists. The large majority of the senior and junior officers from units throughout the country either asked to become members of the League or agreed to back the program. The clique of Crown Prince Constantine disintegrated, as several members, among them Colonel Sapountzakis, worked closely with the usurpers. Other officers, whose loyalty to the League's policies remained questionable, found themselves transferred to insignificant posts in the provinces. In order to curb the threat of possible counterrevolt, men loyal to the Military League soon commanded the most important positions.[13] Ranking army officers in the League organized a section within the army under the presidency of Colonel Zorbas, while Captain John Miaoulis headed the naval group. Similar sections were formed among the junior officers who signed membership lists.[14]

The Greeks had progressively demonstrated their dissatisfaction with prevailing conditions but had been unable to articulate their grievances forcefully enough for their parliamentary representatives to initiate vital reform. Thus the public was psychologically prepared for drastic measures, and it warmly received news of the military's intervention in politics. The press and many citizens characterized the officers for their "revolution" as heroes of the day and saviors of the nation. Athenian newspapers printed telegrams of support from many towns, trade guilds and societies throughout Greece in the weeks following 28 August. The Hellenismos Society, an influential patriotic organization, and the newly formed Military-Civilian League, among other groups, praised in glowing terms the goals of the rebellious officers. George Karaïskakis founded and headed the Political League to spread the gospel of reform-nationalism and often colored his speeches with anti-dynastic statements. Prior to the demonstration at Goudhi most Athenian editors had advocated drastic action and change in one form or another; after the momentous trek up the hill by the army, all newspapers expressed a pro-Military League editorial policy with *Chronos* the most outspoken oracle. There is evidence, however, that some of this journalistic backing was coerced from reluctant editors threatened by the League, an explanation for the plethora of propagandistic editorials.[15]

Despite these early indications of public acceptance, the Military League soon encountered reaction from important quarters. On 7 September, Crown Prince Constantine left Athens on a four-to-six-week trip to Germany. Constantine's train from the capital stopped shortly at Aighion where an enthusiastic crowd greeted him. Later that day at Patras, Greece's third largest city, a cheering throng besieged the train, yelling "Do not leave us!" The prince, visibly moved by the hearty reception, addressed the gathering from a hotel balcony, thanking the people for their warmth and confidence in his person and in the monarchy, even though "a section of the community had not behaved well." He went on to reiterate a former statement by his father that the king and people were one, with the interests of the one the interests of the other. The

77

following day en route to Brindisi on an Austrian steamer, Constantine disembarked at Corfu where the Corfiotes reenacted the previous day's events. The mayor of the town and George Theotokis, the most prominent citizen-politician of the island, accompanied Constantine, who was encouraged by the warm greeting. He refused, however, to receive the officers on Corfu on the grounds that they had signed a protocol advocating the abolition of the post of commander-in-chief.[16]

The British consul in Patras described the reception as "entirely spontaneous."[17] *Chronos* insisted, to the contrary, that members of the old political parties rigged the demonstrations. Other newspapers, probably under pressure from the League, agreed, adding that careless statements from members of the court might create problems. The persons of the king and crown prince were beloved in Greece, but this did not affect the measures demanded by the officers whose movement was not directed against the dynasty. The provinces, it seemed, did not support the Military League to the degree which the capital did. Immune to pressure from the Athenian garrisons, several provincial newspapers came out directly against the Military League. An enraged editor from Pyrgos in the western Peloponnese protested against the tyranny of "Sultan Zorbas," an officer who failed to perform honorably in the 1897 war.[18]

The administrative committee of the League, rankling at such expressions of opposition, called upon the Mavromichalis government to stop receptions for the prince in the provinces. It also demanded that Constantine be prevented from returning to Greece before the Chamber decided on the question of the commander-in-chief position. Mavromichalis yielded. The situation then cooled with the receipt of a telegram from Brindisi containing news that the prince's aide-de-camp had informed an Italian newspaper correspondent of Constantine's decision not to return to Greece until issues personally concerning him had been resolved.[19] Such a statement by Constantine did not, in actuality, imply another setback for his position. It had been determined by advisers prior to his departure from Athens that "in case the King should abdicate and the crown devolves, by unopposed succession or by public wish, upon his eldest son, the Prince's absence would give him a more advantageous position for treating with the government and people of Greece."[20]

Originally, the *Boule* was scheduled to reconvene on 13 September for deliberation of the League's program. Mavromichalis considered the period too short to prepare the legislative bills and requested a postponement. The officers, anxious for quick legislative action, opposed him. Pressured by the officers, the prime minister nearly gave way, until Nicholas Triantaphyllakos, his minister of interior, threatened to resign on this issue. Whether from fear of ministerial crisis or in the spirit of compromise, the officers eventually agreed to 3 October for the opening session. The king, desiring an early end to the crisis, at first balked at a delay but later expressed pleasure at the stiff stance taken by the government toward the officers.[21]

In its attempt to maintain the appearance of legality, the Military League experienced difficulties and steered an unsteady course. The Mavromichalis ministry represented a distinct minority in the *Boule*. George Theotokis, the leader of the majority party, had remained politically silent since 28 August, although his presence with Constantine during his sojourn on Corfu implied opposition to the League. Then, on 11 September, *Athenai* published an interview with the Corfiote politician that created a sensation throughout Greece. In bitter terms, Theotokis spoke of the impossibility of holding a Chamber session with the nation in the throes of revolution. He regarded the officers' program impracticable because of planned economies in very vital areas and overambitious military reforms. Theotokis opposed dissolution of the office of commander-in-chief, a law which he had originally sponsored. And how could he favor pardoning the noncommissioned officers whom he had personally punished? If the revolutionaries had any program, they should carry it out, but without the Chamber. As the preferred alternative, he proposed that elections be held. Furthermore, he believed the best course for his party to follow was abstention from the Chamber.[22]

The former prime minister's comments created a new crisis. Whether his position resulted from party interests or from what he considered national concern, he threatened to create the unconstitutional conditions which the Military League had tried to avert. Without the Theotokis party in the Chamber a quorum was impossible, the proposed legislation could not pass, and a quick return to a normal political atmosphere would become increasingly difficult. Some observers feared that the officers might consider Theotokis's stubbornness the perfect excuse to establish a military dictatorship, thus igniting civil war.[23] *Chronos* dutifully expressed displeasure with Theotokis, labeling him "The Judas of Corfu" and "The Cholera of Hellenism"; "Let him go and may he not return."[24]

Theotokis apparently aired his views without consulting party colleagues, many of whom publicly disagreed. On learning of this disunity, the former prime minister announced he would resign the party leadership. On the heels of these intraparty complications, five party members, three ex-ministers and two deputies, traveled to Corfu. Impressing upon Theotokis the possible consequences of a complete boycott of the *Boule,* the politicians reached a compromise. Theotokis withdrew his resignation and allowed party members to attend Chamber sessions and to vote according to conscience, although he would not himself take any part in the proceedings.[25]

Evidence of Public Approval

Anti-League elements had neither the strength nor the unity to resist effectively. The Military League appeared to control the army and navy, without whose support the monarchy could not assert its opposition. More significantly, hundreds of telegrams and letters streaming into the Military League office in downtown Athens indicated widespread acceptance of its methods and goals. The parties and their leaders, under constant fire in the Athenian press for past corruption, could not garner enough backing from their traditional constituencies to contest the officers. Most politicians considered a conciliatory policy the sensible route out of the crisis; to resist actively, many feared, might lead to civil strife. Theotokis's antagonistic attitude thus found little encouragement from his fellow politicians, who cowered at the thought of boldly challenging their military foes.

Influential citizens outside party politics worked together in Athens to demonstrate support for the events of 28 August before the Chamber of Deputies convened. Leaders of the Athenian trade guilds solicited the cooperation of many associations, clubs and societies throughout the capital and Piraeus for a large public meeting on 27 September. Newspapers publicized the event, describing it as urgent for the execution of national rebirth. Many of the organizers, fearful of a possible violent reaction from supporters of the parties, sought protection from the Military League. Colonel Zorbas attempted to dismiss these apprehensions, but assured the planners that groups of three to four officers would be distributed throughout the crowd to insure order.[26]

The public meeting, conducted under a bright, late afternoon sun, assumed tremendous proportions. Stores and offices closed for the afternoon both in the capital and Piraeus. Estimates for the throng, the largest in the memory of experienced onlookers, ranged from 60,000 the 110,000. The numerous trade guilds, associations and student groups marched in a long procession with their banners to the Champ de Mars where a large gathering, including clergy, had assembled.[27] Here, Papaphotis, chairman of the trade-guild presidents, delivered the only speech, administered in the form of resolutions. His remarks struck out against the abuses of good government by the nation's legal representatives and expressed approval of the Military League's actions. The old politicians had changed into ". . . a self-seeking oligarchy, supplanting the law by its own will and allying itself with an untaxed plutocracy, while the people groan under the burden of most unjust taxes, that is, the taxation of objects of consumption, without enjoying in exchange security for their life, honor, or property." The resolutions sanctioned the military's program condemning jobbery, usury, the abuses of the civil service, judiciary, prison administration and sought relief of the Greek workers' hard lot. They urged the strengthening of the military and naval forces "upon which the national future depended" and for this goal advocated important economies and tax reforms. The resolutions carried by acclamation, after which one of the priests, Papadrakos, identified as a former guerrilla band leader in Macedonia, administered an oath to the large gathering:

> We swear by our holy faith that we decide from today to serve our country as her devoted and faithful soldiers, above all personal interests, far from all party views, and to fall if need be in behalf of the regeneration and the greatness of our country.[28]

After demanding the support of the king in one of the resolutions, the crowd dispersed in an orderly fashion for the

Palace Square. There the masses, densely packed, waited as a deputation of the meeting requested and received admittance into the king's chamber. George cordially accepted the resolutions, believing them an expression of the people's desires. He promised to forward the proposals to the government and hoped it would give them serious consideration by voting appropriate laws. The king emphasized that the interests of the nation were also the interests of the throne; he would never throw obstacles in the way of any measures which might contribute to the advancement of the nation. He added this policy would constantly be followed ". . . always within the limits of the constitution which I have sworn to maintain." The deputation withdrew and Papaphotis, its leader, informed the crowd that the king had graciously accepted the resolutions. After many shouts for his appearance, George stepped onto the palace balcony where he was greeted with prolonged cheering and cries of "We want an army and a navy!" and "Long live the king!" His remarks were brief:

> I congratulate you in that you proceed in so law-abiding a manner to the manifestation of your feelings and desires. I have just heard what your wishes are from your deputation, to whom I have replied. I am convinced that the Chamber of your representatives and the government which I invest with my absolute confidence will wish to vote the laws you demand. I now beg of you to disperse quietly, crying with your king: 'Long live the nation! Long live the people! Long live the constitution!'[29]

The people's cries of "Resurrection!" and "Greece has been resurrected!" combined with those of "Long live the king!" to present a picture of national unity. *Chronos* covered its front page the following day with "Long live the rebirth" and a large Greek flag. Summary accounts and editorials stated the huge public meeting revealed that the revolution was national and popular, not solely military as some critics had misrepresented. Many villages and towns in the provinces held similar demonstrations of support on 27 September and the days following.[30] For the Military League the crowd's tumultuous endorsement erased much of the bitterness left by the receptions for the crown prince in Patras and Corfu. The officers, however, did not gain complete satisfaction from the monarch's remarks about working "within the limits of the constitution." The king thus implied the possibility of unconstitutional rule at their hands, whereas they had publicized their desire to pursue a peaceful, legal course for reform. Moreover, the Military League wished the monarch would either deny or affirm rumors of abdication, since they posed a potential obstacle to the execution of the reform program.[31]

The results of the large public assemblage might have been entirely different had not King George reversed an earlier decision to leave Athens. The press and participants had assumed it a matter of course that the king would receive the deputation of the meeting. But he harbored too many grievances against the League and held that, although ostensibly organized by the guilds, the demonstration was instigated by the League. The troubled ruler did not publicize his resolve but Gabrielle Deville, the French minister in Athens, learned of it from a member of the king's suite. Realizing Britain's minister, Sir Francis Elliot, had "the privilege of access to His Majesty," Deville relayed his fears to his English colleague that a boycott by George would be a disastrous mistake. Elliot concurred and visited the ruler on the afternoon of 25 September at his Tatoi summer palace where he underscored the effect on the king's personal position if the crowd did not see him; its disappointment could easily be turned into dangerous resentment. The king reluctantly yielded to the argument, reiterating the unfortunate nature of the situation. He stressed that there were limited prospects for shaking off the pressure of the Military League. When the present Chamber lost its authority early in 1910, it was almost certain that the people would keep on electing the same politicians imbued with all the corrupt traditions. Elliot countered by saying that having begun a policy of concession, the monarch must continue for the time being until the Military League should dissolve itself. The king finally conceded the diplomat's reasoning for receiving the deputation, but only as long as he could agree with the resolutions and would not be required to deliver a long address to the crowd from the balcony—the king recognized his oratorical limitations. Indeed, his eloquent speech, if short, had averted a potential crisis.[32]

Possible Alternatives for the League and King

Despite the Military League's resolve to utilize parliamentary institutions for pushing through its program, there was division among members over the possible success of this

83

tactic. A group of younger and more militant officers advocated, in case the Mavromichalis ministry faltered, the establishment of a *cabinet d'affaires* to execute the orders of the League's administrative committee. If this approach failed, these more radical officers would then advocate a military dictatorship. After the *Boule* sessions finally began, rumors and press reports circulated around Athens about the imminence of a strong-armed dictatorship.[33] Publicly, the Military League maintained the position of its moderate majority that all necessary programs could be passed by the deputies. The threat of coercive methods and tighter control over activities in the Chamber worked against any semblance of true parliamentary democracy since most deputies reluctantly responded to the officers' demands, fearing, if they did not, an even worse situation. The officers were interested in new laws while the politicians desired the early dissolution of the Military League.

Official statements by the rebels stressed that their movement was not meant to be anti-dynastic. King George, spilling out his feelings to an English diplomat, called it a "great piece of humbug" to pretend the events of 28 August were not anti-dynastic.[34] The League had acted against officers suspected of loyalty to him by transferring them to insignificant provincial posts and called for the dismissal of the princes from their military positions. Moreover, Lieutenant Colonel Metaxas and the other officers who attempted to halt the march to Goudhi faced stiff penalties.[35] Several newspapers, strongly supporting the "revolution," ran a series of editorials critical of the Royal Family.[36] Insults also came from unexpected sources. Demetrios Rallis, in an impudent manner, divulged and exaggerated the contents of an agreement between him and the king prior to his acceptance of the prime ministership in mid-July. These disclosures in the Athenian daily, *Athenai,* angered the monarch, who complained: "How can I ever again have confidence in a man who professes to reveal to the press his confidential communications with me, and not only that, but distorts them into a tissue of lies?"[37]

Although George considered the great powers partially responsible for his debacle because of their lack of support in the Cretan question, he still depended on them as a source of strength. He requested and received an extension for the anchoring of British ships in Phaleron harbor. Even though diplomatic dispatches for this period do not reveal such an intention, it was generally thought in Greek circles that any of the powers represented on the International Finance Commission would have the right to land armed forces for the protection of the IFC and of the National Bank of Greece which held some of its funds. The two British ships in the harbor symbolized for many observers in the capital the omnipresence of great power interests.[38]

The fear of the powers intervening, whether for their interests in the IFC, the Eastern Question, or the Greek dynasty, no doubt held in check some of the more impulsive Greek officers who sought elimination of all obstacles to their reform program. Yet such reservations did not inhibit the Military League from investigating possible candidates for the Greek throne in case circumstances led to the voluntary or forced abdication of George. The League's policy endorsed royalism over republicanism, but it did not, as the Glücksburg monarch rightly assumed, wholeheartedly support his dynasty. Informed people in Athens learned that the League had contacted Italy's Duke of Abruzzi regarding his possible candidature but had received a negative reply. An alternative scheme, backed by those officers opposed to the succession of Crown Prince Constantine, supported Prince George under the regency of his mother, the Crown Princess Sophie. Aware of these plans, the king did not fear the proposed alternatives to his rule since he thought the Duke of Abruzzi would not accept the offer and knew Crown Princess Sophie had lost much of her former popularity. Furthermore, no Regent was necessary since Prince George had attained his majority, although his education had not prepared him for kingship at so early an age. The French particularly feared abdication since Sophie, as Kaiser Wilhelm's sister, represented the Prussian branch of the Greek Royal Family, and might throw some influence towards one of Wilhelm's sons to fill a vacant throne.[39]

Problems in the Chamber of Deputies

Incertitude characterized the Greek scene in which no group with influence felt entirely confident about the future. The political system of Greece which had survived many crises under the Constitution of 1864 and its monarch, George, now faced its stiffest test. The Military League hoped to achieve the political and spiritual regeneration of the nation within the existing governmental framework, believing that the politicians would have to sacrifice temporarily some freedom of political initiative. The responsibilities of national leadership were naturally difficult, but especially for the military, unversed in the intricacies of law-making, the national economy and foreign policy problems. During the remaining months of 1909, the officers exercised their coercive potential, generally within moderate limits, to ensure enactment of their reform program. Yet no one group—sections of the armed forces, the dynasty, politicians and citizenry—was to be completely satisfied with this approach of the officers and the resulting legislation.

The Chamber of Deputies first convened on 3 October. Besides the unusually large number of deputies present, an even greater gathering of officers attended the opening session. Nondeputies were allowed on the floor of the *Boule* on such occasions, and approximately 120 officers found seats while a similar number scattered themselves throughout the Chamber. Their presence emphasized the unusual circumstances in which the parliamentary session was to be conducted. Customary procedural matters dominated the first day, and the Chamber immediately adjourned until 7 October. During the interim Theotokis reversed his earlier position by returning to Athens and informing the officers that he intended to support the government in the Chamber. At first this changed attitude startled many observers, but soon rumors circulated that Theotokis's life had been threatened if he did not attend parliamentary meetings.[40]

When the Chamber reconvened, the first order of business was the election of its president. The question arose whether this officer would be chosen from the small governmental party or from the Theotokist majority. Colonel Theodore Lymbritis, deputy from Tyrnavo and the first to speak, surprised the session by commenting on the excellent motives of the officers but stigmatizing their action as illegal; the leaders of the revolt themselves acknowledged this fact by demanding an amnesty from the king. No speaker followed this daring outburst and in the ensuing vote, Alexander Romas, the government's minister of justice, won the presidency easily. The next two sittings dealt with the elections of the vice president, other officers of the Chamber and the formation of different committees. On 9 October the king presided over a cabinet council held at the palace at which he approved the program Mavromichalis proposed to the deputies.[41]

A week passed casually with nothing but ordinary business. The Athenian rumor-mill churned out reports of the officers' dissatisfaction with this dilatory progress and the possibility of their closing the *Boule*. Whether valid or not, this hearsay had an apparent effect. No deputy followed the precedent of Colonel Lymbritis, and on 11 October the prime minister addressed the deputies, announcing the composition of his government and explaining his programs. After preliminary remarks about the difficult conditions under which he assumed office, he stressed the need of strictest economies, reforms, and improvement of all branches of the public service, civil and military. Such objectives required much hard work and each minister would present his individual program before the Chamber. Under existing pressures for quick action, Mavromichalis continued, the Chamber regulations had to be amended. The government had no desire to restrict freedom of speech, but the *Boule* had to remember that of its two chief duties, criticism and legislation, the latter must not be sacrificed for the former. Indeed, party differences should be cast aside for the sake of patriotism and common national goals.[42]

Nicholas Triantaphyllakos, the minister of interior, followed by introducing his amendments to the Chamber regulations, designed to prevent the customary waste of time by questions, obstructions and motions for counting of the house. Afterwards Leonidas Lapathiotis, the minister of war, outlined in general terms his military reorganization plans. He referred specifically to three bills which he considered the most urgent and probably the most sensitive. The first amended the 1887 law relating to the service and promotion of officers. Henceforward, the princes were to be denied command slots and service in the post of commander-in-chief, established in 1900. Divisional commanders under the authority of the minister of war would share the responsibilities formerly held by the commander-in-chief. The third bill asked for disbandment of the general staff set up in 1904.[43]

The Military League and the trade guilds voiced their discontent with the desultory progress of business through statements to the newspapers, the former implying that ser-

87

ious measures might be taken if the Chamber did not mend its ways. On 13 October, Athanasios Evtaxias, the finance minister, spoke for over five hours on the government's economic projects, revealing much hard work for such a short period of preparation. After an elaborate introduction stressing the patriotic reasons for drastic changes in the financial practices of the nation, he itemized his reforms which aimed at a greatly expanded outlay in military expenditures. He suggested economies of close to 3,000,000 drachmas by cutting government grants for refugees from Bulgaria and approximately another 7,000,000 from a severe reduction of expenses incurred by different administrative departments. Evtaxias recommended new sources of revenue and reforms of old sources to yield an estimated 10,000,000 drachmas. For the purposes of serving a loan for military and naval preparations, the finance minister urged increased taxes on alcohol and tobacco and new duties on certain raw materials. The lengthy speech concluded with a plea for national unity and for a departure from the half-hearted programs of the past which had helped create the country's humiliating conditions.[44]

Subsequent sessions revealed an air of uncertainty as to the future course of legislative proceedings. On 14 October, the minister of war presented bills concerning the staff service, the engagement of foreign officers as instructors and advisers, and the reestablishment of the postponed 1904 army organization laws. After the first reading of the bills excluding the princes from the army, the government received sharp criticism from two unexpected sources. Both Constantine Koumoundouros and Stephen Dragoumis had opposed the original passage of the bill naming the crown prince as commander-in-chief and had, on several occasions, been labeled as antidynastic, charges they had not denied. Now, however, both spoke out openly against the government's bill, claiming it unconstitutional. They proposed amendments applying to the princes the ordinary regulations regarding appointment and promotion in the army but which would still bar them from sensitive high-command positions. Mavromichalis countered with a cautious statement about his government's commitment to resolve the critical situation and the importance of this bill, adding that he and his followers had rendered the nation a great service by accepting office and preventing anarchy and bloodshed. Action on this controversial draft law, the two other military bills, and several other government proposals was then postponed for second readings.[45]

The increased legislative activity did not completely satisfy the Military League which frowned upon the independence of Koumoundouros and Dragoumis. In their test of the League's strength, however, the two idealistic politicians failed to muster even token support. The League's principal journal, *Chronos,* responded the following day with a scathing editorial stating: "The demands of the revolution are not subject to the criticism of private individuals." The newspaper repeated the claim that the army imposed the revolution, and the people officially sanctioned it with the 27 September demonstration. The League informed Mavromichalis that if the crucial bills did not pass without amendment, government and Chamber would be swept away. Operating under this threat which the prime minister relayed to Theotokis, the Chamber quickly approved the military legislation. Later it was learned that troops waited in their barracks to receive prearranged orders in case the *Boule* did not act satisfactorily. On 16 October the deputies considered several other bills with virtually no discussion. Confusion concerning the whims of the officers again revealed itself as they informed the government that while the deputies were not allowed to discuss the three military bills, they were expected to debate the other laws. If they did not, such an act would be considered antithetical to the spirit of the national movement.[46]

The parliamentary majority led by Theotokis, despite its opposition, had acknowledged the existence of the powerful forces lurking in the barracks. Most Theotokist deputies agreed to cooperate with the government by passing the prepared measures, but were not anxious to enter into debate which could only be a simple formality. Moreover, strong resistance to specific bills seemed out of the question. Demetrios Rallis had denounced the military leaders as seditious but thought the movement might still be used for cleaning up the problems of the state. He suggested the formation of a *cabinet d'affaires* under Colonel Zorbas, believing such a government would carry all the necessary measures so that the country could then witness the restoration of true parliamentary rule. Amidst all this muddle Mavromichalis attempt-

89

ed to maintain a certain degree of personal integrity while carrying out the League's program. He had the opportunity to complain to Zorbas of the extreme pressure under which his government was forced to work, and that if the officers were not satisfied, he would resign. In reply, Zorbas stated that basically he endorsed his leadership. Too much emphasis had been placed on *Chronos* articles written by some younger hotheads in the League without the sanction of the hierarchy. A moderate majority still prevailed over an extremist minority. And for a short period after mid-October, the tone of the *Chronos* editorials became milder.[47]

The king continued to yield. At first unwilling to confirm the courts-martial of Lieutenant Colonel Metaxas, Captain Kalinskis and the other officers loyal to him on 28 August, the king signed the documents at the request of the accused officers. George suffered a deep affront when the League pressed for the publication in the *Official Gazette* of the laws signed by him excluding the princes from military service. The king's sons had earlier resigned their positions, and he had signed the decrees, but the Military League wished to make it appear the princes had been forced out of the army rather than having left it of their own accord.[48]

The Typaldos Mutiny

To preserve their predominant role, the officers had to keep the opposition divided, retain popular support from the lower classes for their national goals and insure unity within the League. The officers had coped effectively with the first two conditions and with the third in the weeks following 28 August. But since its inception, the League accommodated two factions, radical and moderate. The latter prevailed until a small segment of the extremist element emerged to confront the League's leadership with its stiffest challenge to date.

During October, reports spread of discontent among younger naval officers. Led by Lieutenant Constantine Typaldos, one of the Military League's earliest and most energetic participants, this group claimed that the revolution had stalled, and that the desperately needed naval reforms were not forthcoming. It was also felt that senior officers, posing obstacles for any true reform programs, had to be removed from their positions of influence. Initially, Typaldos forwarded a letter to Captain John Damianos, the minister of marine, communicating these opinions and stressing the urgency of naval legislation.[49]

Increasing tension and tempers contributed to the confusion of subsequent events, reports of which frequently conflicted. Nevertheless, it seems apparent that Typaldos ran into opposition from several quarters that refused to accept the complete list of demands signed by fifty-four officers. The controversial letter called for the compulsory retirement of all senior officers—except for three captains—ostensibly for reasons of age and economies; in this manner, one rear admiral, seven captains, and twelve commanders would be affected. To reinforce their arguments, the letter provided detailed accounts of poor performances on the part of these ranking officers. In addition, there was a demand for the compulsory retirement of four other officers who did not cooperate with their colleagues during the demonstration at Goudhi. The document emphasized that the younger officers sought not to profit materially by filling these positions, which should remain vacant. In order to correct the glaring problems confronting the navy, a foreign mission had to be summoned as soon as possible to reorganize and retrain the sea forces. And if these demands were not accepted, the junior officers would refuse to serve their incompetent senior commanders.[50]

In an attempt to resolve these sensitive issues, Typaldos accompanied Colonel Zorbas on a visit to the minister of marine on 26 October. Damianos, unwilling to make a hasty decision, promised to reply within 24 hours. The following day Zorbas and Typaldos again met with Damianos in his hotel room, at which time the minister declared he could accept only some of the points and even those with certain modifications. Offering to resign if his proposals proved unsatisfactory, Damianos also implied that the entire government might follow his lead. Upon leaving the session, Typaldos, naturally dissatisfied with this response, was temporarily reassured by Zorbas who told him that perhaps the Mavromichalis ministry might have to fall and that, in the meantime, he should consider the choice of a new minister of marine. But while Zorbas appeared amenable to a change in government, cavalry Captain Epaminondas Zymbrakakis, in a street corner conversation with Typaldos, expressed his concern over such a turn of events.[51]

During the late afternoon of 28 October Typaldos addressed a meeting of the administrative committee. The lieutenant argued that because of the League's structure the interests of the navy had been largely disregarded while those of the army had been receiving greater attention. Furthermore, the possibility of war in the near future required the departure of incompetent officers from command positions. After some committee members remarked that the Mavromichalis government had responded quite well in most matters, Typaldos reemphasized the patriotic and nonpersonal objectives of the younger officers. In angry terms he blurted out that these officers might act to assert their position and to find a cooperative minister of marine, even if "he is a wooden statue." Tempers cooled only when Zorbas intervened and commissioned the naval lieutenant to confer with his colleagues on a candidate for minister of marine.[52]

It appears that the administrative committee members then persuaded Zorbas that Typaldos's supporters had to be checked in their potentially seditious activities.[53] As Typaldos conversed with some of his colleagues at a centrally located Athenian restaurant, reports reached him that opponents to their cause were organizing units of the navy to resist them. The aroused Typaldos decided to head with his followers to Salamis. The island with its arsenal soon fell under their control along with four destroyers, several torpedo boats, and the nearby island of Leros which stored the powder magazines. Concurrently the police and gendarmerie, supplied with arrest warrants, sought to capture the conspirators. At this point, Typaldos had with him about twenty-five officers, including midshipmen, and about 200 enlisted men. Typaldos persuaded the latter that he was only pushing forward the reform movement of the revolution by the demonstration.[54]

The Military League determined on decisive measures to suppress this mutiny. It ordered three battleships anchored in the Bay of Salamis, three miles from the arsenal, to prevent Typaldos's destroyers from leaving. Most of the Athenian garrison positioned itself from Old Phaleron to Eleusis in order to prevent any communications between the rebellious sailors and the shore. Nauplion and Chalkis sent reinforcements. At 4:30 in the afternoon of 29 October, two of the destroyers controlled by Typaldos tried to pass the strait between the arsenal and the mainland. A short engagement of about twenty minutes with the battleships followed, after which the destroyers retreated to their original positions. A second attempt by the destroyers about 9:30 in the evening also failed.[55]

After the first attack many of the sailors on the destroyers deserted Typaldos upon realizing they were involved in combat with their own comrades. With the second attack the leading mutineers recognized their mission could not achieve its goals. Fourteen officers surrendered to the authorities, but nine, including Typaldos, changed into civilian clothes, slipped onto shore near Eleusis and fled into the mountains. Both sides, in what can hardly be considered a violent confrontation, tried to limit casualties and damage to the fleet. Even so, six men were killed and several wounded. Two of the destroyers and one battleship suffered minor damage in this "new battle of Salamis."[56]

By 3 November, the authorities captured Lieutenant Typaldos and the remainder of his confederates. The firmness of the Military League and the government and the demonstrations of loyalty by the greater number of naval officers and sailors served to stifle the mutiny before it could make any advances. The issue of the mutiny, however, did not die out immediately. *Chronos* published an official League statement which declared:

> The Military League saw nothing but lunacy in these demands of [Typaldos], but they were convinced that other impulses, on the part of individuals, foreign to the army and navy, were exploiting this madness, and had contributed to his decision to attack the fleet and to mutiny.[57]

Some newspapers referred to Nicholas Stratos and Apostolos Alexandris, two Rallist deputies, for their part in spurring Typaldos to attempt to install a new government. Zorbas in his memoirs mentioned that during these eventful days "three politicians" and some newspaper editors sought the formation of a new government, "supposedly under the king, and the disbanding of the Military League." Typaldos, in turn, later stated that he had received a visit from Stratos, Alexandris, and John Tsirimokos. These three deputies complained about the faulty economic measures proposed by Evtaxias and the urgency for correcting the situation before too much time passed. They then suggested the formation of a party composed of the newer deputies in the Rallist and Theotokist parties who shared the League's reformist ideas. Zorbas, they went on, should become prime minister, retaining the present ministers of war and marine and securing the remaining ministers from the ranks of sympathetic deputies. Typaldos maintained that he relayed these proposals to Zorbas, who responded that involvement with deputies and parties should be avoided lest the officers expose themselves to trickery by politicians.[58]

When Stratos and Alexandris, the two incriminated deputies, questioned the validity of the journalistic accusations in the *Boule,* Mavromichalis claimed he could not waste the Chamber's time in passing judgment on every controversial newspaper editorial. Although the mutiny had been quickly suppressed, many observers expected the affair would become a sensitive issue in the *Boule.* The prime minister instead made a few summary comments, relegating the affair to the proper courts. Alexandris, when called upon, withdrew his interpellation, and the Chamber resumed discussion on proposed legislation. Evidence indicated that the Military League had exerted pressure to silence discussion. On 3 November Alexandris reportedly left Athens.[59] It can be conjectured that Alexandris and Stratos, as civilians, assumed a scapegoat role for the officers by being blamed in large part for accentuating divisions within the Military League.

The Mavromichalis ministry decided on a criminal court trial for the conspirators rather than a court-martial. They were to be charged with sedition, for which the death penalty was not proscribed in the ordinary penal code. Mavromichalis explained to the British minister in Athens the logic of this procedure. The military movements of 28 August had been declared a political offense because the demand for an amnesty acknowledged this point; it was therefore illogical to treat the Typaldos mutiny otherwise, it being an outcome of the August events. Also, before a military court composed of superior officers, the defendants could claim the judges were all prejudiced.[60]

94

The Military League, and along with it the Mavromichalis ministry, survived the mini-rebellion. Zorbas stated in his memoirs that the great majority of the League disapproved of the mutiny and that this occasion did not induce a change in the program of the revolution. Pangalos differed with the League's leader by emphasizing that Typaldos's sedition benefitted the general development of the revolution. He claimed that the prestige of the Military League and the cohesion of its members both increased. Pangalos implied, and diplomatic reports indicated, the presence of a considerable body of opinion in the army sympathetic to Typaldos's views. Consequently, a bill was introduced in the *Boule* similar to the navy's, reducing the age limit for army officers. Noncommissioned officers also applied pressure for repeal of the law which prevented officers rising from the ranks to achieve a grade higher than captain. The noncommissioned officers had provoked a crisis the previous May over a proposed law to prevent completely their promotion into the officer corps. Bearing this experience in mind and the danger of inciting the noncommissioned officers, Mavromichalis's ministry decided to reconsider this issue.[61]

Some Athenian circles spoke of the possible dissolution of the Military League when the present *Boule* session closed. Still other observers considered the dissension in the League between radicals and moderates as too great for effective, unified action.[62] To dispel rumors, *Chronos* on 4 November placed the following pronouncement from the Military League on its front page:

We are compelled to announce in the most categorical fashion that the Military League has not dissolved, nor is it going to dissolve, nor has any such discussion arisen among its members. Particularly now, agreement, unanimity, and accord prevail in the League, and since the great mission to which it owes its origin is still unfinished, it has neither considered dissolving, nor can it do so, as long as its whole national program is not realized.[63]

Boule Activities

Attracting much popular support during the days immediately following the march up to Goudhi, the Military League found it that much easier to force its program through the *Boule*. The emphasis upon reform and national regeneration sparked many Greeks who sensed that such a policy held

95

many potential benefits for them. Furthermore, no patriotic Greek could dispute the stress on strengthening Greece militarily.

Some optimistic politicians believed the Chamber of Deputies might finish its business in several weeks, apparently disregarding the constitutional stipulation that the session could not be prorogued within less than three months of its convocation. After his initial recalcitrance Theotokis and his parliamentary majority generally cooperated with the Mavromichalis cabinet in its legislative efforts. But the Rallis minority at times daringly posed obstacles.[64]

The military continued the facade of constitutional rule. The government presented a long list of legislative proposals during the first two weeks of November which indicated that the Chamber might be working longer than originally anticipated. Both the Austrian and British ministers reported to their respective governments of their inability to keep track of the large number of bills laid before the legislature, and the German minister referred to the quantity as perhaps approaching a *"Weltrekord."* The deputies seemed anxious to end the humiliating pressure from the military as soon as possible. With virtually no debate and near lightning speed the deputies pushed on to advanced stages and passage bills dealing with, among other issues, primary, secondary and university education, judicial reforms, amendments to the penal code and taxation of wines.[65]

An indicator of the longstanding, unhealthy state of Greek politics came with the introduction of a bill for electoral reform. This proposed legislation sought to reduce the number of prefectures from twenty-six to sixteen, thereby enlarging each district.[66] Of the numerous bills placed before the *Boule* in the hectic weeks of November, only this measure provoked heated debate. Many politicians pronounced vociferously against the proposal, mainly because their influence in the small constituencies would be eliminated. As local potentates in restricted electoral areas, they were able to secure their own election or that of their favorites. These deputies by practice sold their support to the cabinets in exchange for the power to control the local dispensation of governmental patronage. This reform thus struck where it hurt most.[67]

For a short period these deputies, previously silent on issues of national importance, but now driven by self-interest, toned down their opposition. But when the bill came up for a third and final reading, they increased their resistance. The Military League made it known that it sanctioned the bill, while the Mavromichalis cabinet stated that it regarded the vote as one of confidence. Theotokis supported the bill but could not guarantee that all his party members would back it. A parliamentary crisis appeared imminent, spurring the League into action. Four members of its administrative committee approached the prime minister and stressed the urgency of immediate passage without amendment as an essential part of the army's campaign to purge parliament of its self-serving representatives. The dissenting deputies received word of the League's determination, and reports spread of a possible blockade of the *Boule*. On 16 November the galleries of the Chamber filled with noncommissioned officers. Virtually all resistance melted. The reading carried without division. The following morning *Chronos* released a firm reiteration of the Military League to carry through its mission and to insist upon the passage of all laws considered indispensable for the reform not only of the military but also of the nation as a whole.[68]

Signs of Declining Popularity

The widespread wall of popular support for the Military League revealed signs of cracking in November. Various groups with regional and personal interests began to express antipathy to some of the new governmental measures. Public meetings were held at Kyparissia, Levadeia, Corfu, Larissa and other towns to protest the proposed abolition of local courts and courts of appeal for reasons of economy. Upon the intervention of the trade guilds, the government withdrew the plan to impose heavy penalties on those participating in strikes. Several educational bills directed at saving money had to be withdrawn because of the outspoken criticism of students and teachers. From the neighboring countryside approximately three thousand villagers and townspeople carrying olive branches and black flags converged on Volos to demonstrate against a proposed tax on olives. Local authorities summoned military assistance from Larissa while Athens ordered the arrest of mayors accompanying the demonstrators; the crowds dispersed without causing serious damage after their stormy gathering. The government also tried to pass an emigration bill to hold back the flow of Greeks leaving their homeland. One clause stipulated that Piraeus was to be the only port of departure. To protest the bill the populace of Patras, Greece's other large port, staged several noisy demonstrations during November.[69]

Its momentum cresting, the Military League seemed incapable of avoiding controversy. The officers sought now to push through a "purification" of the public services. *Chronos* launched this campaign with a blistering attack on 22 November against Panagis Kavvadias, the Inspector-General of Antiquities. The article accused him of poor administration and embezzlement of funds, implied that he favored the interests of the foreign archaeological schools over those of the Greek Archaeological Society, and demanded his immediate dismissal. Athenian academic groups, some politicians, and the heads of the foreign archaeological schools expressed dismay at what they felt to be unjustified attacks against the inspector-general. Some circles conjectured that the animosity of some of Kavvadias's colleagues and subordinates in the Archaeological Society had influenced the Military League. The League, realizing its error in involving the foreign archaeological schools in the condemnation of Kavvadias, retracted any implications that foreign interests had any role in the case. In spite of this reversal, representatives of the British, American, French, German, and Austrian archaeological schools protested to the prime minister the charge that their activities had injured Greek national interests. On 25 November Kavvadias suddenly departed Athens. Several reports claimed threats to his life, while a section of the Greek press interpreted his flight as an admission of guilt.[70]

On 23 November, the day after the first attack on Kavvadias, *Chronos* published in the column reserved for policy proclamations of the League, "The Need of Sincerity," a general statement on its "purification" program. The League did not reject the concept that only a revolution employing violence could really regenerate and reform Greece. It felt, however, that other means might be utilized to achieve similar ends. The article went on to attack the incompetence of many important members of Greece's diplomatic corps stationed in European capitals. The failure of these diplomats in Paris, Berlin, Vienna, and Rome to defend Greek interests had undermined national security and allowed the growth of anti-

Hellenic feeling in the countries to which they were accredited. Since Greece had long been forced to live on the charity of the powers, she needed able representatives to advance her interests abroad. Having brought out this aspect of a purge, the revolutionary officers promised to reveal in succeeding issues of *Chronos* the measures necessary for rendering healthy, one by one, various branches of the public service. These attacks would center also on companies, banks and corporations associated with state interests and which exercised "an immoral and disgraceful influence upon Greek society."[71]

Mavromichalis rejected these high-handed methods and summoned members of the League to his house for a discussion of tactics. The agitated prime minister emphasized the necessity of maintaining tranquillity and confidence in the political situation, particularly since very sensitive legislation, including the budget, was scheduled shortly for consideration by the deputies. If the League toned down its attacks, his government promised to pursue the program of purging the state apparatus of incompetent officials at a more appropriate time. Mavromichalis obviously succeeded in arriving at a compromise. *Chronos* did not, as threatened, embark upon a campaign against specific individuals in high public positions. But the officers did not drop the purification program completely, relegating dismissals for a later period.[72]

Controversy next hit the Church. The Holy Synod in Athens charged Ambrosios, Bishop of Larissa, with simony and other malpractices. The Bishop, popular with lay and clerical communities under his jurisdiction, defiantly refused to receive a bishop sent from Athens to investigate. Ambrosios, in turn, claimed the Church needed to be purged and threatened to make important disclosures. The military forces in Larissa and surrounding districts vigorously supported him. For a period it appeared the Military League might back Bishop Ambrosios, especially after he refused to travel to Athens at the request of the Holy Synod. The League did not intervene, however. Although newspapers regularly printed headlines on the squabble, the Holy Synod did not depose Ambrosios until the following February.[73]

Problems within the Military League

After the Typaldos embarrassment the Military League diligently attempted to maintain a public front of unity

99

through pressure on the *Boule* and articles in *Chronos*. Internal discord indicated, contrariwise, that various tensions were testing the League's leadership. Reports spread that naval officers protested their limited voice in policy making and, in fact, considered the formation of a separate Naval League. Legislation on age limits for naval officers proposed two exceptions, but naval officers objected. It was said that they then threatened a movement against the League along the lines of the Typaldos sedition. Members of the League conferred with the government, and the naval law passed on 23 November without the two exceptions. Relations between the navy and Military League continued to be strained until the latter agreed to accept three demands. The navy was to be consulted on purely naval questions such as the future of the fleet and also on important legislation of a political nature. Moreover, the large majority of naval officers opposed Typaldos and recognized that the more radical wing of the Military League supported him. They, therefore, asked that no pressure be placed on the civilian court trying Typaldos and his fellow conspirators. By all appearances, the League and navy arrived at an agreement when Colonel Zorbas was entertained at a luncheon on the flagship of the fleet on 2 December.[74]

Signs of dissatisfaction with the membership of the administrative committee increased in late November. Many younger members of the League thought the ranking officers dominated in decision making, and that they had taken too severe a stand towards the Typaldos group.[75] Most important, after Goudhi the League's membership had increased considerably so that the administrative committee, chosen before 28 August, did not represent fairly the expanded constituency.[76] Reacting to this discontent, Zorbas inquired of the various sections of the Military League whether the administrative committee retained their confidence. In general, the replies indicated widespread approval of the leader, Zorbas, but reservations about several officers. The colonel resolved to hold elections in late December for new committee members.[77]

Available sources provide little information about this election. Although new members were chosen, it was decided that officers of the old committee could join the renovated group in recognition of their valuable service. The reorganized body under Zorbas's chairmanship now included over twenty new members. Pangalos alone stated in his memoirs that a basic issue in the balloting centered around the calling of Eleftherios Venizelos from Crete for possible participation in Greek politics.[78]

The Budget

The grand and chauvinist ambitions of the Military League and its backers received partial satisfaction when the Chamber approved the purchase of an armored cruiser of 10,120 tons on 23 November. Considerable debate among naval officers preceded the final decision. Naval Lieutenant Tsoukalas maintained that the acquisition of a large cruiser would not be in the country's strategic interests. To counter this argument, Typaldos and his followers in their statements to the League administrative committee had accused Tsoukalas of serving French naval interests seeking sales in Greece. Finally, the large majority of officers, as in 1908 in their negative response to the proposals of Vice Admiral Fournier for a fleet of smaller craft, backed the acquisition of a large warship.[79]

The vessel, sold by the Orlando Company of Italy, cost 23,678,768.20 francs. The legacy of George Averoff, a wealthy Greek businessman in Egypt, provided for 7 million francs, while the rest of the sum was to be raised from a loan to be concluded by the state. The purchase of this armored cruiser, christened *Averoff,* represented one phase of the intended military and naval regeneration. All patriotic Greeks supported this ideal, but they also shared another—the unwillingness to succumb to heavier taxation.

Athanasios Evtaxias, the minister of finance, planned a series of economic measures to accommodate the buildup of defenses. Tentatively, he projected a minimum annual increase of 10,000,000 drachmas in the budget and the service charges for a loan of from 150 to 200 million francs, all to be directed for army and navy expenditures. The prospects of acquiring this loan from foreign sources appeared slim since Greece's international credit was still recovering from its earlier failures. The International Finance Commission (IFC) in Athens continued its close watch on the Greek economy and its ability to indemnify foreign lenders. It seemed highly unlikely the IFC would guarantee repayment of another large loan. Furthermore, the Greek government was in no position to pledge that budget surpluses could cover services for any loan.[80]

Preliminary negotiations with British, French, German, and Austrian financial interests failed to produce positive results. Alban Young, the British delegate on the IFC, predicted such rebuffs, basing his opinion on the "state of revolution" which existed in Greece and its accompanying complications for the economy:

> If any capitalists should be so ill-advised as to lend money to Greece for the maintenance of armaments disproportionate to her strength and resources, they should surely do so at their own risk and without moral claim on the consideration of the [IFC] in the performance of its sole duty—the execution of the law of control in the interests of the guaranteed debt and the holders of the old Greek stock alone.[81]

In a similar vein Sir Edward Grey noted: "We should discourage further loans to the Greek government as long as the money is wanted for armaments. If they get money to spend on armaments they will rush into war and bankruptcy."[82]

Although Evtaxias spoke publicly of a projected budget with surpluses, current revenues were falling below expectations. With the treasury virtually empty, pensioners and other creditors of the state could not be paid. Greek ministers abroad had not received their full monthly salary since August. Even the pay of the army, navy and governmental officials fell into arrears.[83]

The Constitution of 1864 stipulated that the budget had to be submitted to the *Boule* during the first two months of the session. Evtaxias, in passing this deadline, had to deal with stiff pressure from the Military League for innovative changes in the nation's financial structure. The minister of finance hoped to impress favorably opposing elements within the League. Controversy already centered around his proposal for the taxation of alcohol, upon whose revenues he intended to rely heavily for military reorganization. Some members of the League, however, wished to lower this proposed tax as a favor to the leaders of the Guild of Spirit Merchants whose efforts contributed to the success of the demonstration of 27 September. Reports indicated that the rival forces in Athens-Piraeus, those for and against the added tax, planned demonstrations for 8 December. The government took special military precautions to protect the *Boule,* but the protests did not occur. Publicly, the League assumed a neutral stance, waiting to see which way general opinion drifted since it did not wish to risk the loss of popularity.[84]

On 7 December, as a preliminary to the budget, the beleaguered Evtaxias submitted a series of financial measures to the *Boule.* They included bills altering the land tax upon large estates, terminating the land tax on vineyards, and establishing a vine-growers' defense fund. There were also draft laws imposing a consumption tax on acetylene, modifying certain classes of the customs tariffs, and taxing carts, carriages and automobiles. Another measure proposed the setting up of a sugar monopoly by which the government would buy out existing factories. On the following day the Military League, voicing its opinion in a *Chronos* editorial, stressed emphatically the necessity of passing these bills as soon as possible.[85]

With an intended tone of gravity Evtaxias finally presented his budget for 1910 on 16 December. He calculated revenues at 148,561,000 drachmas and expenses at 146,041,000 drachmas. These totals, nearly 25,000,000 drachmas more than in the previous budget, would result from economies and revenues each estimated at about 12,000,000 drachmas. This extra amount would accommodate the increased expenditures of the ministries of war and marine (947,000 and 2,548,000 drachmas, respectively), the interest of a new loan to cover the existing Treasury deficit of 39,000,000 drachmas, and charges for the anticipated large loan from foreign sources for military and naval purposes. The practice of taking extraordinary and supplementary credits against which no resources were designated had contributed much to the expanding deficit.[86] Evtaxias, to meet contingencies and extraordinary expenses, allocated another 7,000,000 drachmas.[87]

To the bills presented one week earlier, the finance minister added other proposals. He wished to reform the personnel of the customs house, hoping to recover around 3,000,000 drachmas previously lost to contraband. Other bills sought to establish a special customs police to impose more severe penalties on taxpayers in arrears and to eliminate clandestine consumption of tobacco without paying a tax. Evtaxias also proposed to decrease funds for the settlement of refugees from Macedonia and Bulgaria.[88]

The Lapathiotis Episode

Despite its much publicized mission, the League influenced little military legislation from mid-October to mid-December. One new law concerned the calling out of untrained reservists, while another sought to develop a program of preliminary military training for men before conscription. In late October the government authorized the engagement of Commandant Lacombe of the French army to direct and organize a School of Artillery in Athens. A bill passed the *Boule* in early November providing for the employment of a foreign lieutenant general or major general with a suitable staff to help reorganize the Greek army. Athens made arrangements to purchase 30 million Mannlicher-Schönauer cartridges to fill a nearly empty arsenal. Then in late November a minor crisis arose during the Chamber's discussion of the bill limiting the period of active duty for army officers of specific grades. One deputy proposed a special exception should be granted to General Smolenskis, the only real hero during the 1897 war. Colonel Leonidas Lapathiotis, the minister of war, insisted no alterations to the bill could be made, but confronted opposition from many deputies. The Military League, which had sanctioned the original bill, expressed support for the amendment. An angered Lapathiotis stalked out of the meeting, but Mavromichalis declared his government's support for the amended bill which finally passed. The minister of war then retracted an earlier threat to resign.[89]

The plucky colonel did not wait long to provoke a much more serious crisis. During the evening session of 20 December, Lapathiotis presented his military reform legislation in the Chamber of Deputies. Hardly beyond his introductory remarks, he stated that on assuming his position he had found only the ruins of an army, ruins which the Mavromichalis government was trying to rebuild. Nicholas Stratos, a deputy of the Rallis party wishing to make political capital of the situation, pointed to the Theotokist benches and accused them of responsibility for the events and aftermath of 28 August. At this juncture the insulted Theotokist deputies left the Chamber. Undaunted, the minister of war exclaimed: "I am completely indifferent to their departure. I shall address myself to the galleries; it is from the people that I receive my mandate." The galleries responded with loud applause which the president did not order stopped. Rallis, whose turn it was to protest, rebuked these insults to the Chamber. After a ten-minute adjournment, Rallis called for a count of deputies to establish if a quorum were present. The president did not take the required roll call but adjourned the meeting, declaring that there was no quorum.[90]

Theotokis had not been present at the turbulent session, but he quickly forwarded a message to Mavromichalis. The party leader complained about the offensive language and added that as long as Lapathiotis remained minister of war his deputies would stay away from the Chamber. Although the prime minister apologized for Lapathiotis's actions, Theotokis failed to be satisfied. Greek parliamentary life had frequently witnessed the exchange of abusive remarks, but the extraordinary political conditions did not allow for conventional procedures and attitudes. Mavromichalis depended upon the Theotokist majority for passage of legislation, and had to be careful not to alienate the base of his government's support.[91]

At a meeting of the government later that evening, Colonel Lapathiotis offered to resign and then to resume his position after the Chamber concluded its session, but the League's administrative committee, discussing the matter at length, ordered the cabinet not to yield. The following day the Theotokis party also announced its decision to stand firm. *Chronos,* that same morning of 21 December, published a lengthy statement which stressed the need to have the minister of war, as the drafter of the military bills, present these measures before the *Boule* and, by boycotting important sessions, the Theotokis party created irregular conditions which threatened the desires and will of the nation as well as Greece's military preparation.[92] The polarized positions reflected the lack of any compromising spirit.

The Military League again determined to assert its strength and received varying degrees of support from several quarters. On the evening of 22 December university students demonstrated before the League's offices, demanding establishment of a military dictatorship and expressing their willingness to shed blood in this cause. The navy backed the League's position but would withdraw if anything were done to bring on a military dictatorship. The artillery expressed a similar opinion. The trade guilds, too, spoke out against dictatorship, but assured Zorbas of their support in finding solutions to general problems which were also hurting business. The guild leaders then consulted with Theotokis, hoping that he might contribute a plan of compromise and adding that they had become tired of following the League's lead. George Karaïs-kakis, leader of the League of Noncommissioned Officers, stated that his group, for whom the Military League had done little, would resist establishment of a military dictatorship.[93]

Opposing the Military League from its onset into political prominence, King George had indicated his displeasure by absenting himself from Athens for many weeks at a time. In early December he returned for several days and was again in Athens during the height of the Lapathiotis controversy. On the afternoon of 21 December the monarch summoned Sir Francis Elliot. The English diplomat disagreed with George's contention that the war minister's action was deliberately designed to create a crisis in order to heal divisions within the League. The distraught king hypothesized that the League would allow Lapathiotis neither to apologize nor resign and that Theotokis would continue his boycott of the Chamber. If neither party yielded, the Mavromichalis cabinet would have to resign, and in such an instance, he would have no one left to form a parliamentary administration. The king then felt he would be faced with a League demand to govern without a *Boule* by means of Royal decrees proposed by the military. "Rather than consent to such a military dictatorship, he would leave the country as he now wished he had done at the beginning of the trouble," noted Elliot. The British envoy suggested the alternative of dissolving the Chamber and ordering a general election even in light of the possibility that the Cretans might send deputies. George responded pessimistically by stating that although no one in Greece desired war with Turkey, no government would have the courage to turn back the Cretan deputies dispatched to Athens.[94]

Although most Athenian newspapers pleaded for moderation and compromise, *Chronos* continued to publish inflammatory statements defending the League. In the meantime, Mavromichalis and Theotokis nearly arrived at a compromise, but when Theotokis realized the prime minister intended that Lapathiotis should reacquire his portfolio after passage of the bills, he withdrew his consent.[95]

In an attempt to break the crisis at another level, arrangements were made for Colonel Zorbas to confer with King George on the morning of 23 December. This meeting, the first between a Military League representative and monarch, had both parties carefully avoiding use of the word "League." When George asked the colonel whether the army retained confidence in him as king, Zorbas protested its allegiance and its determination to respect all constitutional forms. The monarch refused, however, to concede Zorbas's wish that he personally intervene to moderate Theotokis's stance towards Lapathiotis. Disappointed, Zorbas left the palace for a meeting with his colleagues, who asserted that in this test of strength they would permit neither the temporary nor permanent withdrawal of Lapathiotis. Returning to the palace in the afternoon, Zorbas declared he could not guarantee order during this critical period. He then asked the king to dismiss the Mavromichalis ministry and to form in its stead a *cabinet d'affaires*. The colonel offered a list from which the king might choose a ministry. Without looking at the roster, George retorted that if the army had confidence in him, he should be able to practice his prerogative of selecting his ministers without outside help. And if he had to designate a prime minister, his choice would be Alexander Zaïmis, the Cretan high commissioner. Zorbas conceded the likelihood of no real opposition to the king's preference.[96]

That evening the League's administrative committee conducted a turbulent meeting. Reports indicated that the extremist faction advocated forceful tactics, directing action against the Theotokist deputies and including the military occupation of public offices. Provincial regiments from Chalkis, Nauplion, and Patras had already been confined to their barracks to insure military control during any outstanding events. But suddenly, a unique solution to the Lapthiotis debate presented itself. Or as the German minister, Baron von Wangenheim, aptly telegraphed Berlin: "Crisis during the past night has found a characteristically Greek solution."[97]

It became known that the minister of war had acquired the king's signature several weeks earlier for a long list of officer promotions and that this information was currently at the printing presses ready for publication in the following day's *Official Gazette*. The promotions included the names of Colonel Zorbas, who was to attain the age limit for his rank on 1 January (old-style), and that of Colonel Lapathiotis. The committee quickly decided to censure this action of the minister of war which, if it were confirmed, would imply that the officers sought their self-aggrandizement in time of crisis. Several officers rushed to the printing presses in order to break up the type. Colonel Zorbas, in turn, interrupted a cabinet meeting at Mavromichalis's house and requested the removal of Lapathiotis from his position. The cabinet readily accepted this demand with little argument. Mavromichalis agreed to administer temporarily the duties of minister of war, and so the emergency passed.[98]

Once again assuming a strong, uncompromising position during the Lapathiotis incident, the Military League did not receive unqualified backing from its customary sources. The trade guilds, and even the artillery and navy voiced their antipathy to extreme measures such as the establishment of a military dictatorship. The League determined, however, that it could not display any weakness before parliamentary adversaries. Lapathiotis's list of promotions provided the outlet from the embarrassing situation. The Military League, by sacrificing the controversial minister of war, saved face and possibly enhanced its image for having refused the opportunity to benefit from promotion.

Some question has centered around whether Zorbas and the administrative committee had knowledge of these promotions prior to 23 December. Pangalos in his memoirs denied the revelation of General Leonidas Paraskevopoulos, then a major and personnel officer in the ministry of war, who claimed that Zorbas knew of the promotions. According to Paraskevopoulos, Zorbas and his cohorts held back until their position became untenable and then used the condemnation of Lapathiotis's measures, which compromised the spirit of reform, as an exit to avoid humiliation.[99] There is good reason to accept Paraskevopoulos's contention, since on 12 January (new-style), less than three weeks after the furor subsided, Zorbas and five other colonels quietly received the grade of major general in order to avert retirement according to the new law on mandatory age limits for ranks. The importance of such an advancement could not have escaped the League's leader in preceding weeks, despite his protestations of no knowledge regarding Lapathiotis's promotion list.

Military Pressure for More Legislation

Many critics hoped that the passing of the Lapathiotis incident might usher in normal parliamentary proceedings, so conspicuously lacking in Greece during recent months. Chamber meetings resumed on 25 December, but there remained considerable doubt whether the session would draw its business to a close before the Greek Christmas on 7 January (new-style). The Military League revealed its intentions quickly enough. On the morning of 1 January, Colonel Zorbas addressed similar letters to Mavromichalis, Theotokis and Rallis:

The Military League, looking to the fact that the sittings of the Chamber, as they are conducted, waste valuable time, and thus tend to frustrate the League's work of reform, requests you to use all your influence with your friends in order that they may vote, without selection or evasion, all the bills upon the order of the day submitted by the government, before any interruption of the labors of the Chamber. In the contrary event, the Military League proposes to proceed to extreme measures in order to carry out the program of reform, and throws upon you and upon the Chamber the responsibility before history and the country for the consequences of those decisions.[100]

That same afternoon Theotokis replied that he was astonished at the accusation of wasting time because in three months the Chamber had passed 163 bills. He went on to say that his party agreed from the *Boule's* first sittings to support the work of the government, and it continued to do so. The party leader stressed that he wished to see the government's program approved as quickly as possible and awaited information on which legislation was considered most essential. Rallis, in his reply, also referred to the Chamber's productivity and to the many amendments achieved through debate without which many laws would have been unworkable. The minority leader agreed to continue holding sessions even through the holidays until all necessary legislation passed.[101]

109

The following day, although a Sunday, found the Chamber acting on regular business. The prime minister promised to outline which laws his cabinet considered indispensable. That same morning *Chronos,* speaking for the League, listed twenty-seven areas for legislative action in addition to the necessary military and naval measures. They included public works, mining concessions, restriction of public appointments, emigration, municipal government, the Archaeological Society, university appointments, insurance companies, and education at the elementary and high-school level. Three days later on 5 January *Chronos* in another "Need of Sincerity" column claimed that although 169 laws had been approved in 82 days, only fifteen were of a progressive and reforming nature. The fulfillment of the revolution's goals required much more reform legislation.[102]

Pressures on the King

On 30 December John Konstantinides, a colonel in the infantry who was supported by the Military League, became the new minister of war. No sooner had this new minister assumed his duties than another ministerial crisis erupted. Nicholas Triantaphyllakos, the minister of interior, during a spirited debate concerning mining concessions, levelled some disguised sarcasm against the League. The interior minister had never been a favorite with the officers because of his close ties with the palace, and a demand for his dismissal quickly found its way to Mavromichalis. The prime minister called on Demetrios Stephanou, the king's private secretary, and stated that Triantaphyllakos was ready to resign. Mavromichalis concluded that his government could no longer endure these taunts from military overlords. Rather than see the minister of interior dismissed, he thought it best for his cabinet to resign as a unit. Stephanou replied that if this ministry departed, King George would be left without a government, without anyone to call on, and this would lead to chaos. With Mavromichalis continuing to complain about the intolerable situation, Stephanou telephoned King George at Tatoi who promised to drive to Athens the following morning.[103]

Stephanou next revealed his fears to Sir Francis Elliot. They both agreed that conditions had reached their most serious stage to date primarily because League actions appeared more

110

directly aimed against the king himself—Triantaphyllakos was the only minister in the confidence of George. Apparently the two interviews with the king had disappointed Zorbas. On the following morning of 2 January, however, the Chamber met without incident and without the interior minister. That afternoon it became known Triantaphyllakos had resigned, his responsibilities being assumed by Athanasios Evtaxias, the finance minister.[104] The League won its demand.

Still another point of concern during these hectic first days of January came with the Military League's renewed request for the immediate recall of the Greek ministers at Paris, Rome, Berlin, and Vienna. The king and prime minister conferred about this matter on 1 January. George, quite enraged, admitted that he had submitted all too often on internal questions, but in the sphere of foreign affairs the constitution outlined his extensive authority, and he would not retreat. The proposed measure, in his estimation, would damage Greek interests abroad and lower his dignity in the eyes of the foreign powers. Nonetheless, the monarch suggested that the government might work a superannuation bill through the *Boule* under which two of the four ministers would have to retire for reasons of age. The League, when informed of the proposal, agreed to compromise.[105]

The Palace Fire

Misfortune struck the Royal Family on 6 January, the Greek Christmas eve. At approximately 9:30 p.m., a fire broke out at the palace, noticed first from the nearby French legation. The French notified the proper officials who dispatched fire equipment and then telephoned King George at Tatoi. The king, queen, and Princes Andrew and Christopher hastened to Athens, arriving at 10:30. The fire in the meantime had spread very quickly in the center area of the large building.[106]

Concurrently, partygoers regaled at the British Legation where naval officers from H. M. S. *Cornwallis* and *Aboukir* of the Mediterranean Fleet anchored off Athens were among the guests. The two captains from the ships rushed with Sir Francis Elliot to the blaze and volunteered the resources of the two vessels. Greek authorities, struggling with their soldiers and sailors from the naval station at Salamis, accepted the English offer. Approximately one hour later, about 400 men

111

arrived from the British ships. Shortly afterwards, another 80 men appeared from the Russian ship, *Oleg,* also moored off Phaleron.[107]

Because of the poor water supply, a chronic Athenian problem, the fire raged out of control for several hours until the scattering of dirt and sand over neighboring sections of the palace contained the flames. The authorities simultaneously organized salvage operations. The king and his sons joined the lines of soldiers as they emptied the rooms adjoining the blazing sections of the Royal Archives, relics from the War of Independence, furniture and pictures. In the early hours of the morning the fire was finally placed under control, but not before the whole of the center block of the palace was burned out. Mavromichalis and King George sent Sir Francis Elliot official notes of warm thanks for the assistance of the British navy.[108]

The causes of the conflagration were unknown and remained unknown, but rumors quickly circulated. The English minister reported: ". . . in this country of wildly impossible stories I was not surprised to hear, before I had been one-half an hour on the spot, that it was being said that the king had the palace set alight in order to attract sympathy." A later story maintained that it was known beforehand the palace would be burned down on Christmas eve. The Austrian envoy, Baron von Braun, heard another version that the enemies of the king started the blaze at the order of the radical wing of the Military League.[109]

One particular incident created considerable commotion. The English landing parties that headed for the palace had brought with them a boat flag and twenty marines with their weapons. On arrival, this force stirred up a disturbance among the Greeks. Prince Andrew soon sent a message to Elliot asking that the armed men be withdrawn; the English immediately complied with this request and the marines returned to their ships. Several Athenian newspapers criticized this landing of troops and the "armed occupation of the palace" as wounding the dignity of the nation.[110] One blistering editorial aimed its wrath against Elliot:

> In the political crisis which Greece is traversing, the English minister, Mr. Elliot, shows excessive zeal, and maintains an atti-

tude which sensibly diminishes English influence in Greece and in the East, where Greece predominates. In every disorder, in every military or parliamentary proceeding, Mr. Elliot mixes, running about himself like an enquiring scout. Consequently, these proceedings of his scandalize the Greek people. . . .[111]

Athenai tried to counter these extreme positions with a statement of the minister of interior which claimed the British detachment landed to give a helping hand, carrying the flag as a distinguishing mark. Armed men accompanied the sailors since this was required by British regulations. Elliot stated that if the English sailors had been told to dismantle the wing of the palace, they would need to guard the property for which they would be responsible.[112]

At least two British ships had regularly anchored off Phaleron since late August. Rarely had Greek journals referred to their presence, but after the fire, *Esperini* and one other newspaper stated the obvious—that the British fleet was meant to protect the king.[113] In the months following the Military League's assumption of political influence, London periodically reviewed its policy of keeping two units of the Mediterranean fleet off Athens. The last dispatch by Elliot concerning this issue prior to the fire was similar to those which had preceded. Telegraphed on 11 December, it stated:

> I am unable to report any change in the situation so far as essential details are concerned, since the crisis began [i.e., 28 August]. At any moment disorder may arise out of the opposition to the government's proposals for raising revenues, and the next fortnight, during which the Budget is to be discussed in the Chamber, may be a critical period for the Government. I do not think there ever has been or ever will be, any danger to the person of His Majesty the King, but there is no doubt that His Majesty's ships materially contribute to the maintenance of order by their presence.[114]

In light of this information, Sir Edward Grey thought it desirable for the ships to remain some time longer, but he hoped that "circumstances may soon make it possible to remove them definitely." Elliot after the palace fire reaffirmed this policy when he wrote London: "The continued presence of the ships has exercised a restraining influence, and has therefore been galling to the forward spirits of the League."[115]

Over the span of four months the cloudiness of the Greek political scene was only slightly dispelled. The vague, idealistic goals of the Military League's original memorandum had unfortunate consequences. The officers had not precisely determined the approach to implement their objectives, and their tactics often appeared improvised. The leaders still adhered to a moderate course when it is recognized that they could have instituted a military dictatorship—although Greece might have lost a king and confronted pressures from the powers in such an instance. Nonetheless, citizens did not appreciate their methods which often consisted of armed threats to specific groups and individuals who did not agree with their programs. The court and politicians had been alienated from the first days of the military's intervention. Slowly, various elements of the population realized that the officers had not effectively assumed the role of national savior as expected.

Resurrection and regeneration of the country had not come about. A large number of bills had passed through the *Boule* but, although ambitious, many of the laws proved ill-digested. In spite of all this legislative activity executed at its orders, the Military League professed its dissatisfaction at the results which indicated a program rich in desire and generalities but poor in specific objectives. Even towards their particular interest, the military arm of the nation, the officers had failed to enact effective measures.

As 1909 drew to a close, critics questioned the ability of the armed forces to maintain its dominance. Mavromichalis endured the taunts and pressures of the League for many weeks, but it was hardly expected that he would continue to do so. The 1910 budget had not passed, the economy sputtered, and the much-needed loan had not materialized. Few citizens welcomed the prospect of new taxes so vital for a military buildup. Factions within the League expressed dismay at the lack of progressive action. Still, the appearances of constitutional rule had survived, and this fact, by itself, could help facilitate the restoration of normal parliamentary procedures.

January 1910—March 1910
WITHDRAWAL OF THE MILITARY
FROM POLITICS

The Military League rightly recognized that it had not exhausted alternatives. Disenchanted with their political performance, the officers were willing to solicit advice from a source in which they had confidence. They received no comfort from Greece's traditional leaders who sympathized little with their goals, or anticipated political and economic complications in pursuit of them. Recognizing this problem, the Military League looked beyond Greece's borders and summoned Eleftherios Venizelos from Crete. This politician redirected the uncertain course of the Military League's reputed "revolution" in the first weeks of 1910. Upon the counsel of Venizelos and after much deliberation, the officers decided to disband their extraparliamentary organization on the satisfaction of certain demands. For a newcomer to Greek politics, Venizelos was to play an auspicious role, and he was to assume an even more prominent position in succeeding years.

The Summoning of Venizelos and His Role as Adviser

Eleftherios Venizelos in late August 1909 came out in strong support of the Military League's intervention in politics. Writing anonymously a series of articles for *Keryx* in Chanea, Crete, he claimed that the people demanded a revolution, having grown tired of the selfish interests of the court, political factions and the plutocratic oligarchy which disregarded the general welfare of the nation. It was hoped that the political parties would exploit the opportunity to correct bad conditions which they helped create; the *Boule* session should be substantially a "National Assembly" convened for revolutionary goals in order to create the basis for a new Greece. He added that if

King George were not sincerely disposed to place himself at the head of this national restoration, he should allow Crown Prince Constantine to assume the throne.[1]

In early September, Venizelos suggested the possible use of stronger tactics by the Military League:

> If the political putrefaction, which produced excesses for decades, is so far advanced that it is not possible to accomplish the program of reconstruction through the present political parties and traditional means, the Military League, by using its material and moral strength in the service of its most noble purpose, should, if necessary, impose a temporary dictatorship for an interval strictly determined beforehand, in order to institute its program, summoning the people upon its cessation to the election of a National Assembly for the purpose of determining how the nation is to be governed in the future.[2]

On 15 October Captain John Phikioris, representing the administrative committee of the League, wrote to Lieutenant Xenophon Kontaratos on Crete. The latter was to contact Venizelos, inviting him to visit Athens so that the League could tap his opinions on Greek political conditions. The Cretan declined the trip but did record his impressions in a letter written on 24 October. As in his articles, he expressed wholehearted support for the League, but in planning the revolution he would have solicited the cooperation of politicians willing to pursue the same goals. In this manner the League could almost guarantee enthusiastic support if a dictatorship had to be instituted. Such a regime under good leadership would eliminate many old evils and execute the reform program. But the Military League had instead pursued a more moderate tack. Consequently, the reform program had to be less radical, less bold, providing fewer responsibilities for the leaders of the revolution. In any case, the revolution would be a success only if the army and navy were built up to proportions capable of fighting the Turks and finding a solution to the Cretan question. These minimum goals might elude them, though, if the old politicians provided stiff resistance.[3]

For several years reform-minded elements in Greece had regarded Eleftherios Venizelos highly and sought his leadership. His active participation in Cretan uprisings, his bold struggle against Prince George, and his generally progressive policies in the island's government helped mold the image of a liberal nationalist. It will be recalled that Lieutenant Theodore Pangalos and several confidants considered calling Venizelos from Crete to head their nascent protest movement during the autumn of 1908. And in the early summer of 1909 Kostes Hairopoulos, editor of *Chronos,* had conducted a "Panhellenic Plebiscite for Salvation," seeking to create public support for Venizelos to come to Athens. In a 1933 interview, Venizelos revealed that Nicholas Bouphides had visited him in Crete in the summer of 1908. Bouphides, expecting that Theotokis would step down from his party leadership, confidentially and tentatively extended this position to Venizelos. The Cretan politician declined, believing his presence on the island too important to leave. But he also added that he would never allow himself to be absorbed into the old parties; he would instead try to create a new political movement.[4]

In late December Venizelos's name began to dominate political conversations of the Military League. The administrative committee, evaluating the achievements and failures of the Mavromichalis ministry, concluded that it could not continue in office much longer. The main difficulty lay in finding a suitable replacement, since the prestige of the League was directly related to the performance of the cabinet. Zorbas refused to become prime minister and there would be no advantage in relying on any of the old politicians. Captain Constantine Sarros formally introduced the name of Venizelos on 29 December. The members of the committee well appreciated his political background, but realized that many people viewed him as anti-dynastic because of his campaign to oust Prince George as Cretan High Commissioner, and he would thus face much opposition from the old parties. But, for the absence of another appropriate candidate, the League's administrative committee resolved to ask Venizelos to form a new government.[5]

Captain Ioulianos Kontaratos of the administrative committee carried a letter of invitation to Crete.[6] On 4 January, Venizelos replied. He thanked the officers for the offer of the prime ministership, but he could not accept it outright until he carefully examined conditions in Greece. Moreover, he had to consider his service to Crete first in any decision. Within the week he planned to leave for Athens; in the meantime, he requested that his journey be cloaked in secrecy.[7]

117

On 10 January at 3:00 in the afternoon, Venizelos sailed into Piraeus on the Italian steamer *Singapore*.[8] His secret trip had become public knowledge, but Venizelos avoided any statements to the press. Shortly after his arrival, the Cretan statesman found himself before a meeting of the League's administrative committee. The proceedings of this important session helped determine the League's future policy.[9]

Venizelos first expressed his gratitude to the Military League for the honor of being able to express his opinions and referred to the praiseworthy goals of the officers. Zorbas then summarized the activities and accomplishments of the League since late August. Venizelos began his evaluation on a critical note by censuring the direction which the revolution had taken. The officers had decided wrongly to rely on the old political leaders to push through new laws for the correction of bad conditions. Rather they should have attacked those groups responsible for the unfortunate state of national affairs. The officers had been masters of the situation, but they handed over the task of their program's fulfillment to those guilty of creating unfortunate conditions. The proper course would have been prompt establishment of a dictatorship to govern the country through decrees for at least one year. Then a National Assembly could have been called to reform the government and to curb the irresponsible politicians of the past. Zorbas listed the dangers which convinced the League not to establish a dictatorship, particularly the threat of the king's abdication. Venizelos dismissed this fear, for if George left, there should have been no apprehension of violent domestic or foreign reactions "because everyone accepts a *fait accompli*." Besides, the present dynasty had many branches from which to choose an heir.[10]

Several of Venizelos's good friends and admirers requested that he assume the responsibilities of a dictator to push through the reform program. He responded that according to his information the Military League did not command the strength and popularity it formerly had and that declaring a dictatorship at this point would prove difficult. The officers protested these rumors, but Venizelos insisted that the appropriate time for a dictatorship had passed. Now the Military League should seriously consider measures to terminate the abnormal conditions because it was absolutely necessary for

the officers to return to their prime duty: the military preparation of the nation and the solution of the Cretan question.[11]

Zorbas and other officers defensively stated the League's
determination to carry out the program for strengthening the
armed forces, but that certain events and the government had
prevented execution of these plans. The administrative committee, therefore, resolved to replace the Mavromichalis ministry, preferably with one Venizelos would form. Again, the
wary Cretan refused the offer of leadership, claiming that as
an outsider he would meet considerable opposition from the
political parties and from the Royal Family which considered
him anti-dynastic. He also insisted that he was very much
needed on his home island and that he had to return as soon as
possible. His supporters once more attempted to persuade
Venizelos to head a government and, failing in this, hoped he
would at least express his ideas on what direction the future
course of the revolution should take. After some hesitation,
Venizelos answered that the officers must replace the Mavromichalis government and call for the convocation of a National Assembly as soon as possible. Only then could the Military
League expect to correct the irregular situation.[12]

Some conservative committee members feared unfortunate
complications from a constituent National Assembly. Venizelos countered that in order to avoid conflicts the Military
League should consult and arrive at an agreement with political leaders for a revisionist, not a constituent, National
Assembly—one which would reform specific articles of the
1864 Constitution. In this fashion, the king could also be
persuaded to accept the proposal. A caretaker government
should replace the Mavromichalis ministry in order to pave
the way for such an assembly. Individuals on the committee
conceded that it was highly unlikely they could receive the
support of the political parties on this issue of the National
Assembly. Venizelos, after convincing arguments by the officers, finally agreed to negotiate this issue with party leaders
and also, he stressed, with Stephen Dragoumis and Stephen
Skouloudis. He deemed the latter two men as the only candidates for leading a new government.[13]

Although Venizelos critically evaluated the League's record,
his reputation and commitment to reform made him popular
with many members of the administrative committee. In a

very short time he became the close adviser, entrusted with the task of placing the "revolution" on a more effective track. During his first days in Athens, however, few people knew the closeness of Venizelos's association with the officers. The Athenian newspapers, in their characteristic manner, contrived several theories as to the purpose of the Cretan politician's presence in the capital. Until the journals from Athens reached Crete, the islanders continued to think Venizelos had traveled to the mainland for private business.[14] Initially, he sought to maintain this unofficial front. Thus J. B. Bourchier, the distinguished Balkan correspondent of *The Times* (London), reported:

> Venizelos assured me that the rumors regarding his arrival here as the chosen candidate of the Military League for the Greek premiership were wholly devoid of foundation. He had not come to Athens by the invitation of the League, but entirely on his own initiative, and he will return to Crete in a few days. While sympathizing with the patriotic programs of the Military League, he regards the situation here as chaotic . . . .[15]

Chronos, probably under orders from the League, provided only limited mention of Venizelos's presence, but on 14 January the newspaper offered a translation of the Bourchier article for its readers.[16]

Unquestionably a leading figure in Crete, Venizelos shrewdly extended his influence into Greek politics—but at a gradual rate in order to prevent a political reaction against him. His proposal for a National Assembly, quickly espoused by the Military League, had been suggested earlier by other individuals and discussion of such a recourse had appeared on occasion in newspapers. However, no group with widespread prestige and authority promoted it seriously. Venizelos, having sold the concept to the League, then began to persuade the politicians of its merits. He visited Rallis and Theotokis who both initially opposed the calling of a National Assembly. They did agree, though, to investigate the issue more deeply, with Theotokis adding that he would consent only if the Military League disbanded beforehand.[17]

Venizelos's maneuvering stalled when Lieutenant Thanos Loidorikis, the administrative committee's general secretary, published a controversial article in *Chronos* on 22 January. Loidorikis wrote that the League did not consider the summoning of a National Assembly essential to its program. Whether out of misunderstanding, personal beliefs, or outside influence, Loidorikis succeeded in creating great confusion.[18] Theotokis quickly disassociated himself from his tentative pact with Venizelos. The latter drafted a letter on 24 January to Zorbas asking if the administrative committee had indeed altered its position.[19] That same day Venizelos, through a note, inquired of Theotokis whether his earlier comments to him should be disregarded as a result of his later declaration.[20] Theotokis retorted that a lack of concrete information on the officers' program and the declaration of Loidorikis led him to make the statements.[21] Venizelos, in frustration, informed the League by letter that instead of ameliorating conditions, his intervention in Greek politics had only stirred up more problems; he prepared to leave for Crete.[22]

On learning of Venizelos's plans, Zorbas called a meeting of the administrative committee, which concurred as to the necessity of convoking the National Assembly and retaining the Cretan politician as mediator. His close friends on the committee visited Venizelos at his hotel, the Hermes, stated the League's resolutions and confidence in him, and prevailed upon him to remain in Athens. At a meeting on 26 January, the committee outlined its proposals in positive terms so there would be no misunderstandings. A new government had to be formed which would hold the absolute confidence of the Military League. This ministry would work to pass necessary reform legislation and in time arrange for the convocation of a revisionist National Assembly upon agreement among the leaders of the political parties and the League. A protocol would limit the prerogatives of the assembly which would then be officially summoned by Royal decree.[23]

Venizelos relayed this information to Rallis and Theotokis. The minority leader accepted the terms without reservation. Theotokis, however, insisted that the officers had to abandon their political functions and return to the barracks before he could sanction the plan. Venizelos again checked with the League, which, in turn, declared that it would disband only when the new ministry came into power, the *Boule* passed certain laws, and a Royal decree convoked the National Assembly. Theotokis consented to this succession of political maneuvers.[24]

Zorbas in his memoirs remarked that the administrative committee had for some time seriously considered breaking up the League after a National Assembly had been summoned.[25] There is little available information to establish whether this decision was reached before or after Venizelos's arrival. In any case, the League's willingness at this juncture to divest itself of a political role underscored the limited achievements of the officers. Approved in principle by a small circle, the projected assembly still had to be accepted by other Greek politicians, the king, and the public. The administrative committee determined to put the troops on alert from 28 January to insure public order and to impress upon the citizens the severity of the situation. The committee also proceeded to inform sections of the League in the provinces of the latest developments in the capital.[26] By this time the press had more accurate information, and readers followed events closely.

Venizelos and the League, assuming that Mavromichalis had outlived his usefulness, had not kept the prime minister abreast of developments. The Chamber, after enduring several crises and busy holiday meetings, had adjourned for the Greek New Year on 12 January. Mavromichalis proposed the resumption of parliamentary duties for 18 January, but actual business did not commence until 24 January when a quorum finally gathered. Deputies requested additional pay for attendance at these extra meetings, while Mavromichalis appeared in no great hurry to push legislation. Furthermore, the prime minister stated in response to rumors that he opposed a National Assembly because of its many inherent dangers and unconstitutionality. During the very early morning hours of 27 January, Athanasios Evtaxias, the minister of finance, disclosed to several reporters that Mavromichalis would submit his resignation to the king later in the day. The prime minister balked, though, and did not depart as expected.[27]

King George strongly resisted convocation of a National Assembly in the manner being contemplated. First, George considered this procedure unconstitutional, since Article 107 as drafted in the Constitution of 1864 deliberately made revisions and amendments difficult. Revision of the entire constitution could not take place, but particular provisions, with the exception of fundamental articles dealing with the basic powers of the monarchy and *Boule,* were subject to modification. Article 107 provided for a National Assembly with double the number of usual representatives only if a three-fourths majority voted favorably in two successive legislative periods—that is, elections had to intervene. The monarch feared that such an assembly would present troubles for the nation and for himself if it met unconstitutionally after only one resolution in favor of it by the present *Boule*. Furthermore, no one seemed to have a clear idea which articles of the constitution required revision. George, resolute in his stand, ordered his yacht on 28 January to be ready to leave Piraeus at a moment's notice. If driven to opposition, George planned a short trip either to Patras or Corfu from where he could issue a proclamation to the nation asking it to declare its wishes. He thought such an act would demonstrate that if the people did not support him, he would be ready to leave the country. Since elections were out of the question at this time, George implied that the citizens must express their positions through public meetings. He conceded, however, that such an approach would probably be futile since there were no groups to organize these gatherings. George also learned that attempts by pro-royalist cadres within the armed forces to mobilize against the League's program were ineffective.[28]

On 28 January Sir Francis Elliot conferred with the king who expressed his frustrations. Although plans called for a revisionist assembly, George felt that once it met, there could be no guarantee it would not depart from its predetermined program. The monarch told the British diplomat that the Assembly

> . . . was certain to be composed of demagogues, journalists, and numbers of officers . . . [from] the League, all ready to vote for anything, including his own dethronement, which might be recommended to them by M. Venizelos, who was now master of the situation, and was actuated by personal ambitions and by hostility to himself and the Royal Family, dating from the time of his quarrel with Prince George on Crete.[29]

The ruler's apprehensions about the potentially unlimited powers of the assembly also lay behind his statement to George Moses, the American minister: "It was a National Assembly that brought me here." But George recognized that if Theotokis and Rallis backed the League's strategy, he would be criticized for posing obstacles to the wishes of the people.

123

The troubled monarch decided to preside over a meeting of Greece's leading politicians.[30]

Mavromichalis, Alexander Romas (the *Boule* president), Theotokis, Rallis, Dragoumis, and Alexander Zaïmis, the High Commissioner of Crete, conferred with the king on 29 January. Theotokis stressed the route of the National Assembly as the safest one back to normal procedures. He argued that although the constitution would not be followed to the letter in summoning the assembly, such a procedure was still a lesser evil than the continued existence of the Military League; rejecting this proposal could provoke greater complications, perhaps another coup d'état by the League. Rallis concurred with Theotokis and added that infringement of Article 107 would help lead the nation back to traditional parliamentary practices. The four year term of the present Chamber was to end on 9 April and, if elections were not held soon afterward, this action would also be a breach of the constitution. But if Greece conducted elections prematurely she would have to face serious diplomatic problems when Crete tried to send deputies to Athens. Elections for a National Assembly could be conducted toward the end of the year when conditions might be more suitable. Zaïmis then spoke in support of the National Assembly, but only if summoned according to the stipulations of Article 107. Crete's fate depended upon the will of the powers, and islanders should respect the status quo; only then might union with Greece be realistically considered. Athens should take the unwelcome initiative to order the Cretans not to hold elections simultaneously with Greece. Although an unpopular decision, all Greeks would benefit in the long run. When his turn came, Dragoumis reiterated his position expressed since September, that a National Assembly should be convoked. Mavromichalis, in contrast, produced a strong indictment against an assembly, and Romas supported him in this stand. Both felt there were too many inherent domestic and foreign dangers.[31]

After hearing the politicians, the king delivered his own opinions. George expressed his original reservations about a National Assembly summoned on unconstitutional grounds. He sensed that any caretaker government composed generally of independents would exist only on the confidence of the monarch and not of the parties, a relationship which could encourage internal and foreign crises. Also, unstable political conditions dulled any prospects of procuring the much-needed loan from abroad. Theotokis and Rallis disagreed with the monarch, who refused to pass judgment on the issue until later.[32]

Regarding the situation as highly sensitive, the administrative committee during a late evening meeting on 29 January determined to suppress the spread of any false rumors contrary to its official stand. The committee dispatched troops to the telegraph office to censor telegrams; similarly, the League was to censor issues of the *Official Gazette*. Officers drafted a public telegram to military and police units in the various cities and large towns stating that conditions remained quiet and under control in Athens. Believing that the Mavromichalis government had been spreading false interpretations of events in order to reinforce its weakened position, the administrative committee directed officers the following morning to check newspapers for any disquieting information. One story alleged that Mavromichalis retained armed supporters from Mani, his home district, ready to defend any decision by the king not to approve the National Assembly. No doubt to impress upon the Athenians the solidarity of the League, Zorbas ordered the troops, on alert and confined to barracks for three days, to parade along one of the main thoroughfares of Athens on the afternoon of 30 January. During the demonstration King George rode by on his way to the palace.[33]

Later that afternoon the king invited Theotokis and Rallis to confer with him. The monarch considered the judgment of these politicians more important than that of the other four present at the meeting the day before because Theotokis and Rallis controlled the large majority of deputies in the *Boule*. The two leaders repeated their justifications for a National Assembly, perhaps more freely in this smaller circle. They counseled the king to allow Stephen Dragoumis to form a *cabinet d'affaires* to conclude the business of the present Chamber and to arrange a vote for the convocation of a National Assembly. The king yielded to their case and sent for Dragoumis on the morning of 31 January.[34]

Venizelos from his first days in Athens had considered Dragoumis and Skouloudis, personal acquaintances of his, as the best candidates for prime minister. Both had long and distinguished careers in Greek politics. Originally from Macedonia, Dragoumis had served as a minister several times under Trikoupis, but pursued an independent course when Theotokis assumed the party's leadership after Trikoupis's death. More recently, he led the small, reform-minded Japan party. He had boldly criticized the Military League for unconstitutional measures against the princes even though he had been accused many times of anti-dynasticism. Skouloudis, approaching eighty, was known for his close ties with the monarchy, his strong support for the Cretan cause, and his knowledge of finances. He had at first been the choice of the League for prime minister, but Venizelos, upon speaking with him, reported that he did not approve the proposal for a National Assembly. Dragoumis, on the other hand, had publicly advocated a revisionist assembly since the previous September. Venizelos contended that despite Dragoumis's earlier defiance of the League, he nurtured the "revolutionary" spirit necessary to pass important reform legislation and to set the stage for the forthcoming assembly. In conversations with Venizelos, Dragoumis expressed a willingness to assume this burden of leadership. At a meeting of the administrative committee on 28 January, the members voted for Dragoumis to head a new ministry. Theotokis and Rallis accepted this decision of the officers without argument since they knew that they could not take on the responsibilities of a caretaker government. The king, in turn, recognized the dearth of alternatives. Zaïmis, Crete's high commissioner and George's preference for prime minister, had to be eliminated due to the wish of the powers not to disrupt the status quo on the explosive island.[35]

The committee assembled in the late afternoon of 30 January to draft a list of individuals in whom the League had confidence for membership in a new ministry. It was determined that Venizelos would carry this roster of candidates to Dragoumis, who could then make selections from it. After much persuasion, Zorbas yielded to his colleagues who insisted that he enter the cabinet as minister of war. They believed the interests of the "revolution" could best be served in this manner even after the League disbanded. For minister of marine, the League designated one of its number, Commander Andreas Miaoulis, member of the distinguished naval family.[36]

126

Dragoumis neither protested nor departed from the League's list of candidates. The officers desired either Skouloudis or John Valaoritis, president of the National Bank of Greece, for minister of finance, but both declined. Because of the importance placed upon procuring a foreign loan, the administrative committee deliberated at length the candidates for this slot. Unable to arrive at another choice, Dragoumis assumed the position himself, also taking on temporarily the ministry of interior. On 4 February, General Theodore Petmezas was named to this latter post. Demetrios Kallerges, career member of the Greek foreign service and strong supporter of the Military League from its inception, became minister of foreign affairs. The ministry of justice went to George Phikioris, former deputy, lawyer and relative of John Phikioris of the administrative committee. Andreas Panagiotopoulos accepted the ministry of public instruction and worship. King George swore in the new government the evening of 31 January.[37]

Within a relatively short period of three weeks, the Military League significantly overhauled its program and policies. Frustrated by their limited accomplishments, the officers willingly listened to Venizelos who became their political guide. Baron von Braun, the Austrian minister in Athens, cogently assessed the Cretan's important role: "Der Mephisto Griechenlands ist jetzt Herr Venizelos."[38] Mavromichalis, long the political tool of the League, had been manipulated for five months and then abandoned. Leader of a small party in the Chamber, he had hoped to distinguish himself and his followers during this critical period, yet he could never perform any better than his masters allowed. In January he foresaw his impending dismissal and attempted to assert his position by rejecting the League's proposal for a National Assembly. Reports indicated that an infantry regiment prepared to desert the League on notice and that Rear Admiral John Miaoulis (related to the new minister of marine) had assured King George that the navy would back him in defense of the constitution. In his memoirs Zorbas implied that Mavromichalis was actively involved in this plotting.[39] But the king did not gamble and reluctantly followed, as Theotokis and Rallis had also, the moderate path of concession, yielding once again to the threat of force.

The Military League skillfully maneuvered to perpetuate its

power during this transition period. Only three of the new cabinet members came from the *Boule* and two, Zorbas and Miaoulis, held important slots within the League. The officers also found it to be good politics to sanction as prime minister Stephen Dragoumis, a bold, outspoken opponent of earlier League practices whose attitudes now largely coincided with the altered program of the League.

The Cretan Question

Venizelos boarded a ship for Crete on the morning of 4 February, leaving behind him a scheme for solution of the imbroglio. He had also created some political enemies. For example, in conversations with Sir Francis Elliot, Mavromichalis expressed hostility for Venizelos, whose motives were deemed base and whose interference would inevitably prove disastrous. Zaïmis similarly regarded Venizelos's intervention as tragic, motivated by personal ambition and animosity towards the king.[40]

Politics in Crete were traditionally volatile and divisive, much more so than in Greece. Whereas Venizelos had elicited a positive response from the leaders of the two largest parties in Greece, his own countrymen in Crete criticized his activities. Michaledakis, Koundouros, Polygeorges and Manos, leaders of Venizelos's rival parties on the island, drafted a telegram to Athens in late January protesting the proposed National Assembly.[41] Reasons for this opposition ranged from mere jealousy to dismay at the indefinite postponement of Cretan representation in Athens. Other politicians claimed that elections for the Greek National Assembly would be held before military reorganization reached levels adequate for successful resistance against the Turks.[42]

Alternating periods of low and high tension had characterized the Cretan problem for several decades. After the turbulent events of mid-summer 1909, the issue slipped into relative quiet immediately following the Military League's revolt. Still, the Greeks could never be satisfied until Greece annexed the island, while the Turks, resisting any further diminution of their influence, demanded a definitive settlement on Crete's form of administration. The powers merely wished to maintain general peace; hence their efforts to maintain the status quo. During the autumn Cretan politicians restated their desire to dispatch deputies to Athens after the next Greek election. In late December the Cretan Chamber convened and selected another executive committee of three nonpoliticians who, like their predecessors, took an oath of loyalty to King George. The Chamber also reaffirmed the applicability of Greek laws to Crete.[43]

January 1910 witnessed another period of increased Cretan tension. The Sublime Porte voiced alarm at the Cretan Chamber's resolutions and particularly at renewed talk of forthcoming elections in Greece, which would grant the islanders an opportunity to send deputies to Athens. The suspicions of Constantinople understandably increased because of the significant role played by Venizelos, a Cretan, in Athenian affairs. In addition, Demetrios Kallerges, the new foreign minister, had served as Greek consul in Monastir, Macedonia, where he had been accused of complicity with Greek guerrilla bands. Suffering from political failures at home, the Turkish government asserted itself diplomatically on the Cretan issue and informed the powers that they should consider reoccupying the island if the Cretans insisted on sending deputies. If the powers did not act, then Turkey would have to express forcefully its displeasure with the Greeks.[44]

British, French, Russian and Italian diplomats exchanged opinions on the Cretan situation. Intent on maintaining the status quo, the powers did not wish to see the Porte forced into bold action which might end in a Greco-Turkish war. They also did not care to reoccupy the island, a costly and controversial venture which would label their departure the previous summer as a mistake. The four governments decided to warn the Cretan and Greek regimes against any attempt to send Cretan deputies to the mainland.[45]

Athens did not react sharply during this period of diplomatic wrangling. The adoption of the project to summon the National Assembly would, in fact, postpone elections for at least five months, thus deferring any opportunity for Crete to act. By autumn the powers might resolve the longstanding Cretan question to the satisfaction of all parties. Many Greeks, moreover, considered this delay in elections vital for continued military preparations. Venizelos hinted through his comments that it would be unwise for the island to elect deputies and that the Cretans should conform to the dictates of the protecting

129

powers to whom they owed everything. The new Dragoumis government in February affirmed that it sought to restore domestic tranquillity and to avoid complications abroad. There was no question of Cretan deputies sailing to Athens for the National Assembly, and the Greeks hoped that neither the powers nor Turkey would make any hasty threats.[46]

In case the islanders did act impulsively, the various representatives of the powers discussed seizing Crete's customhouse or reoccupying the island. The powers agreed to submit a warning to the Cretan government on 12 February. The joint statement stressed that they would not permit the island's population to participate in Greek elections; if the Cretans attempted to do so, the four powers would take effective measures to prevent such efforts (" . . . elles prendraient des mesures effectives pour en empêcher la réalisation").[47]

The Greeks could only hope to be compensated for good behavior, the lure held out for them in the note of the powers dated 28 October 1908; realistically, they had no other alternative. Yet, as in earlier instances, the powers tended to place Greece's interests behind those of Turkey. Theotokis in conversation with Elliot lamented that Crete had become a useful card in the hands of the powers for their dealings with Turkey. "He was aware that Greece was out of favor in the councils of Europe, and that there was no likelihood of that being done for her now which was refused to her a year and a half ago." Acknowledging its disadvantageous position, the Greek government sustained its policy of proper diplomacy. Crete toned down her intent to send deputies to Athens, and Constantinople relaxed its threats.[48] The Cretan question lapsed again into a state of decreased tension by March.

The First Weeks of the Dragoumis Ministry

Many deputies during the lethargic Chamber sittings of mid-January believed that after the frantic lawmaking of the preceding three months an extraordinary session was appropriate. Under such an arrangement, according to practice, the legislators could vote themselves a supplementary allowance. The Dragoumis ministry resolved to call the Chamber into an additional meeting on 3 February to ratify the minutes of the previous gathering, allowing bills that passed their third reading to be submitted for the king's signature.

The government then declared the ordinary session closed with the extraordinary session called for 14 February. It was speculated that the vote for the National Assembly would fall sometime in early March.[49] In the interim the League indicated that it intended to remain actively involved in the direction of governmental activities, thereby forewarning the new ministry of a difficult future.

The Typaldos mutiny, for example, persisted as a sensitive issue. Thirty-two trade-guild presidents had presented a petition to the king in late December requesting amnesty for those officers involved. Several newspapers carried editorials which claimed that these men deserved a pardon because they had erred from an excess of patriotism. Since the late October events, the Military League contained a substantial number of Typaldos's sympathizers. The petitions increased, but King George considered amnesty unjustified for legal and moral reasons. The Military League also pressed for amnesty, no doubt taking into consideration public and military support for the mutineers, as well as a particular reluctance to establish a precedent for the punishment of insubordination. Moreover, the League also sought to avert open scandals and embarrassment which Typaldos could foment with statements in a public trial. Dragoumis dutifully relayed the sentiments of the League to King George, who reluctantly bowed to arguments for a pardon. On 8 February King George issued the Royal decree according complete amnesty for Typaldos and his followers. All these men retained their rank while Typaldos and five of his co-conspirators received three years leave to travel abroad for advanced instruction. The intent here, of course, was to avoid possible commotion by their continued presence in Greece.[50] The Military League was now arranging for the release of those officers who had seriously threatened it. More than a few Athenians shook their heads in bewilderment at this reversal.[51]

The new ministry inherited still another problem from the previous government, that involving the diplomatic corps. The League had earlier agreed to a compromise with the king which provided for a superannuation bill. Ostensibly for purposes of economy, Dragoumis resolved to recall the Greek ministers in Berlin, London, Vienna, Rome, Belgrade, Sofia, and Bucharest; Paris and St. Petersburg were already vacant owing to recent deaths. The work of the legations was to be entrusted to chargés d'affaires. John Gryparis in Constantinople and Lambros Koromelas in Washington would remain at their posts. Although Dragoumis had adopted a similar measure when he had served as foreign minister under Charilaos Trikoupis, critics questioned whether there would be a noticeable saving because most of the ministers were entitled to pensions, and allowances had to be granted to the chargés d'affaires. The Military League and Dragoumis no doubt collaborated to enact the former's original demands for a reorganization of the diplomatic corps. Many diplomats, considered incompetent by the League, belonged to distinguished Greek families whose influence remained strong despite the military's pressure. Hence, these few well-connected, but inefficient ministers could be removed only in a clean sweep. The king reluctantly sanctioned these measures and on 22 February the *Official Gazette* published the recall of these diplomats.[52]

Simultaneous with their handling of old issues, the League earnestly sought to create a setting that would guarantee the execution of measures it considered vital. The administrative committee informed Dragoumis in early February that he should appoint *nomarchs* (i.e., department prefects) who supported the goals of the government and Military League. Recognizing the threat of potential opposition to their policies, the officers drafted plans to transfer to the garrison in Athens one hundred men from each provincial regiment and twenty to thirty men from each Evzone battalion. The administrative committee also ordered cavalry units to assemble outside the capital.[53]

The League's tougher tactics were next directed at the press. On the evening of 12 February the administrative committee commissioned Lieutenant Sarros to inform Tsangaris, head of the Athens News Agency, that he should speak with the editors of all the newspapers in the capital on the new policy: the League would not tolerate "reactionary articles" opposing convocation of the National Assembly. If any editors persisted, the League would prevent distribution of the newspapers. Two days later, the officers also forbade articles which referred to any violation of freedom of the press.[54] The editors demanded that Dragoumis intercede, but the prime minister failed to persuade the officers to rescind their dictates. At 2:00 a.m. on the morning of 15 February, the League sent officers to the individual newspapers to enforce its decree. Some of the army reinforcements ordered to Athens joined large units patrolling the streets and occupying strategic spots that tense night. In the morning only *Chronos, Akropolis, Athenai,* and *Proïa* reached the normally crowded kiosks. Thereafter, the editors submitted to pressure and printed only articles favorable to the concept of the National Assembly.[55]

The willingness to use the threat of force together with other methods short of violence again minimized public opposition. Success in these endeavors obviously depended upon unity within the armed forces. The League periodically dealt with internal challenges, although there were several fissures which had the potential to induce larger cracks. Thus did some of the younger officers continue to demonstrate greater radicalism which, except for the Typaldos mutiny, Zorbas and his moderate majority contained satisfactorily. In mid-February the new minister of war forwarded a long list of promotions for junior officers to the king for his signature, a crucial measure to sate the professional ambitions of the younger officers. Meanwhile, many noncommissioned officers considered their interests ignored by the League. And while the Typaldos amnesty appeased the younger elements, many senior naval officers added this action to a growing list of grievances against the League.[56]

The public became aware of strained relations between the two services when *Esperini* published a protocol drafted and signed by Rear Admiral John Miaoulis and many senior officers of the fleet. Publicized on 14 February but dated 5 February, this document emphasized that the signatories would follow the lead of King George and that they would neither allow the king nor the politicians to be forcefully coerced nor the constitution to be violated. This revelation naturally embarrassed the League. Shortly after, however, the newspapers printed a notice that the date of the protocol was actually 29 January, just before the king agreed with Theotokis and Rallis on the National Assembly.[57]

The administrative committee expressed its concern over the increased dissension to the ministers of war and marine, suggesting that officers not sympathetic to its program should

133

be transferred to provincial posts where they might be less obstructive. At a later meeting the committee listed five naval officers involved in criticism of the League that it wanted placed in noncombat service. There were also attempts, not very successful, to break up the leadership of the destroyer squadron and to disarm it so that these units might not be employed against the League. Within the army the committee recommended to Zorbas that he keep newly-appointed Generals Koumoundouros and Kostantinides and Colonel Vakaloglou from any post where they might effectively generate opposition.[58]

Another verbal thrust to the Military League's prestige came from a source which it could not easily muzzle. General Constantine Smolenskis, the only highly regarded ranking officer of the 1897 war, had uttered anti-League sentiments to close friends, and they soon became public knowledge. On 24 February *Embros* published an interview with the general, in which he stressed that the League should dissolve immediately, inasmuch as the justification for its existence, the strengthening of the armed forces, was not being carried out effectively; involvement in political matters only hindered this mission. He claimed that many army and naval officers had complained of these conditions and encouraged him to intervene. If the proper moment for action arrived, he would work to aid King George and to preserve the constitution. Once the League disbanded, the general expressed his willingness to cooperate with its former members to help build up the nation militarily. By ironic coincidence *Chronos* that same morning printed a strong editorial stating that the Military League would crush any reactionary movements.[59]

Venizelos had returned to Athens on 14 February for further consultations with the League. The administrative committee commissioned its Cretan adviser to visit Smolenskis, and the results of the interview, which appeared in the 25 February issue of *Kairoi,* served to ease the tension produced by the general's pronouncements. Venizelos declared all the rumors circulating around Athens represented a situation that did not exist. The National Assembly would be voted on, and the fundamental articles of the constitution regarding the monarchy and parliamentarianism would be maintained. General Smolenskis and some other comrades were apprehensive about the officers' intention to dissolve the League, but Venizelos assured them that it would disband on the same day of the Royal proclamation.[60]

Boule Passage of the Bill for a Revisionist Assembly

The extraordinary session of the *Boule* began on 14 February but dealt only with minor business at that sitting. Three days later, the deputies voted 109 to 3 for General Nicholas Tsamados as president of the Chamber. This election of the retired general, a Theotokist and former minister of war, by an overwhelming majority indicated an understanding among party leaders that the prime object of the *Boule* was to terminate the present crisis as soon as possible. Doubt, however, pervaded the political atmosphere since some Theotokist deputies expressed an unwillingness to vote in favor of the National Assembly. Moreover, the public displayed a lack of enthusiasm, though not outright opposition, for the assembly. Nevertheless, the espousal of the National Assembly by Theotokis and Rallis and the Military League's stiff methods combined to convince a growing number of deputies that the League should disband quickly—such action, the League insisted, was contingent upon a favorable vote for the assembly.[61]

On the evening of 18 February, Dragoumis addressed the *Boule* in frank, urgent terms, citing the abnormal political conditions which had required the formation of a government composed of essentially nondeputies. Exceptional circumstances, both domestic and foreign, had led the political leaders to support the summoning of a National Assembly. Those who initiated the reform movement in late August desired to return to their proper occupation, wishing at the same time to see the affairs of the country improved. The political leaders had admitted the necessity of modifying Article 107; there was no other acceptable alternative for a return to normal conditions. If the proposal for an assembly met defeat, the nation would be exposed to political chaos.[62]

Aware of such a possibility, King George on 15 February had telegraphed Crown Prince Constantine in Germany and Prince Nicholas in Russia to return home. The monarch wished to preside over a family council to determine action in case the Chamber did not provide the three-fourths majority for a National Assembly. George presumed that rejection would push the League to demand a Royal decree, a request he seriously considered denying on constitutional grounds. Resistance on his part meant a struggle with the League; and in such a circumstance not only his own future but that of his family would be involved. The monarch was also concerned about renewed rumors that he would be forced to abdicate, to be succeeded not by the crown prince but by Constantine's eldest son, Prince George.[63]

Neither George nor Dragoumis, who had approved the decision to summon the princes, expected controversy. But various sections of the Greek press reacted quickly and strongly urged that the crown prince not return. Editorials stated that a premature arrival by Constantine might encourage reactionary demonstrations similar to those in Patras and Corfu in September. Such activities would disrupt progress toward settlement of the crisis. The Military League also expressed its own displeasure at reports of Constantine's reappearance to Dragoumis. Assessing the unfavorable conditions, the prime minister and Sir Francis Elliot convinced the king that if the crown prince presented himself in Athens, it would be difficult for the government to remain in office. George then decided to telegraph Constantine in Brindisi, and on 21 February Prince Andrew traveled to the Italian port to explain the changed plans to his brother.[64]

Constantine accepted his father's decision to postpone his return and instead journeyed to Paris for a short stay. In Milan the crown prince delivered some astute remarks for the *Corriere della Sera* which silenced any further journalistic outbursts in Athens. The prince declared that he had decided not to return home because he wished to avoid possible demonstrations. He criticized the Military League's actions for infringing standards of discipline, but conceded the good intentions and patriotic aims of the officers. Every loyal Greek desired increased military strength and, indeed, many of the League's proposals coincided with his own past plans for reorganization of the armed forces. The prince offered an optimistic forecast for the country's politics and military capabilities. After Paris, Constantine planned to travel to Frankfurt where he would await the proper moment to return to Greece.[65]

Amid this mid-February clamor over the League's problems with the navy and General Smolenskis and the controversy over the crown prince's proposed arrival, the deputies handled their regular business. In the first days of the session the *Boule* amended several laws passed by the previous government which in practice were found to be unworkable. The government also introduced a bill for the creation of a ministry of agriculture, commerce and industry. Otherwise, little of an outstanding nature occurred as the political leaders prepared for the crucial resolution on the National Assembly.[66]

At the meeting on 21 February of the administrative committee, Venizelos presented a list of twenty-nine articles in the constitution which, in his opinion, required revision. Among other points he stressed that Article 71 should be changed so that an officer in the armed forces could not run for political office. Moreover, all members of the army and navy should be deprived of the vote in national elections as long as they were on active duty. Acceptance of these proposals by the Military League indicated its sincere desire to alter traditional practices by neutralizing and eliminating any military affiliations with political parties.[67]

The administrative committee approved Venizelos's suggestions and passed them on to the prime minister, who already had Nicholas Saripolos, a distinguished legal authority, working on a similar project. The list, produced by Saripolos and publicized on 25 February, resembled that of Venizelos's plan in most aspects. The fundamental articles of the constitution, including the privileges of the king, remained untouched. Essentially, the list slated for revision those articles dealing with the composition and rules of the Chamber and with the method of electing deputies.[68]

Relative tranquillity marked the political scene during the last days of February. The king received the president of the *Boule* on 26 February, and on his own initiative the monarch introduced the subject of the National Assembly, underscoring its importance for the nation. When George inquired whether the required number of deputies to vote for the proposal were available, Tsamados answered in the affirmative. This positive attitude of the king, widely publicized by the press, contributed even more supporters for the assembly among the deputies.[69]

Moderation and compromise carried over into March, as Dragoumis met with Theotokis and Rallis several times to discuss the final form of the resolution to be placed before the Chamber. The two party leaders offered a number of minor alterations and suggested some of the government's recommendations be dropped. Dragoumis arranged for the assembly vote on 3 March. The Military League had slipped quietly into the background during the days preceding the vote, but the administrative committee on 2 March ordered the troops in Athens placed on alert while deputies debated the resolution.[70] Since no disturbance was expected, one can only surmise that the League, overly nervous, reacted out of habit when it confined soldiers to their barracks.

On the evening of 3 March, Dragoumis introduced the resolution enumerating the proposed changes in the constitution. The National Assembly would be composed of twice the usual number of deputies and was to convene within six months. Mavromichalis opened debate with a series of negative comments, maintaining that the constitution was not at fault for poor conditions, but that the blame lay with the politicians who for the past thirty years ruled the country for selfish purposes; he concluded by stressing the dangers which an assembly posed for the nation. The prime minister countered with the now familiar argument that this proposal represented the easiest and most peaceful road away from the present crisis. Prior concurrence among deputies would guarantee that the spirit of the constitution would not be transgressed. Theotokis and Rallis also aligned themselves against Mavromichalis and the small number of deputies who rose to speak against the resolution. The debate provided few ideas other than those thrashed around in earlier weeks, although tempers did flare toward the end of the sitting.[71] Dragoumis succeeded in calming the furor and shortly afterwards moved that the deputies cast their votes. The resolution passed easily with 150 votes for and 11 against.[72]

The articles subject to revision included Article 71 covering the right of members of the armed forces to vote and run for office. In addition, the proposals sought a change in Article 3 which excluded non-Greek subjects from public service. This correction would allow foreign advisers to reorganize the nation's military and civil services and to qualify Greeks with

Ottoman citizenship or that of other nationalities for service in any public position. It was felt that Article 14, which covered the seizure of newspapers and printed matter if they attacked the Church or the person of the king, was insufficiently broad to protect other "national interests" from printed assaults; a modification of the article would provide against injury to these national interests (to be defined later). Quorum rules had hindered effective parliamentary proceedings and so Article 56 was to be altered to lower the number of deputies required for general discussion, but for decisions by vote, the quorum level of more than half would continue. Articles 83 to 86, providing for a Council of State, had subsequently been abolished, but now many politicians believed that this council should be reinstituted for the purposes of parliamentary efficiency in the framing and examining of law drafts and executive decrees and for deciding in cases of contested administrative questions. Experience indicated that Article 66 dealing with voting by the use of colored balls demanded modification. The remainder of the list contained proposed revisions for education, parliamentary procedures, tenure of public officials, and a series of minor issues.[73]

Protocol required King George to deliver a Royal proclamation convoking the National Assembly at the final sitting of the extraordinary session, approximately four weeks away. Seeking to demonstrate good faith in future political plans, the king sanctioned the departure of British ships moored off Piraeus. Even after the controversy stirred up by the presence of the English at the Christmas eve fire at the palace, no Greek politicians had pressed for their departure. In late January Elliot had suggested to the monarch that the vessels should be withdrawn, pointing out that no nation had the right to maintain ships of war indefinitely in the ports of another state. Their continued presence, he added, might damage the prestige of the king by implying, as had been pointed out by Greek newspapers, that the crown depended upon the protection of foreign arms. The monarch resisted these arguments and claimed the ships checked the boldness of the League. By early March the pressure of the League on the king had diminished so that Elliot's repeated efforts to withdraw the ships succeeded, although with some reluctance on George's side. On 8 March, the *Cornwallis* and *Suffolk* of the British

Mediterranean Fleet lifted anchor, leaving Athens without a British vessel for the first time in over six months.[74]

New League Demands and Agrarian Dissent

The Military League soon revealed it had no intention of surrendering prematurely any of its influence. On 9 March the officers delivered to Dragoumis a series of proposals which they wanted to see passed before the extraordinary session concluded. These demands, some of greater importance than others, aimed at administrative efficiency and eliminating corruption. In its proposals the League frequently used the word *ekkatharisis,* which literally translated means a "purification," "cleaning up," or "purging." The list included: (1) the purging of the public service by the dismissal of the higher officials, of whom the more competent might be reappointed; (2) the purging of the university by the dismissal of all the fifty-eight professors, some of whom might be reappointed, while the places of the others would be taken by Greek professors in foreign universities; (3) the purging of the army by a committee which was to decide without appeal on the fitness of officers to serve; (4) the disqualification of directors of public companies and banks from sitting in the Chamber; (5) the election of delegates to the National Assembly on the basis of smaller electoral districts rather than the larger districts recently established by law at the League's insistence; (6) the establishment of a ministry of commerce and agriculture; (7) the solution of the agrarian question in Thessaly by the purchase of the landlords' estates and the distribution of the land to peasant cultivators.[75]

By far the most difficult of the demands to satisfy concerned the agrarian problems in Thessaly. Whereas peasant proprietorship characterized the system of land tenure most prominent throughout Greece, feudal principles still prevailed in Thessaly. During the period of Ottoman domination, Moslem landowners presided over large estates, or *chifliks,* from palatial residences which dwarfed the thatched mud houses of the peasants. Under the Turks the peasants lived essentially as serfs, subject to the will of their Moslem overlord. In 1881 upon Greece's annexation of Thessaly, wealthy Greeks purchased most of these large estates, although the Turks retained control of some *chifliks.* Only about one-quarter of the land in

1882 belonged to small peasant proprietors. Quite commonly the wealthy Greek owners of the *chifliks* resided in distant urban centers as Athens, Constantinople and Alexandria, leaving supervision of the land to trusted overseers. When Thessaly fell under Greek control, the former serfs became free men in the sense that they acquired political privileges. But the new Greek owners, wishing to recover money paid for the estates, administered their land on strict business principles which degraded the status of the peasants. With written contracts, ejections, middlemen, and lawyers, the peasants probably suffered more than they had under the Turks. And the Thessalian peasants working for the remaining Turkish owners after 1881 lived under relatively better conditions.[76]

Although the number of free villages (*kephalachoria*) increased before 1910, the state of the peasants on the *chiflik* improved little. Repeated requests by these downtrodden farmers for financial help and land reform met little sympathy from politicians in Athens. The large landowners, few in number but wealthy and influential, successfully exerted pressure on legislators to remain virtually inactive on land reform. Some limited government loans had been extended since 1890 under a program initiated by Trikoupis, and amounts increased with the establishment of the Agricultural Bank of Thessaly in 1907. Much of this new money, inadequate to begin with, went toward settlement of Greek refugees from Bulgaria and Rumania. The Convention of Constantinople on 2 July 1881 between Greece and Turkey, however, provided perhaps the greatest obstacle toward alleviating the plight of the Thessalian farmer. According to this agreement, the compulsory expropriation of Thessalian proprietors could only be carried out for the purposes of public utility, in a legal manner, and after adequate indemnity had been assured the landlords. Furthermore, no proprietor could be compelled to sell the whole, or part, of his property, nor could any modification be introduced into the relations between proprietors and cultivators except by means of a general law applicable to the entire nation. Any massive land reform, therefore, required large sums of money which the nation's coffers could not supply.[77]

Low market prices for their produce and the precarious political atmosphere in the country spurred the Thessalian peasants into considering bolder protest in early 1910. Local schoolteachers, lawyers and politicians in Karditsa, a regional center in Thessaly, earnestly went about organizing ways to pressure Athens for action. A deputation traveled to the capital insisting on a compulsory expropriation law to institute universal peasant proprietorship. In late February Dragoumis declared that his government could not deliberate this very sensitive question, because the problem required extensive debate along with vast funds not available; moreover, Greece's treaty obligations with Turkey restricted any legislation. The delegation from Thessaly did succeed in persuading the Military League to include its request among the latter's demands to the government on 8 March. Shortly afterward, Dragoumis repeated to representatives of the League his case against solving the Thessalian issue at that time. The prime minister convinced these officers, and the administrative committee in a communique published in the 10 March newspapers stressed that rumors of dissension between the League and government were entirely false.[78]

Members of the Thessalian delegation returned to their troubled province. George Karaïskakis, deputy from Karditsa and constantly associated with reformist causes and antidynastic statements, joined them. Large public meetings and isolated acts of violence occurred, driving some *chiflik* owners and administrators off their estates. While tension increased, Thessalian deputies introduced a new bill on 16 March which took into consideration Greece's obligations to Turkey. The modified proposal provided for the extension of compulsory expropriation of estates under similar tenure in all of Greece. Only land actually under cultivation would be involved and only two-thirds of the landlord's estate could be transferred. The Agricultural Bank of Thessaly was to supervise these sales. Backed by party leaders, Dragoumis refused to support the new legislation, reiterating that the short time remaining in the *Boule* session did not permit serious consideration of such an enormous problem. To complicate matters, the Turkish minister in Athens delivered a stiff note which insisted that the Greek government respect the rights of the Moslem proprietors. If Athens did not respond properly, Turkey threatened to regard other conventions with Greece as not binding.[79]

The peasants' dismay at the government's decision, fired by Karaïskakis and his colleagues, led to increased violence. The most tragic incident took place on 19 March when a combined total of about 500 peasants twice stopped a train destined for Larissa. The peasants demanded the right to board at the village of Kileler, but after some minor scuffling a detachment of troops on the train fired into a crowd, killing five men and wounding fifteen. Some demonstrators boarded the train to join the planned demonstration in Larissa, where a large crowd assembled under a black flag. Serious rioting followed, after which governmental authorities, attempting to hush up the matter, declared there were no casualties; unofficial reports, however, indicated about twenty wounded. Related incidents occurred throughout Thessaly with military units bolstering local authorities. The peasants, who formerly thought the Military League supported their goals, now found the army opposing them with armed force.[80]

In the *Boule* the prime minister responded to accusations that the military authorities on government orders had caused unnecessary slaughter. Dragoumis maintained that drastic measures were imposed to prevent more serious evils since he had received reports that a general uprising was imminent in Thessaly. He went on to criticize those individuals who had led the peasants to believe that the agrarian problem could be solved in a few days. His request for the support of the Chamber in restoring law and order met with widespread approval. The ardor of the peasants for violent demonstration died out during the last week of March for several reasons. Poorly armed themselves, they recognized that they could not successfully cope with the repressive tactics of the army executing government orders. Some mayors who acted as organizers of protest meetings in their localities had been arrested. A drenching rain which continued for five days contributed significantly to dampening the revolt, as the wet peasants remained in their villages.[81] Yet bitter memories of bloodshed could not be washed away.

The Royal Proclamation and Dissolution of the Military League

Dragoumis found himself in a position similar to that of his predecessor.[82] The League exerted pressure on him for the passage of legislation which the political parties in the *Boule* often deemed undesirable, if not impractical. The prime

143

minister, as the beleaguered intermediary, had first to employ persuasion to push through his government's legislative program. If that method did not work, Dragoumis attempted compromise with the conflicting parties, that is, League and deputies. On occasion, he threatened resignation which, if carried out, would have fomented even greater problems because of the limited legislative period remaining to treat unfinished business. Despite the League's commitment to disband after the Royal proclamation for the National Assembly, rumors spread around Athens that the extremist officers welcomed a crisis as an excuse to launch a temporary dictatorship. It was reported, too, that Zorbas, upon his promotion to general and his appointment as minister of war, had lost considerable authority within the administrative committee. With his moderating influence diminished, stronger voices held the potential to disrupt the forces striving for a return to normal conditions.[83]

If the Thessalian question defied solution, satisfaction of the other League demands did not come easily. For example, the officers placed considerable weight on their desire for reform within state services and the university. *Chronos,* parroting the League on 11 March, stated that the revolution could not expect success merely through laws which the old, inefficient officials would fail to carry out effectively. The nation required competent administrators to execute new laws and programs.[84] Some "purification" had already been instituted in the navy, diplomatic corps, and judiciary, but the League stressed now the necessity for more widespread action.

The call for purging the civil services and the teaching staff of the university confronted stiff resistance from the deputies. This opposition stemmed partly from principle, but also from the personal ties of deputies with leading officials whose careers were threatened. It was only natural that a society plagued with chronic patronage would combat any threat to this practice. Eventually, however, the pressure for reform resulted in a compromise which probably satisfied the officers more than the deputies. During heated debate in the last hours of the extraordinary session on 26 March, Dragoumis requested a vote of confidence on the university bill. The law finally passed, authorizing establishment of committees composed of faculty members and specified nonacademic personnel to rule on the qualifications and competence of professors. The Chamber voted legislation organizing similar committees to pass judgment on members of the civil service.[85]

Purging the army was a more immediate concern of the League. On 19 March *Chronos* published a lengthy memorandum addressed to Zorbas on 20 February. Signed by members of the administrative committee and a large number of officers, this document contained a series of demands for purging the army and for better training of officers. The League requested immediate passage of a law creating a committee of higher officers appointed by the government. This group would remove from the army those officers guilty of poor performance or immoral behavior. The memorandum repeated the army's commitment to reform—if purification were not implemented by the government, the military would attack the problem on its own authority.[86]

Theotokis and Rallis both resisted this proposal, fearing that the League would use such a committee to purge its opponents. Dragoumis, however, argued for the exigency of this legislation and denied that the army would wield it vindictively. After the League clarified that only a small number of officers generally considered unfit for duty would be expelled, the party leaders on 22 March agreed to vote for the law as long as its wording excluded any possibility of abuse. General Constantine Sapountzakis was to head a committee composed of the inspector of artillery, commanders of three infantry regiments, senior ranking officers of the cavalry, and a superior officer of the engineering corps.[87]

The demand for smaller electoral districts presented a complete reversal from the League's earlier stand which had provoked heated debate the previous November. The officers then expected that larger electoral districts would diminish the influence of local politicians, and the bill had passed only after stiff pressure from the army. The administrative committee anticipated, as did the law's supporters, that election of new candidates backing widespread reform would be facilitated by these larger prefectures. But in March the League, reportedly under the prodding of Venizelos, requested the restoration of smaller electoral districts. The officers now regarded the election of new deputies not affiliated with the old parties more likely under a system of smaller electoral districts.[88]

Theotokis and Rallis defiantly combatted any return to the older system, not wishing to appear foolish in light of their previous endorsement of the November law. The political leaders most likely acknowledged the League's revised position that new independent candidates might attract votes more readily in smaller areas. Under such an arrangement it would be easier for a fresh political figure to make his program popular in a smaller district. The administrative committee pressed Dragoumis to force this bill through the Chamber, but Theotokis and Rallis would not retreat. The followers of Karaïskakis and members of George Philaretos's Radical party sponsored a demonstration in Omonia Square for 23 March for the limited electoral areas. Only a disappointing group of about 500 people assembled and later delivered a resolution in support of the League's measure to Zorbas. The minister of war replied that the responsibility for the passage of the necessary law remained with the Chamber. Dragoumis, however, failed to budge Theotokis and Rallis. Probably realizing that too much pressure at this late stage of the session might create unfortunate consequences, the administrative committee quietly withdrew this demand.[89]

Although plagued by the interventionist tactics of the officers, Dragoumis concentrated on some longstanding legislation. With the resignation of the Mavromichalis government, Evtaxias's plan for a loan had been dropped. Greece required added funds to ease her chronic economic problems and to subsidize public works and the buildup of military forces. Dragoumis, as minister of finance, presented to the *Boule* a loan bill on 7 March, and it passed on 19 March. The law authorized the Greek government to conclude a 4 percent loan for 150 million drachmas to be directed for public works, railroad construction, the covering of budgetary deficits to 1909 and "other needs of the state," the latter expression implying defense expenditures. Article 9 of the law allowed an increase in the amount of the loan from 150 million to 240 million drachmas, the supplementary funds to be utilized for redemption of the forced paper currency.[90]

The Greeks still faced the difficult task of finding foreign financial groups willing to underwrite the loan. Earlier efforts by Evtaxias had failed to generate a satisfactory response from European capital primarily because of doubts concerning the political climate and Greece's ability to guarantee payments.

The last regular meeting of the hectic extraordinary session convened at 10:00 a.m. on 26 March and continued, except for short adjournments, until 5:00 a.m. the following morning. Thirty-six bills passed, dealing with, among other issues, education, administrative and purging procedures for the various ministries and indemnities to currant growers for the uprooting of their vineyards; this last measure aimed at reviving the currant trade. During this sitting the deputies also approved the long-delayed budget for 1910. Greek law required only one reading for passage of a budget, and Dragoumis presented it in its final form after several revisions. Financial matters customarily stimulated heated debate in the *Boule,* but the representatives conceded that obstructionism could only foment greater problems. The level of Dragoumis's budget was approximately six million drachmas lower than that of Evtaxias's but considerably higher than that of 1909. Many of the new imposts proposed by the former finance minister had been diminished or repealed primarily because of popular opposition. Dragoumis now fixed receipts at 142,166,215 drachmas and expenditures at 142,031,079 drachmas. He offered no provision for the service of the proposed foreign loan on the assumption that the new Chamber would vote necessary funds when it assembled later in the year. League pressure resulted in an increased expenditure from the 1909 budget of about 8,500,000 drachmas for military and naval purposes.[91]

At the close of this final session the prime minister thanked the deputies for their cooperation and announced that the Royal proclamation for the convocation of the revisionist National Assembly would be delivered by King George on 30 March. In the interim, rumors circulated that the League might not disband before the king's trip to the Chamber. Dragoumis consulted George who wished to be assured of the officers' intentions. The prime minister informed his war minister, Zorbas, of the king's request for a formal statement on the League's dissolution prior to the Royal proclamation. The administrative committee debated the query on 29 March and finally agreed to the king's overture. Dragoumis delivered the response to the ruler the evening before his public announcement, but, on the League's request, it was not to be published by the newspapers until after the monarch's speech.[92] The contents of the document eased whatever apprehensions the king might have had:

> The administrative committee of the League, bearing in mind the fact that the government has carried out the mandate which it received from the revolution, considers its work terminated, and entrusts to the government the conclusion and completion of the work commenced until the Greek people shall send its representatives to the revisionary National Assembly. The League cherishes the conviction that the government will remain intact until the advent of the National Assembly, and it releases its members from their obligations [of 28 August].[93]

Nineteen members of the administrative committee placed their signatures at the bottom of this public announcement.

Thus assured, the king, accompanied by Queen Olga, left the palace at 10:00 a.m. on 30 March. Notwithstanding the beautiful weather and the importance of the event, the crowds en route to the Chamber were only average for a public ceremony. Upon arrival George walked into a *Boule* crowded with spectators, deputies, approximately fifty officers, and all the foreign representatives except for Baron Hans von Wangenheim, the German minister.[94] The king, greeted by Dragoumis, proceeded to the president's tribune from which he read the Royal proclamation. The monarch declared the deputies were summoned "in accordance with the spirit of the constitution" on a task of reform destined to make more effective the provisions of the constitution. Reviewing the political crisis of recent months, he concurred in the necessity for change in political methods and in the urgency of "restoring the course of the country's affairs and strengthening the regime with which the national aspirations are indissolubly bound up." Fortunately, the politicians had agreed on a path out of the crisis which he could sanction: the proposal for the revision of the nonfundamental clauses of the constitution. His Royal proclamation would summon this revisionist Chamber. The monarch concluded:

> Gentlemen, I express to you my Royal thanks for the noble zeal and devotion to your country and my dynasty with which you are inspired for the accomplishment of your labors in the course of the extraordinary session. You have thus seconded my government in its efforts for the definitive restoration of the affairs of the country and the return to us of the peace necessary for the welfare of the nation.[95]

After his address the king, accompanied by the prime minister, departed from the Chamber amid cheers which were not, however, universal on the part of the deputies. Dragoumis returned into the legislature to deliver several concluding remarks, emphasizing that the work of reconciliation had been accomplished due to the support which the *Boule* had granted to the government. The minutes were accepted and the formal proceedings, which consumed scarcely fifteen minutes, ended.[96]

On the following day *Chronos* published a final communique of the Military League to the public. In temperate terms it stated that the Royal proclamation had crowned the campaign of reform "to which the army and navy have devoted themselves for the last seven months." But this did not mean that the campaign had terminated or that the nation had embarked on the path of definite reform. On the contrary, the Military League was well aware how small the fruits of revolution had been so far, and how many opportunities for national regeneration still lay ahead. The officers' action resulted from fifty years of pain and sore humiliation to the fatherland. The Military League conceded that it had committed some mistakes, but was convinced that considering dangerous conditions and the needs of all Hellenism, "it will be found to have served them with sincerity by military moderation." The manifesto went on to state:

> The Military League, aware that the interests of the fatherland require the return of the army and navy to their own duties, and, on the other hand, certain that nobody will think of frustrating all that the revolution, in the name of the Greek people, has placed on the road to improvement, declares that after the Royal decree, it considers and agrees that the intervention of the army in the

149

affairs of the state is at an end. Judging, however, from the difficulties, from the corruption, and from the opposition which it has had to encounter during seven months, the League urgently directs the attention of the Greek people to everything connected with their future fate and registers the conviction that although dissolving today, the Greek army remains a vigilant guardian of the national honor and ideals.[97]

The newspapers of the same day printed a statement by Dragoumis to the League that he would carry out faithfully the program set up for him and actively pursue a purging of the nation's administration.

Revolution or Coup d'État?

Although in Greek lexicons the word *epanastasis,* "revolution," has a definition quite similar to that found in English dictionaries, semantically the word's usage fluctuates. Instead of restricting "revolution" to its most common application as "an attempt to make a radical change in the system of government,"[98] *epanastasis* has been employed by many popularizers of Greek politics to categorize the broad range from actual "revolution" to very dramatic political events or demonstrations. Hence, the events of 28 August 1909 and their aftermath have been represented by a majority of Greek writers covering the period as the "revolution of 15 August" (old-style calendar) or the "revolution of 1909." Several books bear these titles and still more refer to it as such.[99] And, of course, the rebellious officers and their supporters maintained from the start that the actions of the Military League constituted a "revolution." Only a minority of commentators interpret the affair as a "coup d'état," "pronunciamento," or "uprising."[100]

On reviewing the immediate events surrounding 28 August, one has to classify the incident as a coup d'état. By no means was there a violent overthrow of an existing political-social system with the intent of substituting another. The officers emphasized, threats of violence notwithstanding, that they wished not to upset the constitutional system but to eliminate the ingrown obstructions to progress. The Military League overthrew one ministry, yet substituted for it one which differed little in terms of political identification. The Mavromichalis ministry was an attempt by the conspirators at maintaining constitutionality. The new prime minister, another member of the maligned old political school, was charged with the responsibility of pushing through a program more reformist than revolutionary in scope. Ideologically, the "Memorandum of the Military League" supported chauvinistic goals intended to strengthen the armed forces and therefore bolster the nation in its quest of the *Megale Idea*. Reflecting essentially military concerns, the document intended neither to express principles of late nineteenth-century liberalism nor to seek the advancement of specific class interests. Whatever general socio-economic reforms the officers proposed were designed to facilitate the military buildup.

The public and press generally hailed the "revolution" and considered the Military League the appropriate medium to inaugurate a new era of greatness for Greece. Remaining in the background the officers curbed the inevitable opposition of the political party leaders and deputies to reform proposals by employing various means of coercion. The administrative committee also sponsored an extensive journalistic campaign to discredit the past practices of the politicians. Formerly accused of aloofness to the nation's problems, King George now wished to express his concern, but found his position too weak. The forced removal of his sons from their leadership posts in the armed forces was but one of several humiliations for the dynasty.

Under the leadership of Colonel Nicholas Zorbas, the League's administrative committee steered an essentially moderate course. Although threats usually cowed civilian opponents, certain elements of the League deemed more radical and forceful methods necessary for success of the "revolution." Some officers even favored establishment of a dictatorship and the consideration of alternate candidates for the throne. Such extreme policies and authoritarian attitudes did not reflect the thinking of the majority, which did not aspire to rule the nation directly and which advocated the maintenance of parliamentary procedures—albeit under strained conditions.

Anti-dynastic attitudes, not republicanism, characterized the policies of the League. In general, advocates of a republic remained few prior to World War I, never numbering more than five members of the *Boule* at any one time during

151

George's long reign from 1863 to 1913.[101] Publicly the officers expressed their loyalty to King George, reluctantly acknowledging the concern of the great powers for the Glücksburg ruler, an interest which the League could not consider challenging. Even republican France supported George, obviously fearing that in the confusion following the king's abdication, a pro-German successor would emerge. Greece's diplomatic position, already highly dependent on the will of the powers, could only worsen if the officers forced George to abandon his throne. Two units of the British fleet off Phaleron served as constant reminders of vested great power interests. Moreover, Athens had to negotiate a loan with foreign financiers which, even under normal conditions, would have proven difficult. Not having reaped many diplomatic rewards with George on the throne, as the officers recognized, did not mean Greece would fare better without him.

The political function of the Military League became an uncomfortable one for its members. Vague reform proposals and pressure on beleaguered deputies resulted in a long list of well-intentioned but ill-conceived legislation. Some of the potentially most effective bills aiming at economies or increased revenues struck at the vital interests of important groups whose opposition often checked passage of the laws. Collectively this disenchantment at certain reforms diminished the League's popularity. Increasingly the officers realized chauvinism and sincerity were no substitutes for political experience. Even regarding their immediate concern—the armed forces—only limited advances had been made because of a lack of funds and preoccupation with other political issues. In his "Annual Report, 1909," Sir Francis Elliot commented: "... the state of the Greek army at the end of the year was probably worse than it was at the beginning."[102]

As 1909 drew to a close the officers evaluated their few achievements and conceded that the orientation of their political involvement had to change. The League perceived, too, that at all costs the armed forces could not retreat from the political arena with a tarnished image—the nation's expansionist dreams depended upon a powerful, united military backed by a people willing to make sacrifices. Although the League continually criticized the politicians for misguided leadership, it relied on the same men for the execution of a reform program. Progressive forces, few and disorganized, shared the officers' hope that new politicians with fresh ideas might take over the reins of leadership. At this important juncture the administrative committee solicited advice from Eleftherios Venizelos, for several years a favorite among liberally-inclined circles in Greece.

The Cretan leader carried much-needed political insights as well as personal ambition with him to Athens in January 1910. After considerable deliberation the League agreed to accept Venizelos's main suggestion to summon a National Assembly to revise the nonfundamental articles of the constitution. Recommended by others in the preceding months but generally disregarded, the proposal now provided the officers with the appropriate exit. With issuance of the Royal decree assuring the assembly's convocation, the Military League could gracefully divest itself of uncomfortable political responsibilities. Revision of the constitution would revamp weak areas of the Greek political structure and facilitate reform.

By March all concerned parties concurred in the need for the Military League to disband. In its parting communique on 31 March in *Chronos* the administrative committee in muted tones admitted that it had made some mistakes and provided limited achievements. The officers insisted, however, that their policies had placed the country "on the road to improvement" and that national interests demanded "the return of the army and navy to their own duties." Having emphasized dramatically the urgent requirement of reform, the Military League expected the people to maintain the momentum. A frank expression of the League's activities, this final statement nonetheless perpetuated the myth of "revolution" with all of its reputedly positive connotations. The League and its backers consistently used the term as a rhetorical instrument, despite admission of circumscribed accomplishments and moderate policies.

Under the direction of the Mavromichalis and Dragoumis ministries the *Boule* cranked out more than 150 laws which fell into the categories of administrative and general, judicial, financial, educational, and postal.[103] Most of the new laws were directed at increasing the efficiency of existing institutions and practices of the state services. The bulk of financial legislation sought to curb corruption and augment revenue

153

collection. There were no intentional attempts to pass laws aimed at the advancement of bourgeois interests. Moreover, little attention was given to the plight of the worker or peasant who comprised the overwhelming majority of the population. Statutes for the closing of shops on Sundays and certain holidays and the establishment of a ministry of agriculture, commerce and industry were perhaps the most important measures approved for lower class interests. The suppression of agrarian protest in Thessaly provided a harsh indicator that the Military League was not ready to sponsor extensive change in the nation's allocation of wealth and property. Such action or inaction did not imply that the officers deliberately defended the dominant socio-economic groups. Instead, by not pushing for laws directed at redistributing social and economic influence and by utilizing a *Boule* dominated by traditional oligarchical interests, the Military League as a body demonstrated that it did not perceive its problems or aspirations in specific class terms.

The Military League's prime justification for intervening in politics in late August was to strengthen the armed forces. Yet in this area, too, few gains had been made by late winter 1910. Included among thirty-two laws dealing with the army were those restructuring its hierarcy and deposing the crown prince and his brothers from their influential commands. New laws approved purchases of equipment and weapons, better transport and improved recruiting practices. Of twenty-nine bills passed by the lawmakers for the navy, the acquisition of the large armored cruiser, *Averoff,* and plans for buying small destroyers ranked among the most important. Provision was also made to hire foreign missions to reorganize the army and navy.[104]

Despite legislation with projections to increase significantly the peacetime size of the army over seven years, in the early spring of 1910 it numbered less than 20,000 men in uniform—a far cry from the levels mandatory for Greece to defend its national interests effectively. To ameliorate conditions, arrangements were made to noticeably augment budgetary allocations for the armed forces and to seek out foreign loans. More hope than conviction accompanied these measures to strengthen the country. The Military League had to admit, as had earlier ministries, that Greece's limited resources and heavily taxed populace could not support ambitious expansionist programs and only with difficulty could it supply and train an effective army. Greece's vulnerable diplomatic status in Eastern Mediterranean affairs had spurred the officers to revolt, but the nation under their guidance had not remedied its poor condition. The dependency of Athens on great power backing remained high as it solicited aid in the form of loans and diplomatic shoring. To receive help Greece had to demonstrate greater financial stability, or indicate that it could be a valuable diplomatic or military ally.

In evaluating the short-term impact on Greek politics and society, it must be concluded that the Military League's activities spawned, at most, moderate, limited changes. The demonstration of strength of the officers in the early morning hours of 28 August 1909 constituted a coup d'état; subsequently, upon its departing from the political scene on 30 March 1910, its circumscribed accomplishments have to be assessed as those of a reformist coup d'état and not, contentions to the contrary, of a revolution.

V
April 1910—December 1913
AFTERMATH OF REVOLT

Against the backdrop of twentieth-century Greek politics the military revolt of 1909 assumes a highly important role. Yet in order to evaluate accurately the seven-month involvement of the Military League in politics, it is necessary to relate its influence on subsequent events. This approach can confront difficulties, however, because of the complex episodes of the World War I era. Where the eleven years following the 1897 defeat had been relatively quiet, stagnant ones for Greece, the fifteen years after 1909 provided the nation with a succession of domestic and international crises of long-term impact. The comments and analysis in this chapter and the "Epilogue" will serve to place the 1909 revolt in appropriate historical perspective.

Elections, Reforms, Wars

It was only natural that uncertainty should characterize the political scene once the Military League disbanded. The officers had restored the initiative for political change to the people, and the Stephen Dragoumis ministry prepared to lead the country toward elections. During this period rumors circulated regularly that the Military League still existed in clandestine form. General Nicholas Zorbas and Commander Andreas Miaoulis, as ministers of war and marine, respectively, represented the interests of the League in the cabinet even though it had formally dissolved. In his memoirs Zorbas stated that had events drifted into a reactionary direction, the Military League would have re-emerged, "but in another form and its activity would have been very different from that of its predecessor." Zorbas was probably intentionally vague in light of what followed, while Theodore Pangalos commented with no supplementary details that the League dissolved permanently only in late 1910.[1] In any case, the League did not reappear in a public form nor is there evidence that it operated behind the scenes in succeeding months. The main reasons for this quiescent mood in the ranks of the officers, it can be safely surmised, were that events generally evolved favorably for their interests and that a renewed political function would not have been received well by the people.

In accordance with commitments to the League, the Dragoumis ministry continued the policy of purging the state bureaucracy of corrupt and inefficient personnel. The public remained essentially apathetic as the government by the early summer dismissed employees from the ministries of finance, education and interior and seventeen professors from the University of Athens. The committee, organized by the army to inquire into the qualifications of officers, ordered the compulsory retirement in May of 67 officers classified as undesirable. A navy board dismissed a smaller number.[2] The government, army, and navy committees appear to have carried out this purging process in an essentially fair, nonvindictive manner.

Dragoumis also supervised the important task of acquiring the 150 million drachma loan authorized by the law passed on 19 March. A group of French, English and Greek banks agreed to supply the funds and made an advance of 40 million drachmas in July.[3] This money temporarily ameliorated tight financial conditions in the country and permitted the government to divert money to railroad construction, public works and, of course, the armed forces.

In spite of the general concern over the future of national politics, relative calm prevailed during the spring. After the succession of seven nervous months King George and Queen Olga departed Athens on 14 April for a holiday on Corfu. Twelve days later Crown Prince Constantine joined his parents, finally returning to Greek soil after his forced departure the previous September. His reception on the island was warm, and even Athenian newspapers responded cordially to his arrival.

Relations with the Ottoman Empire remained tense. Although the Turks protested Greek guerrilla band activities in

Epirus and Macedonia, Crete continued to be the main point of contention. In response to the irksome behavior of the Greeks, the Turks began a boycott of Greek shipping during May in Trebizond, a policy which soon spread to other commercial centers. Ostensibly the boycott was a popular rejoinder, but officials in Constantinople condoned this tactic which hurt Greek economic interests both in and outside the Empire. And with the forthcoming elections planned in Greece, the Porte emphasized, as so often in the recent past, that war would instantly follow if the National Assembly admitted Cretan deputies.[4]

One of the first signs that the summer elections might depart from customary patterns surfaced with rumors in April of an agreement between George Theotokis and Demetrios Rallis. Rivals for more than a decade, the two leaders planned to merge forces to ensure control of the National Assembly by dividing seats in proportion to the strengths of their respective parties. The pact became public knowledge after 14 July with announcement of 21 August as the date for elections.

Premature revelation of this pact between the two parties encouraged the formation of countermovements. In the region of the capital the Political League, trade guilds, associations of merchants, and the Piraeus Chamber of Commerce compiled electoral lists of candidates advocating reform. Many of these nominees were campaigning for the first time and came from the middle-class ranks of attorneys, manufacturers, journalists, and merchants. In Thessaly, still restless from the riotous conditions of March, candidates representing peasant interests emerged to challenge incumbent deputies, most of whom were wealthy and resided in far-off Athens. Office-seekers with socialist platforms also appeared in significant numbers. Thus for the first time the Greek people were to have the opportunity to choose from a sizeable list of candidates not associated with the old oligarchical groups. These aspirants for office faced elections as "Independents" without a leader and without a formal party apparatus.[5] The name of Eleftherios Venizelos naturally dominated conversations concerning the appropriate chief for a reform party. Venizelos at this time was engaged in Cretan politics, and although his name was placed by supporters on the electoral lists of Attica-Boeotia, he refused to accept formally. Instead, he announced that if chosen and if he could arrange matters on the island satisfactorily, he would serve.

Great Britain, France, Italy, and Russia—the four powers actively overseeing affairs on Crete—placed considerable pressure on the Cretan government during the summer to respect the rights of the island's Moslems and not to hold elections for sending deputies to Greece. Constantinople, among its complaints to Athens and the powers, added a protest over the candidature of Venizelos in Greece. The Cretan politician, in turn, claimed Greek citizenship through his father's naturalization the preceding century.[6] At the time of the Greek elections Venizelos planned to be in Switzerland on a holiday.

The quiet conduct of the 21 August elections belied the surprising outcome. Prior to balloting most observers conceded victory to the Theotokis-Rallis combine. But when the results were tabulated for this National Assembly of twice the normal number of deputies, the two previously dominant parties failed to achieve a majority. In the Chamber of 362 deputies the Theotokists acquired 112 seats and the Rallists 67. Mavromichalists with 24 and Zaïmists with 13 also represented traditional interests. The uncoordinated coalition for reform, dubbed "Independents," amassed an unexpected 146 seats. Since many of the victorious Independent deputies were relative political unknowns, the people had apparently voted against old party nominees rather than with conviction for new leaders. The Greeks responded for the first time to socialists of several different schools, electing ten from their ranks. In Thessaly 46 to 48 deputies received the support of the impoverished peasantry by calling for widespread agrarian reform. The other region outspokenly for change was Athens and its environs. Here Venizelos topped the Attica-Boeotia lists with the most votes, followed by eight other Independents. Dragoumis, the prime minister and also unaffiliated, ranked tenth, ahead of Rallis who customarily dominated this electoral district.[7]

Accompanied by Crown Prince Constantine, King George officially convened the Revisionist National Assembly on 14 September.[8] The monarch stressed the calling of the Chamber to revise the nonfundamental articles of the constitution. This position ran counter to the wishes of those among the new

159

deputies who now sought conversion of the gathering to a Constituent National Assembly with broad sweeping powers. Turbulent debate between the two rival groups followed the king's departure: the one faction supported an oath by the deputies in terms of the existing constitution while the other proposed a pledge to the nation, thereby backing the concept of a constituent assembly. Stormy proceedings on the following day did not resolve the heated issue and the Chamber recessed until the nineteenth. In the meantime an important step was taken towards providing direction and cohesion to the disparate groups advocating reform.

Having returned to Crete after his sojourn in Switzerland, Venizelos resigned his positions in the Cretan Assembly and Executive Committee to enter formally into Greek politics. On 18 September a large crowd greeted him upon his disembarkation from a special steamer at Piraeus. Many of those welcoming the Cretan politician at the port followed him to his hotel in downtown Athens, outside of which a throng swelled to nearly 10,000 cheering partisans. In firm tones Venizelos addressed the crowd, stressing that he had not come to Greece to become a party leader in the old sense; those personal politics had nearly ruined the nation. Although King George had committed errors in the past, he should now place himself at the head of the reform movement. Upon referring to the National Assembly as revisionist, the crowd roared "No! Constituent!" Venizelos replied "Revisionist!" After this exchange occurred three times, the gathering voiced its approval of his stand.

The following day found him in the Assembly where, after orderly debate, he proposed a compromise on the oath: the deputies could reserve the right to determine the assembly's character later but now should take the oath prescribed by the constitution to "the country, the constitution and the constitutional king." His resolution passed. Within a short period Venizelos astutely altered his political image without losing his popular backing which, in fact, increased. He was no longer the anti-dynastic critic nor the revolutionary—he was the reformer who inspired confidence. In checking the nascent radicalism of those Greeks pursuing extensive change with an entirely new constitution, he became their leader, concurrently attracting to his side many who were formerly wary of his intentions.

Preliminary business and the validation of elections preoc-
cupied the Chamber for another three weeks. On 12 October
Prime Minister Dragoumis submitted his resignation to the
king, having effectively fulfilled the mandate of his original
appointment during this difficult period of transition. In the
subsequent parliamentary confusion, George boldly determined to invest Venizelos, formerly the dynasty's bugbear,
with the responsibility of forming a new ministry. The new
government, composed of individuals with no previous ministerial experience, was sworn in on 19 October. Confronted with
the incomplete support and obstructionist tactics of the old
parties comprising the majority, Venizelos convinced the king
on 25 October to dissolve the Chamber. Elections for a new
double Revisionist National Assembly were scheduled for 11
December.

The old party leaders and their deputies bitterly opposed
new elections, calling them ruinous for the country and against
the spirit of the constitution. They criticized the king for his
failure to consider their position in light of past loyalty. In
protest the three old party chiefs—Theotokis, Rallis, Mavromichalis—decided not to participate in the forthcoming
electoral struggle. *Patris,* an Athenian daily, aptly summarized general opinion by claiming that these three leaders
committed suicide in order to escape the guillotine.[9] The trade
guilds, commercial organizations and the Athenian press,
with two exceptions, sided with Venizelos in his decision.
Telegrams and resolutions of endorsement flowed into his
office from the provinces.

During these weeks the Liberal party started taking form
under Venizelos's leadership. Political cadres throughout the
country worked to create a unified party network with slates of
candidates for the forthcoming elections. To launch his campaign for office and to define more precisely the platform for
his new party, Venizelos chose to address the people of Larissa,
in Thessaly, on 27 November. Under a steady rain the prime
minister spoke from the balcony of a local club to a very large
crowd. Among his first points, he dealt with the heavy burden
of taxes, particularly indirect taxes upon the poorer classes.
His government would strive to lessen these onerous imposts
and place a greater responsibility for their collection on the
wealthier classes. The new ministry of agriculture, commerce
and industry would work in a scientific manner to develop the

161

productive potential of the country. Efforts would be made to discourage emigration but not through compulsory measures. He proposed to reorganize communal institutions to eliminate the evils of the old system and to promote public security with a restructuring and training of the gendarmerie. A revision of juridical codes and the system of justice was also mandatory. The question of developing and maintaining the permanency of public officials would be solved by constitutional provision. Educational reforms also loomed important in his party's program. Measures for the reorganization and strengthening of the armed forces with the assistance of foreign missions were of utmost significance. On the sensitive issue most relevant to his audience, the agrarian problem, Venizelos courageously declared that because of its complex nature, the people should hold no illusions. Although part of his policy was the development of peasant proprietorship, he had no intention of confiscating the property of large landholders and handing it over to the peasants. A legislative readjustment of the relations between owners and cultivators would be made on the basis of the written and customary law prevailing in Thessaly before its incorporation by Greece in 1881, and with these considerations further reform would be made. Except for his stand on the agrarian problems of the region, the audience enthusiastically received the speech, subsequently publicized throughout the nation as a detailed statement of the Liberal party's platform.[10]

The results of the elections of 11 December 1910 were a foregone conclusion. With the three old parties boycotting the contest, the Liberals of Venizelos won a resounding victory, garnering nearly 300 of the 362 seats. The larger percentage of these deputies was serving in the Chamber for the first time. In fact, only 117 of the deputies had been chosen in the August elections and only a small number of the remaining 245 had ever served previously in the Chamber.[11] Thus, part of the Military League's hoped for goals had been achieved with Venizelos's overwhelming victory, the large number of new deputies and the elimination of the old parties from positions of influence. The prime minister next proceeded to revision of the constitution, reform legislation, and strengthening the armed forces.

The second double Revisionist National Assembly opened on 21 January 1911. A parliamentary committee with Stephen

Dragoumis as chairman undertook the necessary preliminary work and on 10 March discussion began on the *Boule* floor of articles slated for revision. The issue of a constituent assembly no longer existed as Venizelos's strong stand of the preceding autumn silenced the advocates of radical change. Heated debate erupted over certain articles, but with his large majority Venizelos was assured passage of those modifications supported by him. By early June the Chamber terminated its work on 54 nonfundamental articles of the 110-article constitution, and the king shortly thereafter affixed his signature on the revised document.

Included among the most important modifications were the following articles. To curb obstructionist tactics by opposition parties, the quorum requirement was lowered from one-half plus one to one-third of all deputies. Elementary education became compulsory and the responsibility for financing it shifted from local authorities to the state. A Council of State, abolished in 1865, was revived to function as a consultative body to assist in drafting bills presented to the *Boule* and also as a supreme court to deal with administrative abuses. Foreign officers through special legislation could now serve in the public employment of Greece. Barring some exceptions, civil servants obtained security of tenure to restrain rampant spoils practices. To avoid inherent abuses because of their dual loyalties, military officers on the active list could not run for deputy. The powers of the executive could be substantially increased in times of crisis with the suspension of all guarantees related to arbitrary arrest, the right of public meeting, the inviolability of domicile and private correspondence, liberty of press, and trial by jury. The inviolability of private property was modified so that the state could expropriate land but with proper compensation and for the public advantage. While acknowledging the inherent right of the state to expropriate land the article made clear that the exercise of this prerogative could be barred by international treaties—a specific reference to Turkish rights in Thessaly.[12]

The legislative achievements of this double Chamber, which adjourned on 25 July and reconvened from 25 October until the early winter, were considerable and fulfilled many of the Liberal party's campaign promises. For example, the Venizelos regime restructured communal government and amended penal and civil codes. A new law reconstituted the ministry of agriculture, commerce and industry, renaming it the ministry of national economy, with a special labor bureau. The *Boule* also passed important laws for the settlement of employer-labor disputes, for the health and safety of workers and hours of work, and also regulations for female and child labor. Specific requisitions provided for the drainage of marshes, construction of roads, the establishment of an agricultural school in Larissa, and the purchase of agricultural implements for distribution to peasants.[13]

The nation's financial condition exhibited noticeable improvement and unexampled strength. Instead of customary deficits, ordinary revenues exceeded ordinary expenditures at the end of both 1910 and 1911—an accomplishment attained without the imposition of any extra taxes. Administrative reforms and the more business-like methods of the Venizelos government account for part of the surplus. Credit has also to be given, however, to the additional taxation levied by Venizelos's predecessors, the revenue collection reforms instigated by the Military League, growing commercial activity, and the impact of the foreign loan.[14]

Efforts designed to bolster the military arm of the nation advanced at a rapid rate. The Venizelos ministry arrived at terms with Paris for a military mission, with London for a naval mission, and with Rome for a mission to reform the gendarmerie. Article 3 of the constitution was accordingly amended so as to permit employment of foreign personnel; in order to hasten the hiring process before the conclusion of constitutional revision, the Assembly passed a special law for the French mission in April and one for the British contingent in May. General Joseph-Paul Eydoux had arrived in late January 1911 with a small staff to begin work considerably before the legal formalities were concluded. During the year Eydoux instituted new organizational patterns and training procedures, increasing appreciably the army's fighting capabilities. Seven Greek officers travelled to Paris for schooling at the Military Academy; another group of Greeks received aviation training in France for the new airplanes ordered by Athens. Although the size of the peacetime army remained small (around 25,000), with new organization, equipment purchases and training of reserves, Greece expected to mobilize in time of war over 130,000 men.[15]

Britain's Rear Admiral L. G. Tufnell arrived in Greece at the end of April 1911 to commence his duties with the navy. New organizational plans, regulations, and instruction along British lines revamped the navy within a year. Long training cruises under the admiral's direction provided rewarding results. The government also bought two submarines and proposed to acquire eventually another armored cruiser, six torpedo boats, and two destroyers.[16]

With this feverish activity the Venizelos ministry accomplished many of the general goals which the Military League had outlined but had failed to attain. The Cretan politician had shrewdly consolidated reformist energies under his banner. During 1911 the formerly active military officers had to be regarded as a secondary force in any political reform. There were several minor instances, quickly and quietly snuffed out, of seditious activities by small coteries of officers, none of whom, however, had been prominent in the hierarchy of the Military League.

Perhaps the clearest sign of Venizelos's strong position and determination to promote national unity came when he engineered the return of Crown Prince Constantine to a command position in the army. The prime minister presented a bill creating an inspectorship-general of the army with Constantine as the first occupant. Protest came from several quarters, including opposition deputies and the press. Some army circles quietly expressed indignation and logically so, since a prime motivating factor for the rebellion of 28 August had been just this question of a command position for the crown prince. Venizelos, the dynasty's old nemesis, now argued that conditions were appropriate for the future king to resume responsibilities and to utilize his expertise for the benefit of the entire nation. In order to accent the urgency of this issue, Venizelos designated passage of the bill as a vote of confidence in his ministry. On 28 June 1911 the Assembly approved the law, although Constantine did not assume his duties until the following spring.[17] Assessing accurately the mood of the public, the army remained quiet, recognizing that it could not dare resist the authority and popularity of Venizelos nor threaten the favorable pace of general reform.

Having altered his anti-dynastic image, Venizelos also tempered his formerly passionate advocacy of Crete's union

165

with Greece. Towards this emotional problem Venizelos wished to exercise caution and display patience. Greece, he felt, should avoid impulsive war with Turkey. The nation should complete its military organization first. Bearing in mind the opposition of the great powers to Cretan adventurism, Venizelos, in the face of criticism by fellow Cretans and their supporters in Greece, resisted attempts at demonstrating *enosis* in 1911 and into the summer of 1912.

The double Revisionist National Assembly completed its mission and elections were set for 24 March 1912. The Greeks indicated their general approval of Venizelos's leadership by providing his party with an overwhelming victory—out of 181 deputies, 146 belonged to the Liberals. Ten Theotokists, eight Mavromichalists and six Rallists entered the new *Boule* from the ranks of the old parties. The discrediting of the traditional factions continued. Even Demetrios Rallis, who long had laid claim to Attica-Boeotia as his personal fief, met defeat as the Liberal party captured every seat in the district. Venizelos was thus able to rule the country in the absence of a viable parliamentary opposition.

With the Greek house in the process of being reordered, Venizelos capitalized on the opportunity to pursue the nation's expansionist ambitions more vigorously. The development of this capacity had been the ardent hope of the Greeks for decades and the ultimate objective of the Military League. The Balkan states temporarily shelved their rivalries over territory to align against the common enemy, the Ottoman Empire. Turkey's failure in her war against Italy, which broke out in September 1911, encouraged Bulgaria, Greece, Montenegro, and Serbia to join forces. Hostilities began in October 1912 and the Balkan League quickly demonstrated its superiority. Crown Prince Constantine headed the Greek forces which captured control of the critical port of Thessaloniki on 8 November, beating Bulgarian contingents to the city by several hours. Greek units, again under Constantine's direction, also took over Ioannina in March 1913. With the signing of the Treaty of London on 20 May 1913, Turkey ceded collectively to the Balkan allies all her territory in Europe except for Constantinople with its approaches and Albania. After decades of struggle Greece acquired Crete while the fate of Greek-inhabited islands in the Aegean and of Albania was to be determined by the powers. Conflict over the division of Macedonia ensued and Bulgaria blundered disastrously into the Second Balkan War during July 1913 against her former allies with Turkey and Rumania also joining in the campaign. Greece with her military and diplomatic achievements acquired, besides Crete, Southern Epirus and a large section of Macedonia with its port of Thessaloniki—increases of sixty-eight percent in territory and sixty-seven percent in population.

During the Balkan Wars Greece demonstrated that she had utilized the period from the late summer of 1909 for a profitable revitalization. The Military League had launched this era of national reform and had set the stage for the entry of Venizelos into the Greek political arena. The wily Cretan statesman then placed his own stamp on the direction of politics. He was the effective opposition politician who subsequently became the successful leader working for national unity and reform. Shifting his earlier anti-dynastic stance, he gained the confidence of King George and also the services of Crown Prince Constantine, the former *bête noire* of the Military League. Venizelos's popular support and tactics helped reimpose discipline in the armed forces, concurrently snuffing out its political potential. All these adjustments to the situation created by the antagonisms of the August 1909 revolt appeared to be justified by the Balkan War conquests and with the succession to the throne by Constantine. On 18 March 1913, a mentally deranged Greek (the official description) assassinated King George during his walk in the newly acquired city of Thessaloniki. While George's death was a tragedy for the nation, Constantine nonetheless could not have received his crown at a more propitious moment. His earlier unpopularity had faded away in the light of his military conquests, and both king and Venizelos basked in the glory of the new, larger Greece.

The Extent of Political Change

That the Military League's involvement in politics did not constitute a "revolution" has already been discussed. Nor can the Venizelos years up to 1914 be labeled revolutionary despite all the changes they brought to the Greek scene. The military revolt is better appraised for its catalytic function in inducing an accelerated evolution of national politics. Prior to August 1909 broadly representative elements of the population—trade guilds, merchants, peasants, university students, the press—critically attacked prevailing conditions. But no one political group effectively transferred these grievances from the factories, shops, fields, and offices into the *Boule* where the country's representatives might act on them. The Military League's political intervention increased the tempo of an already growing movement by vocal segments of the populace and the press to place pressure on politicians for reform. The emphasis upon "revolution" in the League's propaganda and the arrival of Venizelos to guide the country on an altered course introduced new individuals into national politics. These fresh figures discarded the generally static and nondifferentiated positions of the old parties. They instead represented a greater cross-section of political and class interests. Greek parties had habitually formed around personalities and in several respects would continue to do so. But the electorate in the 1910 and 1912 elections had the opportunity to choose deputies who reflected varying ideological platforms. The program of Venizelos's Liberal party resembled that of similarly named groupings in other areas of Europe. Moreover, the Greeks elected socialist and agrarian deputies. There is no doubt that these parties would have eventually appeared in the Greek political arena as they had already throughout Europe, but the impact of the League's intervention quickened their emergence.

The predominant role of Venizelos, however, muted the nascent influence of the socialists and agrarians. The prime minister shrewdly attracted support from workers and peasants through his legislative programs which satisfied, at least in part, some of their demands. While commercial groups benefitted by his leadership and from the recovered economy in 1912, labor also received laws to protect its interests. Moderate measures to improve the plight of the peasant and the compromise arrangements of the Thessalian estates pacified the restless region. The strong leadership and magnetic personality of Venizelos drew support to his moderate Liberals and away from more radically-inspired and smaller movements. Therefore, in the elections of 21 August 1910 the agrarian deputies of Thessaly won forty-six of forty-eight possible seats and the socialists captured ten slots. In the interim before the second elections of that year, Venizelos organized his Liberal party and in December the number of agrarians dropped to twenty-eight and the socialists totaled only five. The balloting of 24 March 1912 found the Liberals with a crushing majority in Thessaly, and the few socialists under Alexander Papanastasiou were absorbed as the left wing of the Liberal party.[18]

Influenced more by Western Europe's moderate and revisionist socialist schools, the disparate cliques of Greek socialists never flaunted the revolutionary Marxist banner of violent class struggle in the years before World War I. No equivalent of an advanced ideological conflict of socialist factions occurred as in the split of the Bulgarian Social Democratic party between the "Broads" and the "Narrows." Nor did socialist principles influence the conceptual development of Greece's irredentist program, the *Megale Idea,* which remained faithful to its early nineteenth-century conservative forms. Characteristic of their moderate, nonrevolutionary inclinations, the Greek socialists, alone among their ideological brethren in the Balkans, supported participation of their nation in the Balkan Wars. Greece before 1914 never spawned a prominent leader who combined programs of widespread social reform with those of revolution, national liberation and Balkan federation as was the case in Bulgaria and Serbia. For that matter, had Greece followed the route of her Balkan neighbors and instituted a communist regime after World War II, it would have been an impossible task to commemorate any outstanding socialist-revolutionary heroes from this earlier period—none existed to fit the mold of Serbia's Svetozar Marković or Bulgaria's Khristo Botev.

Politicians representing exclusively agrarian interests had their short-lived heyday in 1910, and they then represented only one geographical region. Greece alone among the Balkan states has never witnessed a strong peasant movement. Several factors worked to deter development of radical agrarian politics. Greek peasants early became involved in the patronage-clientage syndrome, and the pursuit of the *Megale Idea* captivated them. The lure of emigration served as the most immediate antidote to their poverty-stricken status. The unemployed or underemployed of the countryside flocked to

169

American shores, thereby defusing rural discontent. Statistics indicate that from a high of 36,580 emigrants to the United States in 1907, the number dropped to 14,111 in 1909, only to rise again to 25,888 in 1910 and 28,126 in 1911.[19]

When evaluated in the overall context of the twentieth century, the months following the December 1910 elections constitute a honeymoon period for Greek politics. The national unity and the popular backing for Venizelos and his policies were unprecedented, but the real changes did not run very deep. Succeeding years revealed that although ideology tinged political parties, personalities and spoils practices continued to dominate. Voters and politicians still valued patronage-clientage relationships. Beyond the regional level, charisma and rhetoric drew voters to national leaders, frequently over-shadowing exclusively political issues.[20]

Ephemeral Unity

In light of subsequent events, too, the national unity of this era proved to be only veneer. The Greeks during World War I divided between the supporters of King Constantine and Venizelos over the fundamental question of the nation's involvement in the hostilities. The role of the great powers and the basic conflicts in this struggle within Greece should not, however, be confined to the months following the assassination at Sarajevo. The lines of division already manifested themselves in 1909. As so often has been the case in her turbulent history, foreign interests penetrated Greece and gave partial direction to her internal politics.

Crown Prince Constantine's position as commander-in-chief of the army was colored with controversy from the first day it was presented by George Theotokis as a bill to the *Boule* in 1900. With the Military League's demand for his ouster, the dispute also assumed a foreign dimension when German diplomacy sought to buttress Constantine's weakened position. Kaiser Wilhelm's concern for his brother-in-law, the future king of Greece, naturally heightened after this humiliation of the late summer of 1909. King George, in turn, consulted British diplomats regularly and found solace in the presence of British warships anchored off Athens.

Constantine departed Greece in September 1909, followed by his wife, Sophie, who welcomed the friendlier confines of her native Germany. Baron Hans von Wangenheim, Berlin's minister to Athens, kept the crown princess abreast of developments in Greece with regular dispatches. The baron expressed his adamant attitudes against the Military League in his communications which, in turn, reinforced Sophie's own distaste for the rebellious officers, not to mention her critical view of her father-in-law's moderate, compromising tactics; Constantine also shared these feelings. The minister's communications continued in the same vein even after the dissolution of the Military League and the August 1910 elections.[21]

These Royal attitudes, hidden from the public eye, hardened over the decision to commission a foreign mission to reorganize the army. In the late winter of 1910 Prime Minister Stephen Dragoumis and his minister of war, General Nicholas Zorbas, communicated with the French government about the prospect of providing such a military advisory group. King George did not respond favorably to the proposal because he did not wish to antagonize the Kaiser. Apparently in 1908 and 1909 during Wilhelm's annual holiday on Corfu, George Theotokis, then prime minister, arrived at a tentative agreement that upon resolution of the Cretan imbroglio German military organizers would be commissioned by Athens.[22] With the coming of the Military League to political prominence and with its policies directed against Constantine, Germany could not consider supplying the necessary officers. In December 1909 Wangenheim wrote his superiors in Berlin of pro-French sentiment among League leaders, arguing that German officers should not have any associations, official or social, with these rebellious, anti-dynastic elements. Moreover, a reorganized Greek army would only launch an unsuccessful war against Turkey. In later dispatches the German envoy stressed that aiding Greece at this juncture would jeopardize Berlin's growing influence in Constantinople. A compromise solution to secure the interests of the Triple Alliance in Greece might be the approval of an Austro-Hungarian military mission.[23]

This sensitive issue slipped into the background during the late spring and summer of 1910 as the nation prepared for elections. The Germans regarded George Theotokis as a representative of their interests in Greece and naturally hoped that he would regain the prime ministership after the August voting. Long a supporter of Constantine, Theotokis resisted the incursion of French influence, claiming that France's

171

radical politics and links with Slavdom, also Greece's enemy, should draw Athens toward the German diplomatic orbit.[24] It should be recalled that both France and Great Britain rejected Theotokis's proposals for alliances in 1907.

The subject of the military mission again became the matter of concern for the Royal Family in the autumn. On taking over the prime ministership, Venizelos acquired concurrently the portfolios for the ministries of war and marine. He then set into motion the procedures for the summoning of General Eydoux and the skeleton of his staff which would increase in size only after passage of the necessary legislation. King George said he could not trust the French, but the crown prince and his wife expressed graver apprehensions. They suspected that with the coming of the French mission, radical, republican influences would spread within the ranks of an army which had already exerted anti-dynastic pressures. With this expectation Zorbas and his clique, according to Constantine, contacted Paris the previous spring. Where the Royal Family could trust the old parties, they had now to fear the politicians advocating widespread reform. Crown Princess Sophie believed that with the French in Greece all ties between the armies of Greece and Germany would be severed. In one very emotional scene in the presence of Wangenheim, Sophie tearfully exclaimed to Constantine that all associations with her brother would come to an end. She then blurted: "There is no longer any place for us in this country. Let us pack our suitcases and depart."[25] Sophie had thus placed the entire issue on both personal and national levels: German connections in Greece were being threatened by ascendant French interests. The setting was created for Greece's involvement in diplomatic tussles whose scope went beyond the cul-de-sac of the Eastern Mediterranean.

Zorbas in his memoirs cited several reasons for preferring the French. The existing regulations for exercises were translated from those used in France. Many Greek officers knew the French language and a fair number had received some education in France, while those familiar with German or trained in Germany were far fewer. In Zorbas's estimation the national characters of the French and Greeks resembled each other and this factor would therefore facilitate cooperation.[26]

In speaking with King George and Constantine, Venizelos offered more complex explanations for summoning the French. The prime minister revealed that his hands were tied by the earlier understanding of the Dragoumis cabinet with France. Paris had stated it would underwrite the crucial 150 million drachma loan for Greece only if Athens would employ a French military mission. In dire need of the money and unable to find other sources, Dragoumis arrived at such an agreement with France. Venizelos also inferred that Greece could gain with the Cretan question through an understanding with the Triple Entente. Britain, in particular, played an overriding role in determining the island's future.[27]

Expressed otherwise, Greece required assistance, and Paris provided with certain stipulations that which Berlin was unwilling to extend. In actuality Wilhelm had agreed earlier with Theotokis that Greece would receive a German loan for the purposes of purchasing an armored cruiser from a German naval yard. The military revolt and the League's decision to buy the vessel elsewhere had angered the Kaiser. In reaction to these developments and to the rough treatment of his relatives in Greece, Wilhelm refused to consider Greece's loan request in the spring of 1910. The Kaiser's advisers also counseled him against damaging German interests in Constantinople.[28]

In his maneuvers to unite the resources of the nation behind him in the autumn of 1910, Venizelos pursued moderate, compromising policies. No doubt with the intention of mollifying Constantine, the Cretan prime minister appointed Captain John Metaxas, a close confidant of the crown prince, as his aide-de-camp. Additional assignments restored some other pro-Constantine officers to important slots from which they had been removed by the Military League. Venizelos's boldest initiative, however, was the scheme to return the crown prince to the army as inspector-general. This conciliatory plan, suggested by Venizelos in mid-November 1910, initially met with the opposition of Constantine himself and then of officers and political rivals. The crown prince stated simply that he could not work with French officers; upon their departure it would be possible for him to accept the post. Sophie also voiced disapproval of Venizelos's proposal. In all probability heavy pres-

173

sure from his father influenced Constantine to rejoin the army.[29] As mentioned, passage of the necessary legislation came in late June 1911 and only after a storm of controversy. A Royal decree on 7 April 1912 designated the crown prince as inspector-general.

Constantine revealed his pro-German sympathies in both public and private ways. Although few in number, the Greek officers trained in Germany, such as Metaxas, had been intimates with Constantine when he commanded the army. Thus in the tense weeks before the revolt of 28 August, Constantine felt he could trust only these German educated officers.[30] He continued to consult these men after the coup d'état. The crown prince and his German-oriented officers revered Prussian education, discipline, and reputed military invincibility, and they regularly expressed their disrespect for the French. For example, during the summer of 1911 Major Agamemnon Pallis, Constantine's aide-de-camp, was sentenced to two months confinement in his house for having criticized the French officers in Greece to a friend, reportedly stating that a mission of Chinamen would have been equally useful. Constantine, in turn, expressed his reservations towards working with General Eydoux to the British military attaché in the late autumn of 1911, adding that the French failed to instill needed smartness into the Greek soldier. During the spring of 1912 Constantine began working with the French mission but nevertheless sniped at its accomplishments. On conclusion of the July 1912 maneuvers as the troops marched past the inspector-general, he remarked to a bystander that the Greek army had gone back three years in efficiency. The resentment of many Greek circles to this comment, later made public, was great, but it could not compare in intensity to that which followed Constantine's elevation to the rank of field marshal in the German army after the Balkan Wars in August 1913. The new king attributed his victories first to the courage of his troops and secondly to the training he and some of his officers had received in Germany. In his "Order of the Day" to the Greek armed forces on this occasion, Constantine declared: "I regard the bestowal of this honor by the Emperor [Wilhelm] as one more indicator of His Majesty's desire to draw this country into the orbit of German policy, and the King's eagerness to share it with his troops as a sign of readiness to fall in with that scheme, and to educate his people into acceptance of it." It required the efforts of the Greek press, explanations of the Venizelos government, and a follow-up speech at Paris by the king to remove the unfavorable impression to the French authorities.[31] With the outbreak of European-wide war in the summer of 1914 the implications of Constantine's pro-German sentiments could not be dismissed this easily.

The large majority of Greek accounts evaluate favorably the military revolt of 1909, primarily because it prepared the nation for its Balkan War victories. This is a valid interpretation by itself. But just because of this aura of national regeneration and exultation associated with territorial conquests, there has been a tendency not to consider the political, social and diplomatic currents beyond the 1909-1913 period. These years may indeed constitute a new era—but one which ended abruptly. Serious repercussions stemming from the coup d'état did not manifest themselves immediately. Initially its opponents were confused, discredited and disorganized. The forces of reaction begrudgingly lay dormant during Venizelos's inspired tenure as prime minister until after the Balkan Wars. Constantine, first as crown prince and then as king, had difficulty accepting the influential roles of Venizelos, the forces of reform and the French military mission. Instead he catered to the old political groups and expressed his admiration and sympathy for Germany. Venizelos, nonetheless, tried to straddle the middle road of conciliation, the route which King George had also adopted on many occasions. This course became increasingly untenable for Venizelos, largely due to diplomatic complications. Almost imperceptibly at first, the rivalries of the Triple Entente and Triple Alliance had entered the Greek political world with Venizelos and Constantine, respectively, to represent their interests. The linkage between great power concerns and Greek politics tightened with the outbreak of World War I. Consequently, as the European powers had earlier divided into two militant camps, so did Greece.

1914—1976
EPILOGUE

The military revolts of 1843, 1862 and 1909 resulted in gains for parliamentary rule and institutions as each coup d'état served to liberalize existing political conditions. Notwithstanding the important political role of the army in these three instances, the period prior to World War I generally had the armed forces outside of or barely on the periphery of the political arena. It should be noted, too, that while military conspirators worked briefly with organized political factions in 1843 and 1862, this was not the case in 1909 when the Military League acted independently.

After 1915 the involvement of the military in politics became more direct and frequent. The political world polarized during World War I to the extent that Greece experienced the effects of this crisis for decades. Individual factions found proponents of their interests within the armed forces which, in turn, split along political lines. Collaboration between sections of the civilian leadership and the politicized military, earlier apparent only on an infrequent basis, became so intimate and constant from 1916 to 1936 that it was hard at times to distinguish differences in their composition or mission. Instead of bolstering governmental institutions as with the first three revolts, the extraparliamentary potential of the armed forces was abused, thereby contributing to confusion and marked instability in national politics.

In the first months after the Sarajevo assassination and after it became apparent that the war would not end quickly, Prime Minister Eleftherios Venizelos began to argue for an alliance with France and Great Britain on the premise that the

176

Greeks would be amply rewarded with new territory for this support. King Constantine warmly backed the objectives of the *Megale Idea* but demanded heavy guarantees in arms, troops and money from the Entente to insure national security. Since this aid was not forthcoming in the amounts requested, the monarch advocated neutrality, a policy recommended by his pro-German military advisers and beneficial to German interests in that area of the Balkans. The dispute sharpened during 1915 with Venizelos maintaining that the king exceeded his constitutional prerogatives in blocking Greece's entrance into the war. Regardless of the motives behind the differing policies, both arguments had evident merits and wide constituencies: the Chamber of Deputies and the populace divided into Venizelist and Constantinist camps as did, inevitably, the armed forces. During these years of turmoil the "old party" politicians, predominant in the pre-1910 period, reemerged with new strength to back the king's program of neutrality.

Greece's international position evolved precariously after October 1915 when Entente detachments landed in Thessaloniki. Staunch adherents of Venizelos in Macedonia, fearing the incursion of Bulgarian forces on Greek soil, formed a Committee of National Defense during the last days of August 1916. With revolutionary designs, a small cadre of officers intended to create a large fighting force which would support the Allied campaign in the Balkans and be independent of the Athens government dominated by Constantinist and apparently pro-German interests. Greece was splitting in two with prodding from foreign interests, but the lines of division had actually been drawn well before war's outbreak—with the events of the 1909 coup d'état serving an important function in the process.

Venizelos, the political beneficiary of one military revolt, that of 1909, now redirected his career behind another sedition. On 26 September 1916 he declared the establishment of a Provisional Government for the purpose of exerting pressure on the royalist government to change its policies. The Committee of National Defense became the military arm of this regime based in Thessaloniki, attracting volunteers and deserters from throughout Greece. In the rapidly developing political schism, the armed forces began their breakdown into

177

three categories: the two groups of officers supporting respectively the Venizelos-Liberal "revolution" or its rival, the monarchist government in Athens, were smaller than the third
and largest segment which tried to remain apolitical.[1] But it
was the polarized wings of the armed forces, like their civilian
counterparts, that dominated the direction of Greek politics
after 1916.

On 13 June 1917 the British and French forced the departure of King Constantine, who was succeeded by his second
son, Alexander. Later that month a triumphant Venizelos
arrived in Athens, thus reuniting Greece with foreign assistance and bringing her into the war on the side of the Entente,
his political benefactor. During the next three years the Cretan
statesman ruled Greece by martial law, dismissing hundreds
of Constantinist and suspected Constantinist civil servants.
More significantly, over fifteen hundred Constantinist officers
were cashiered, and a smaller number imprisoned or exiled
together with royalist politicians. Meanwhile, the loyal officers from Venizelos's Macedonian army received rapid promotions.

The prime minister's persuasive personality and shrewd
diplomatic maneuvering among his patrons, the victorious
powers, almost achieved the elusive *Megale Idea* with the
landing of Greek troops in Smyrna during May 1919 and the
signing of the Treaty of Sèvres in August 1920. But these
accomplishments at the Paris Peace Conference failed to unite
the nation which still divided along Venizelist and Constantinist lines. Weary of eight years of mobilization, a suffering
economy, and increased corruption by his subordinates, the
Greeks defeated Venizelos at the polls on 14 November 1920.
With King Alexander's untimely death from a monkey's bite
and the plebiscite of 5 December restoring Constantine to the
throne, an extraordinary political reversal took place. A large
number of Constantinist officers, cashiered by the Liberal
government, returned to assume leadership posts vacated by
Venizelists who resigned voluntarily or were dismissed.

Disregarding a number of strategic handicaps, including
the drying up of financial and diplomatic support from Britain
and France, the king revived Greek military efforts to control
a larger portion of Asia Minor. Left alone to confront a

rejuvenated Turkish army under Mustafa Kemal, Greece suffered a tragic defeat by late summer 1922. Portions of the battered Greek army regrouped on the islands of Chios and Mytilene where Colonels Nicholas Plastiras and Stylianos Gonatas proclaimed a "revolution" to save the nation from further catastrophe. Constantine, once again discredited, departed from Greece on 29 September, leaving his first son to reign as George II. The frenzied emotions of these months contributed to a military court's decision in late November to execute five prominent royalist politicians and one general for their presumed primary roles in bringing on national disaster.

One day before the executions Colonel Gonatas became prime minister, the first, but not the last, time a member of the officer corps took on the direct responsibility of leading a Greek government without a parliament. The Gonatas ministry had to cope with the thousands of refugees from Asia Minor, a serious economic crisis, a disorganized army, the Italian bombing of Corfu, and the sensitive treaty negotiations with Turkey at Lausanne. Maintaining a moderate or conciliatory path proved difficult as extremism thrived during this period studded with complex issues. The leaders of the 1922 revolt proclaimed themselves above political parties, but their anti-Constantinist attitudes inevitably drew them into close associations with the opponents of the royalist regime. Among the Venizelists a strong anti-monarchical movement mushroomed in the civilian world under the leadership of Alexander Papanastasiou and in the armed forces under the instigation of General Theodore Pangalos and Colonel George Kondylis.

The terms "Venizelist," "republican," "liberal" and "anti-Venizelist," "royalist," "conservative" defied precise definition but designated the individual elements composing the political poles. These two general groupings contained a loose coalition of factions, by no means homogeneous, which contested each other for predominance. The so-called Venizelists were not all ardent republicans in 1923. Many individuals in their ranks supported the dynasty while rejecting Constantinist policies; and, it might be added, some liberals opposed Venizelos who, except for a short interlude in the winter of 1924, kept away from Athens until 1928. On the other end of

179

the political spectrum their rivals unified around their loyalty to the dynasty or opposition to Venizelists-republicans, but, otherwise, broke down into several identifiable parties.

Within the armed forces the supporters of a republic started operating as a forceful pressure group. Simultaneously, a clandestine formation of royalists and liberals, dissatisfied with the military's excessive involvement in politics and its growing republicanism, conspired to overthrow the "revolutionary" government of Colonel Gonatas. Generals George Leonardopoulos and Panagiotis Gargalides (both former Venizelists) and Colonel George Zeras (with no political identity) headed the unsuccessful counterrevolt which erupted on 23 October 1923, and which burned itself out in less than a week. Royalist officers formed the majority of those participating, but former General John Metaxas did not, as was then widely believed, organize the abortive revolt.[2]

Republican leaders prospered in the political reaction to the late October events. The elections of 16 December 1923, boycotted by the royalists, returned an overwhelming liberal majority. The leadership of the armed forces quickly dismissed nearly 1300 officers for reasons ranging from royalist loyalties to poor professional performance. With the ranks purged, outspoken republican officers increased their influence and aligned themselves with republican politicians to forward their program to oust the dynasty. Amid the breakdown of old alignments, anti-monarchical forces claimed their victory. The Republic was declared by the National Assembly on 25 March 1924 and confirmed by plebiscite on April 13.

The fledgling Greek Republic, facing continued conservative-royalist opposition, faltered and did not survive, partly because its fragile institutions could not tolerate the frequent jolts of military intervention.[3] It can be argued, moreover, that those leaders instrumental in establishing the Republic also contributed to its demise. That it was not difficult for the military to leave the barracks for a political role had become quite evident, and this encouraged opportunism and adventurism from certain officers. Within such an environment, some politicians sought to utilize influential and politically inclined allies in uniform.

In the months following the establishment of the Republic, the parliament provided few solutions to outstanding prob-

180

lems in foreign policy, refugee settlements, and the economy; and by the late spring of 1925 only thirty-five articles of the Republican Constitution had been drafted. General Theodore Pangalos, who had associated himself actively with radical-reformist endeavors since 1909, executed a successful coup d'état with minimum of effort on 25 June 1925. Alexander Papanastasiou, the prominent republican leader, aided the general in the political takeover, falsely believing that Pangalos would reward him with the prime ministership or, at the least, support for his legislative program. Acquiring a vote of confidence for his ministry, Pangalos quickly rebuffed Papanastasiou and refused to be influenced by his civilian sponsor.

Pangalos, attempting to present himself as a dynamic leader of political action, methodically consolidated power. A formal dictatorship emerged after a speech before a gathering of officers on 3 January 1926. The general declared that the "revolutions" of 1909 and 1922 rendered important services to the nation, but the mistake of the officers in both cases was to restore power prematurely to the politicians—that error would not be made again. The dictator dealt effectively with several outstanding problems, but concurrently he alienated most of his former republican colleagues in the armed forces and the political world, sending many of them into exile or prison.

General George Kondylis, officer-turned-politician, successfully engineered the dictator's downfall on the evening of 21-22 August 1926. The Republican Guard detachments, which had aided Pangalos in his rise to power, conspired with Kondylis to end his career.[4] The following weeks witnessed the restoration of parliamentary government and the formation of a "national coalition" ministry with representatives from all major political parties. And after more than three years of delays and interruptions, the Republican Constitution became law on 3 June 1927.

In an attempt to create a conciliatory atmosphere between republicans and royalists, the "national coalition" government established a military board to consider the reinstatement of officers cashiered from 1917 to 1923. Many republican officers protested such action which, they argued, would undermine the republican foundations of the military and, in turn, the form of government. These officers also recognized that their advantageous positions regarding future promotions and leadership posts would be menaced by returning royalists. After bitter debates and threats of military intervention, it was resolved that fewer than ten percent of the more than three thousand cashiered officers would be reactivated in 1927.

During the spring of 1928 Eleftherios Venizelos assumed again the leadership of the Liberal party, then divided into several factions. His ministries, which lasted more than four years, brought distinguished achievements in foreign policy but ineffective, sometimes corrupt, internal administration. Moreover, the problems of economic depression created widespread dissatisfaction. Aware of their declining image, republican leaders feared that with the coming of a conservative government, the Republic might fall; many officers also shared these forebodings.

Perhaps exaggerated, these apprehensions nonetheless found expression in the attempted coup d'état of Nicholas Plastiras immediately after the 5 March 1933 elections indicated a victory for the conservative parties. With little prior planning and negligible support, Plastiras's forces failed miserably in their effort to nullify the conservative victory. Old antagonisms flourished anew as anti-Venizelists accused the Cretan politician of organizing the revolt to reverse electoral defeat. An unsuccessful attempt to assassinate the Liberal party leader on 6 June 1933 added to renewed extremist feelings.

A call to revamp the system of promotion in the armed forces so that longstanding advantages of the republican officers would be eradicated also intensified emotions. Although the government arrived at no decision, the committed republican officers viewed this maneuver as still another attempt to undercut their influence which, they maintained, buttressed the Republic. The electoral defeat of the republican parties convinced many officers that they should rely on extralegal action to save the Republic and, by direct implication, their professional security. Whereas he had had a very minimal association with the unsuccessful coup of 1933, Venizelos this time participated in the plans for a forceful takeover by loyal troops. The rebellion broke out on 1 March 1935 with Plastiras again serving as nominal leader. The abortive insurrection attracted little backing within the armed forces, while the populace, as has been the case in all Greek military revolts of this century, assumed a quiescent role.

The events of March 1935 signalled the imminent death of the Republic. The conservative government prosecuted republican officers, politicians, and civil servants, imprisoning or dismissing over one thousand individuals. In an act of belated revenge for a long list of royalist grievances, military courts ordered the execution of three officers and condemned to death Venizelos and Plastiras, both of whom fled abroad. Diehard royalists among the conservatives consolidated their position through an overwhelming victory in the election of 3 June 1935, from which the republican parties abstained. A controversial plebiscite under the authoritarian supervision of George Kondylis, resulted in an incredible 97 percent vote in favor of King George II's return under the terms of the revised 1911 Constitution. The monarch arrived in Greece in late November 1935, but by August 1936 the nation succumbed to dictatorship. Suspending vital articles of the constitution, George permitted John Metaxas to rule the nation with a stiff hand in the hope that Greece might better cope with its outstanding internal and diplomatic problems.

During this faction-ridden era of the Republic, economic and class issues assumed increasingly important roles in politics. The national division, stemming originally from the World War I personality cults surrounding Venizelos and Constantine, became more ideological by the 1930s. The "progressive" camp of anti-royalists included not only liberals but also communists of the radical left, and the anti-republican combinations, in turn, ranged from liberally-inclined royalists to fascists. Extremist rather than moderate interests predominated by 1936. Metaxas claimed that the communists with their tactics threatened to take over control of the nation. With the backing of the monarch and purged army, Metaxas launched his "Fourth of August Regime."

Born out of extreme reaction to monarchist excesses, the short-lived Republic died despite the inherent strategic advantages of its supporters. The republican cliques controlled the governments until late 1932 and still held important posts within the armed forces until March 1935. Accelerating political insecurity, nonetheless, pushed them to the point where they resorted twice to military revolts. The conservative parties, by no means a dynamic focus of popular support at this time, prevailed because the republicans discredited and undermined themselves by their own factionalism, political blunders, and extremist initiatives. Eleftherios Venizelos, whose name was long linked with progressive revolutions and liberalism and whose career advanced with these programs, ended his political life on a humiliating and negative note. Nicholas Plastiras, a prominent leader in the 1922 revolt and directly involved with the events ushering in the Republic, contributed to its downfall with the two attempts at coup d'état. George Kondylis, fanatic advocate of the Republic and instrumental in maintaining it until the late 1920s, but basically a political soldier of fortune, shifted loyalties and masterminded the return of King George.

With Metaxas's fascist-style policies, the armed forces, purged of republican officers, became the preserve of the monarch and dictatorship. But the sequence of events following the Italian invasion of October 1940—early victories, defeat, occupation, and national resistance—temporarily shifted political strength from the right to left. In reaction to the oppressive conditions of the occupation, resistance groups emerged supporting different socio-political programs for the post-war period. The National Liberation Front, or EAM, the popular front coalition headed by communists, proved the largest and most active force against the Axis occupiers. British maneuvering among the Greek brigades in the Middle East and the resistance groups in Greece mirrored London's vital concern for the political composition of the nation after the war. Winston Churchill deemed the return of the monarchy a guarantee that Athens would remain friendly and noncommunist and thereby assure continued British influence in the Eastern Mediterranean.

Bitter fighting erupted in Athens between leftist elements and government forces backed by the British army shortly after liberation in December 1944. The costly civil war in Greece ended only in 1949, but during the interim King George returned and the left lost the power struggle, having been defeated by the reorganized conservative groups, bolstered first by the British government and then more extensively by the United States after the proclamation of the Truman Doctrine in March 1947. The conflict in Greece had become an integral part of the Cold War. The more than two billion dollars of aid to Greece, which joined NATO in 1951, secured this nation for the West and developed an armed forces with a conservative hierarchy.

The problems of political, social and economic reconstruction dominated the 1950s. Relative stability and noticeable economic gains marked the unprecedented eight-year prime ministership of the conservative Constantine Karamanlis from 1955 to 1963, although some practices of his administration and the conduct of the 1961 elections aroused criticism from center and left parties. The Glücksburg dynasty appeared as secure as it had ever been—defended by right-wing parties, the loyal armed forces, and less directly by the United States.

This period of outward stability, attributable in large part to the domineering control of the state apparatus and military by the political right, faced a new, stiff challenge by 1963 from the emergence of a strong liberal center and a vocal left. Feeling his vested interests and those of his staunch supporters threatened, the newly crowned King Constantine II thrust himself into the middle of the disputes. Reformist elements backed the silver-tongued George Papandreou and his left-leaning son, Andreas, against the conservative forces. The young monarch fomented controversy over constitutional questions as he created and manipulated governments for the defense of right-wing interests. The ensuing political battle bore an eerie resemblance to that between Constantine's grandfather and Venizelos during World War I. Then, at a crucial point before scheduled elections, Colonel George Papadopoulos and fellow-conspirators stunned the world by executing on 21 April 1967 the latest in a long series of revolts.

Certain aspects of past military interventions were echoed in the statements and actions of the officers who spearheaded the April 1967 coup d'état. Like their predecessors in 1909, the leaders of the 1967 revolt did not represent the interests or the personnel of any of the traditional political parties. That there were no amicable ties with the royalist right became blatantly evident with the abortive counterrevolt of King Constantine on 13 December 1967 and with the establishment of a republic on 1 June 1973. Both the 1909 Military League and the 1967 "junta" made a call for new political leaders to guide Greece onward to greater progress. The two groups also felt that a change in the constitutional structure would create an atmosphere more conducive to reform and stability. With anxieties akin to those of the republican officers in the interwar period, many officers in 1967 feared that a center-left electoral victory would pose a serious threat to the rightist control of the army and to the ideological fabric of the nation. The George Papadopoulos government emulated earlier patterns by cashiering hundreds of officers whose loyalty was suspect. The rhetoric of the military leadership, as that of General Pangalos in 1926 (but unlike Colonel Zorbas in 1909-10), claimed that it would be a mistake for the armed forces to give up control before the completion of an extensive reform program. It can be argued that the process by which the republic was established in the spring and summer of 1973 bore many similarities to the events of 1923-24. The attitudes and policies of the Papadopoulos coterie paralleled in many ways those of Metaxas, under whose dictatorial regime many of these officers received their military education and training. And more generally, all military revolts in this century have been executed with very little bloodshed and negligible participation of the masses. Rebellious officers frequently acted out of concern for professional promotions and security of tenure. Except for the events surrounding the Pangalos dictatorship of 1925-26, all coups and attempted coups had as a direct or indirect interest the status or influence of the dynasty. In all cases the pronouncements accompanying the revolts expressed the need to save the nation from disaster.

The singular characteristics of the George Papadopoulos administration were many, but several important points should be mentioned. No other military regime maintained itself in power for such a long period, utilized such oppressive methods, or infiltrated to such a degree all levels of the governmental machinery with personnel of the armed forces. In the past, several military revolts pressed for institutional change, but essentially in a more liberal direction. Drafted under strict military supervision the 1968 Constitution (and as revised in the summer of 1973) envisaged the foundation of the most authoritarian system since the 1844 document. The role assigned to the armed forces did not provide for a complete withdrawal from political responsibilities. This new constitution differed from all its predecessors in that it included a separate section of four articles which dealt exclusively with the military. Article 129 stated: "The armed forces . . . have as their mission to defend the national independence, territorial integrity of the state, and the existing political and social system against any threats." Article 130 elaborated: "The mission and capacity of the military is absolutely opposed to ideologies aiming at the overthrow or undermining of the existing political or social order or the corrupting of the national convictions of the Greeks or connected to the principles and programs of parties which have been dissolved or outlawed." These articles in effect legalized the historic extra-parliamentary function of the armed forces which, in this instance, was directed at maintaining the "controlled democracy" envisioned by the Papadopoulos government. Evidence of the diminished political influence of the civilian sector and the augmented responsibilities of the armed forces lay in the presence of the above two articles and in the omission of the final article included in all other constitutions since 1844: "The observance of the present Constitution is committed to the patriotism of the Greek people."

The combined effects of brute force, skill, considerable luck, and a divided opposition provided the junta with several years to prove that authoritarian rule rather than the traditionally turbulent parliamentary system could offer more effective, honest government. But by 1972 the creditability of the regime was rapidly diminishing, and Papadopoulos found that few former politicians could be seduced to participate in the new system outlined in the authoritarian constitution. It was indeed ironic that this former colonel, who had originally denounced the old party politicians for their corrupt ways, now actively sought their cooperation. After the 1967 revolt in the early days of vague promises for a new parliamentary system, the military leaders maintained they would exclude the old politicos and replace them with new figures untainted by past corruption. These fresh politicians were few, however, and outnumbered by loyal hacks of the junta. Thus the military failed to emulate the success of the 1909 revolt, referred to in numerous pro-government newspaper editorials, when a whole new school of able politicians came forward to lead Greece.

During 1973 a skyrocketing rate of inflation, dissension within the armed forces and student disturbances combined to shake the foundations of George Papadopoulos's regime. On

187

25 November 1973, after the brutal crushing of the student demonstrators at the Polytechnic University campus, General Demetrios Ioannides, head of the military police, directed the overthrow of his erstwhile colleague. Once again the people heard an official proclamation stating the armed forces acted "to save the country from danger and chaos." Disapproving of the intended incline toward civilian rule, the Ioannides clique declared that the "country was being dragged into an electoral adventure" by Papadopoulos. Most Greeks welcomed the fall of the colonel-turned-president but had little to cheer in the successor regime which ruled in still harsher fashion, support- ed by the official terror of the military police, some 20,000 strong. The grip of dictatorship had tightened and the rejug- gled military elite, apparently unwilling to yield control to civilians, made not even vague promises to the population for an easing of conditions.

Then, in the span of a few dramatic days in mid-July 1974 a rapid sequence of critical incidents divested Greece of dictator- ship and restored civilian rule. The Ioannides-sponsored plot to overthrow Archbishop Makarios on Cyprus, the Turkish invasion of the island and the chaotic mobilization of Greek reserves totally discredited and diplomatically isolated the junta which quickly exited on 23 July. Seeking to avert national catastrophe, the military leaders dissolved their au- thority and approved the creation of a civilian government under Constantine Karamanlis. By year's end Karamanlis guided the country to free elections and to a plebiscite which approved the establishment of a republic. And in 1975 a constitution embodying democratic institutions was drafted.

Greece during this century has faced a series of complex crises, some of which are longstanding in nature. Parliamen- tary procedures have repeatedly failed to cope successfully with many critical problems, partly because politicians, mon- archs and officers have not always respected the principles of liberal representative government mirrored in the several constitutions. Civilian and military groups have resorted to coups d'état for advancing their goals, even when it has meant going against the verdict or anticipated verdict of national elections. The revolts of 1843, 1862 and 1909 produced changes in the political process with little resistance. In the 1916 to

1936 period elements of the armed forces intensified their involvement in politics within a polarized setting. The military became highly politicized and control of it meant, logically enough, control of the country. But where past military coups had politicians as collaborators or immediate beneficiaries, the officers ruled from April 1967 to July 1974 with unprecedented independence. The "colonels" indicated a definite reluctance to relinquish their power, and the political-social order outlined in the 1968 and 1973 constitutions reflected their dictatorial inclinations. The military, formerly politicized by civilian interests, attempted by its actions to politicize the Greek population in its own authoritarian image.

APPENDIX

Memorandum of the Military League Addressed to the King, the Government and the Greek People

Our Fatherland is in the most difficult circumstances, and the official state, insulted and humbled, cannot make any move in defense of its rights.

The whole of Hellenism, deeply feeling this lamentable situation, has manifested its fervent desire for unremitting measures with the object of avoiding similar danger in the future. For the rest, even foreigners, official and other, have repeatedly pointed out that our nation would not have undergone the misfortunes and humiliations which it has suffered if we had a sufficient military and naval force for purposes of defense.

The Military League of army and naval officers, inspired with the same feelings and sharing with all Greeks the consciousness of the painfulness of the circumstances and the necessity for an army and navy capable of fighting for the defense of the soil of the Fatherland and for the rights of the nation, and knowing that the complete formation of such has been always neglected by the authorities—not from bad motives, but on the unjustifiable pretext that the revenues of the state were insufficient, whereas they have been squandered at random—submits a sacred entreaty to the king, according to the fundamental law the leader of the military and naval forces of the state, and to his government, that they will wholeheartedly devote themselves to the immediate and

This translation is based in large part on that found in Elliot to Grey, Athens, 29 August 1909, FO 371/678, No. 133.

speedy rectification of the evil state of affairs, especially as regards the army and navy.

The Military League does not aim at the abolition of the dynasty or the replacement of the king, whose person is sacred in their eyes, nor does it desire to establish a despotism or militarism or to touch the constitutional government in any other way, as the officers who compose the union are themselves Greek subjects and have taken the oath to maintain the constitution.

Since, however, both the crown prince and the other princes have taken active and administrative service, and exercise, owing to their personal authority, a very great influence upon the carrying out of the service in general, and upon the character of the officers, and necessarily come into personal friction [with them], which contributes to the impairment of the prestige of their exalted persons; and since, on the other hand, although these exalted personages, as a matter of form, are responsible for the management of the duties entrusted to them, as a matter of fact, however, they command with entire irresponsibility, to the greatest detriment of the interests of the service and of individuals, and in contravention of the constitution of the country; for this reason the Military League is persuaded that, in the interests of the dynasty, both the crown prince and the other princes should refrain from active and administrative service in both the army and the navy, and should retain the ranks which they hold and be promoted when the king pleases.

The Military League does not propose a change of government, as it is convinced that the members of the Greek government are patriotic above all others, and that they always labor for the happiness and greatness of the Fatherland. Nevertheless, as the appointment of political persons as ministers of war and marine is opposed to the well-understood interest of the service in general, and especially of the discipline of the army, as long experience has shown, notwithstanding the goodwill of these ministers, the Military League requests that in the future the king who appoints the ministers by the rights accruing to him from the constitution, shall demand that the ministers of war and marine shall be drawn from officers of superior rank on the active or seconded lists.

The Military League does not aim at the increase of the cadres of the army and navy, or at the removal of the superior

191

officers from the service, as it is not working on behalf of base personal interests, but for the attainment of a sacred object.

The Military League desires that our religion be raised to its befitting sacred vocation; that the administration of the country be rendered worthy and honest; that justice be dispensed speedily and impartially, and with equity to all citizens alike, irrespective of rank; that the education of the people be rendered conducive to practical life and to the military necessities of the land; that the life, the honor, and the property of the citizens be assured; and that the finances of the country be put right, and the necessary measures taken for the judicious regulation of the revenues and expenditure of the state, so that, on the one hand, the poor Greek people may be relieved from the hard taxes which it now pays, and which are cruelly squandered in the maintenance of luxurious and superfluous services and officials, owing to the detestable system of jobbery; and, on the other hand, that the limits may be fixed, within which expenditure for the military preparation of the country and the maintenance of the army and fleet in general is possible.

Besides this, the Military League, discerning forthcoming national complications, warmly begs that some measures of military concentration, capable of coping with the situation, be taken immediately, of inevitable necessity.

Such is the prayer of the Military League, with the object of the reform of the different services of the state, of which the army and navy form a slight, but very important, part. As it judges itself incompetent to enter into details which are outside its special sphere and which the government is competent to define in accord with the Parliament of the nation, the League confines itself to submitting the following program containing general and fundamental bases of the organization of the army and navy, and to pointing out the measures to be taken immediately for the speedy military and naval preparation of the land.

The Military League, in submitting this request, has no doubt but that it will be accepted, since the will of the Greek people is such, and the government, with the patriotism distinguishing it, will hasten to the convocation of the Chamber in order to vote the necessary measures for achieving this work of national salvation.

The necessity of the immediate convocation of the Chamber is unavoidable, because the dissolution and the holding of new elections demand a considerable time, and the slightest loss of time under present conditions is a wrong to the nation.

The Military League is firmly determined, in case its request is not taken into consideration, to recoil before no obstacle, whencesoever it may arise, tending to frustrate the patriotic object aimed at. It rejects all responsibility for the creation of any abnormal state of affairs, whether brought about for the professed object of discipline by those who have long ago destroyed discipline from its foundation, or for that of the prosecution of the members of the union, as acting in contravention of the law, by those who have kept no law, and it addresses itself to the pure and patriotic sentiments of the Greek people, and seeks their aid in the noble campaign which it is undertaking.

Program For The Military Organization of the Army and Navy

I. Speedy Preparation of the Army

A. The recruit class now serving to be retained with the colors until the termination of their two years' service, except if circumstances permit their being discharged earlier.

B. The exempted recruits of four or five of the more recent classes to be called out on the 1st of October for drill.

C. At least four classes of the reserves to be called out in February 1910 for grand maneuvers in case of need.

D. The immediate increase of the supplies requisite for the army on a peace footing and for the contingency of a mobilization.

II. Speedy Preparation of the Navy

A. A new battleship, of 10,000 tons at least, to be ordered, with eight torpedo-boats of 150 tons minimum each.

B. The hurried, as far as possible, repair of the three battleships, and an improvised amelioration of their guns by the substitution of smokeless for common powder.

    C. The necessary ammunition for the guns and torpedoes to be ordered.

III. Regular Organization of the Army

    A. Regulation of the organization of the army in a more suitable and economic manner, abolishing superfluous services and posts.

    B. A fuller application of recruiting, those exempted being reduced to the minimum, so that as many recruits as possible may be enrolled in the army every year (15,000 to 17,000 if possible).

    C. Maneuvers of large units of men to be held regularly every year with at least three classes of reserves being called out every year.

    D. Determination of the plan for the defense of the country and the gradual execution of the measures called for thereby.

    E. The commanders of the large units, brigades, and divisions to be appointed so that they may be prepared during time of peace and so that the troops may know their leaders.

    F. Abolition of the General Staff, which does not fully answer its vocation owing to its faulty composition.

    G. A foreign general with a foreign staff to be invited for the organization of the staff service of the army, the direction of the grand maneuvers, and the practical instruction of the army. The staff service to be drawn up at first, and, until officers of all ranks have been trained as shown hereinunder, from officers of all arms, chosen from among the most suitable for such service; in the future the same to be composed of officers instructed in some foreign military school and sent for instruction after a competitive examination at the expense of the state. The international organization of the staff service to be defined by law, together with the term of service of the officers therein, and all the necessary details of the regular working of the service and its single command. The officers of different arms who offer themselves for competition with the object of being sent to Europe for instruction in the above school to possess the rank of lieutenant and captain. In the staff of the general to be invited there must be included a commissary of stores with the object of organizing the commissariat and the financial service of the army, also one officer each of the artillery and infantry, the one to command the school of gunnery and the other the school of musketry.

H. All necessary supplies for the army, in peace and in case of mobilization, to be ordered, and the annual loss by consumption for the needs of the service and the instruction of the army to be fully made up, proper care being taken at the same time to render feasible the ordering, if not of the whole, at any rate of the greater part thereof, especially as regards the ammunition ordered in the country. Care also to be taken for the state to acquire suitable firing ranges for both the schools, in addition to such ranges in the various towns where bodies of troops are stationed for firing purposes.

I. Abolition of the post of commander-in-chief of the army, and the establishment of a supreme Military Council, composed of the commanders of the divisions and of the chief of the staff service, with the senior officer as president. This council to meet once a year in Athens after the general inspection of the army, and to draw up the lists of the officers to be promoted, and settle the general disposition of the officers of the army.

J. If possible the army to be set free from political ministers.

K. Abrogation of the law ΑΥΛΗ′ of 28 May 1887 as superfluous, as the princes who may in the future be desirous of enrolling themselves in the army or navy can acquire this right, and can be promoted to the different ranks of officer by conforming to the respective existing general laws of the army and navy. The princes who already hold the rank of officer in virtue of the above law, to abstain from

195

the execution of any active service in the army or navy, retaining the ranks they now occupy, and being promoted whenever the king desires.

L. For the regular composition and serviceable training of the army on a peace footing, as formed on the basis of the foregoing, it is necessary for 23,000,000 drachmas to be earmarked in the estimates of the regular expenditure of the ministry of war.

IV. Regular Organization of the Navy.

A. New ships to be substituted for the old warships, according to the views of the navy, the torpedo fleet to be completed, the flotilla of the Gulf of Arta to be renewed, and the needs of the arsenal to be supplemented so as to render it adequate for the needs of the fleet.

B. The useless ships and material to be disposed of, and the yachts to be confined to one, for the exclusive use of the king.

C. The navy to be freed if possible from political ministers.

D. Strict economy and retrenchment in the different services of the navy, so that the expenditure already fixed in the estimates for the ministry of marine may suffice for the regular needs of the new fleet.

E. Foreign organizers to be invited for all branches of the fleet.

V. Regular Organization of the Gendarmerie

A. The gendarmerie to be released from political influences, and to this effect to be suitably arranged in respect of its command and council of inspection.

B. The gendarmerie to be more conveniently and more economically organized, upon a military basis, so that in case of need it may serve as an auxiliary military force.

NOTES

Abbreviations

AA: Germany. Auswärtiges Amt (microfilmed by London School of Economics).

FO: Great Britain. Foreign Office Archives, Public Record Office, London.

HHS: Austria-Hungary. Haus-, Hof-, und Staatsarchiv, Vienna.

NA: United States. Department of State, National Archives, Washington, D.C.

Note on Dates

Unless otherwise stated, all dates are according to the Gregorian (new-style) calendar. Greece switched from the Julian to the Gregorian calendar in 1923.

Note on Transliteration

The Library of Congress system for the transliteration of Greek has been adhered to in a general way. Noticeable modifications have been made, however, in order to approximate Greek pronunciation, particularly in the spelling of names, where *i* is generally used instead of *e* for eta in the last syllable. The macron has been eliminated in all cases.

Introduction

1. The best analysis for the first years of King Othon's reign is John A. Petropulos, *Politics and Statecraft in the Kingdom of Greece: 1833-1843* (Princeton, 1968).

2. I. Ch. Poulos, "He Epanastasis tes 3es Septemvriou 1843 epi te vasei ton gallikon archeion" ["The Revolution of 3 September 1843 on the Basis of the French Archives"], *Deltion tes Historikes kai Ethnologhikes Hetaireias tes Hellados* [*Bulletin of the Historical and Ethnological Society of Greece*], II (1956), 223-29; Barbara Jelavich, *Russia and the Greek Revolution of 1843* (Munich, 1966), pp. 24-26, 38; Petropulos, *Politics and Statecraft,* pp. 434-42.

3. Petropulos, *Politics and Statecraft,* pp. 442-43; Poulos ["Revolution of 3 September 1843"], pp. 242-46.

4. Jelavich, *Russia and the Greek Revolution,* p. 38. The Austrian minister in Athens wrote Metternich on 6 October 1843: "Not a hand was raised for

197

him [i.e., Othon] in the entire kingdom." *The Times* (London), 28 September 1843; George Finlay, *A History of Greece* (Oxford, 1877), VII, 173-77; Petropulos, *Politics and Statecraft,* pp. 444-46.

5. Nicholas Kaltchas, *Introduction to the Constitutional History of Modern Greece* (New York, 1940), pp. 96-102; George D. Daskalakis, *Hellenike syntagmatike historia: 1821-1935* [*Greek Constitutional History: 1821-1935*] (Athens, 1952), p. 59. Daskalakis refers to the suffrage laws as the most liberal in Europe at that time: any male at least 25 years of age with property in his electoral district with no restrictions on occupation.

6. Jean Meynaud, *Les forces politique en Grèce* (Paris, 1965), pp. 25-27; Hariton Korisis, *Die politischen Parteien Griechenlands: Ein neuer Staat auf dem Weg zur Demokratie 1821-1910* (Hersbruck/Nürnberg, 1966), pp. 45-47.

7. Barbara Jelavich, "Russia, Bavaria, and the Greek Revolution of 1862/63," *Balkan Studies,* 2 (1961), pp. 126-28; for details: Eleftherios Prevelakis, *British Policy towards the Change of Dynasty in Greece, 1862-1863* (Athens, 1953).

8. Tasos Gounaris, *He Naupliake epanastasis* [*The Nauplion Revolution*] (Athens, 1963), pp. 31-95.

9. George Aspreas, *Politike historia tes neoteras Hellados* [*Political History of Modern Greece*] (Athens, 1963), I, 250-61; Finlay, *History of Greece,* VII, 269-74; *The Times* (London), 19 November 1862.

10. Aspreas [*Political History*], I, 262-95; Finlay, *History of Greece,* VII, 276-305.

11. Alexander P. Couclelis, *Les régimes gouvernementaux de la Grèce de 1821 à nos jours* (Paris, 1921), pp. 100-01; Daskalakis [*Constitutional History*], pp. 62-72. Before 1864 the only other European nations to have instituted universal male suffrage were France and Switzerland in 1848.

12. William Miller, *Greek Life in Town and Country* (London, 1905), p. 23. The author mentioned that Demetrios Rallis, a prominent politician and prime minister several times, had in his district of Attica over one thousand godchildren, "who are doubtless one source of his popularity there." Basil P. Mathiopoulos, "Die politischen Parteien Griechenlands," *Internationales Jahrbuch der Politik,* (October 1955), pp. 308-11; George D. Daskalakis, *Politika kommata kai demokratia* [*Political Parties and Democracy*] (Athens, 1958), pp. 35-36; D. Argyriades, "The Ecology of Greek Administration: Some Factors Affecting the Development of the Greek Civil Service," *Contributions to Mediterranean Sociology,* ed. J. G. Peristiany (Paris, 1968), pp. 342-44; Miller, *Greek Life,* pp. 28-29.

13. Gregory Daphnis, *Ta Hellenika politika kommata, 1821-1961* [*Greek Political Parties, 1821-1961*] (Athens, 1961), pp. 65-79; Korisis, *Die politischen Parteien Griechenlands,* pp. 80-100.

14. Trikoupis served as prime minister from March 1882 to April 1885, May 1886 to October 1890, June 1892 to May 1893, and November 1893 to January 1895. Delegiannis headed ministries from May 1885 to May 1886, November 1890 to March 1892, and June 1895 to April 1897.

15. Harry J. Psomiades, "The Economic and Social Transformation of Modern Greece," *Journal of International Affairs,* XIX (1965), 196; A. A. Pepelasis, "The Legal System and Economic Development of Greece," *The Journal of Economic History,* XIX (June 1959), 180-83; P. B. Dertilis, "Le

problème de la dette publique des états balkaniques: L'endettement de la Grèce," *Les Balkans,* VI (October-November 1934), 572-74; Herbert Feis, *Europe the World's Banker, 1870-1914* (New Haven, 1930), pp. 284-86; for complete coverage of Greece's foreign loans see John A. Levandis, *The Greek Foreign Debt and the Great Powers: 1821-1898* (New York, 1944).

Chapter I

1. Douglas Dakin, *The Greek Struggle in Macedonia: 1899-1913* (Thessaloniki, 1966), pp. 41-42; William Miller, *Travels and Politics in the Near East* (London, 1898), p. 279; William Miller, *Greek Life in Town and Country* (London, 1905), p. 51; George Aspreas, *Politike historia tes neoteras Hellados* [*Political History of Modern Greece*] (Athens, 1963), I, 272-73. For example, King George's sister, Alexandra, was married to King Edward VII of England, and another sister, Dagmar, had been married to Tsar Alexander III of Russia. Crown Prince Constantine was married to Princess Sophie of Prussia, Kaiser Wilhelm's sister.

2. The following are the prime ministers and the dates of their governments for this period: Delegiannis (12 June 1895-28 April 1897); Rallis (30 April 1897-3 October 1897); Zaïmis (3 October 1897-14 April 1899); Theotokis (14 April 1899-25 November 1901); Zaïmis (25 November 1901-5 December 1902); Delegiannis (7 December 1902-26 June 1903); Theotokis (26 June 1903-10 July 1903); Rallis (11 July 1903-17 December 1903); Theotokis (18 December 1903-28 December 1904); Delegiannis (28 December 1904-13 June 1905); Rallis (22 June 1905-21 December 1905); Theotokis (21 December 1905-20 July 1909).

3. Egerton to Salisbury, Patras, 25 May 1898, FO 32/702, No. 104A.

4. Egerton to Salisbury, Athens, 2 December 1898, FO 32/703, No. 167.

5. Egerton to Salisbury, Athens, 17 March 1899, FO 32/712, No. 27; Egerton to Salisbury, Athens, 27 March 1899, FO 32/712, No. 29.

6. Hariton Korisis, *Die politischen Parteien Griechenlands: Ein neuer Staat auf dem Weg zur Demokratie, 1821-1910* (Hersbruck/Nürnberg, 1966), pp. 183-90.

7. Egerton to Lansdowne, Athens, 12 December 1902, FO 32/737, No. 127.

8. Egerton to Lansdowne, Athens, 22 November 1901, FO 32/729, No. 96; Egerton to Lansdowne, Athens, 24 November 1901, FO 32/729, No. 101; Egerton to Lansdowne, Athens, 24 November 1901, FO 32/729, No. 102; Egerton to Lansdowne, Athens, 12 December 1902, FO 32/737, No. 127; Aspreas, [*Politike historia*], II, 18-31.

9. P. Kontogiannis, *Ho stratos mas kai hoi teleftaioi polemoi* [*Our Army and the Recent Wars*] (Athens, 1924), pp. 9-10; Charles Martel, "The Greek Army," *The Army and Navy Magazine,* 82 (August 1887), pp. 333-39.

10. Intelligence Branch, War Office, 13 March 1886, FO 881/5206, "Greece," p. 13.

11. Intelligence Branch, War Office, 13 March 1886, FO 881/5206, "Greece," pp. 13-17; E. K. Stasinopoulos, *Ho stratos tes protes ekatontaetias* [*The First Hundred Years of the Army*] (Athens, 1935), p. 57.

12. Intelligence Branch, War Office, 13 March 1886, FO 881/5206, "Greece," pp. 20-28; Stasinopoulos, [*First Hundred Years*], pp. 55-60; Kontogiannis [*Our Army*], pp. 20-28; X. Lefkoparidis, ed., *Stratigou P. K. Dangli: Anamneseis*

Engrapha—Allelographia [General P. K. Danglis: Recollections—Personal Papers—Correspondence] (Athens, 1965), I, 113-17.

13. Intelligence Branch, War Office, 13 March 1886, FO 881/6206, "Greece," p. 24.

14. Intelligence Division, War Office, 1898, FO 881/7015, "The Turco-Greek War, 1897," p. 21.

15. Greece, General Staff of the Army, Historical Division, *Historia tes orghanoseos tou Hellenikou Stratou, 1821-1954 [History of the Organization of the Greek Army, 1821-1954]* (Athens, 1957), p. 72; "Ho Hellenikos Stratos" ["The Greek Army"] *Eleftheron Vema*, 27 July 1928; Theodore Pangalos, *Ta apomnemoneumata mou [My Memoirs]* (Athens, 1950), p. 34; K. Boulalas, *He Hellas kai hoi synchronoi polemoi [Greece and the Recent Wars]* (Athens, 1965), p. 9; Stasinopoulos [*The Army*], p. 69; L. I. Paraskevopoulos, *Anamneseis: 1896-1920 [Recollections: 1896-1920]* (Athens, 1930), p. 40; V. Dousmanis, *Apomnemoneumata [Memoirs]* (Athens, 1946), p. 29; A. Mazarakis-Ainian, *Apomnemoneumata [Memoirs]* (Athens, 1949), pp. 28, 95; Kontogiannis [*Our Army*], pp. 11-12.

16. Egerton to Salisbury, Athens, 13 November 1899, FO 32/712, No. 96; Egerton to Salisbury, Athens, 18 November 1899, FO 32/712, No. 97.

17. As quoted in E. J. Dillon, "Constitutional Crises in Europe," *The Contemporary Review*, November 1909, p. 630.

18. Egerton to Salisbury, Athens, 10 February 1900, FO 32/720, No. 28; Egerton to Salisbury, Athens, 16 February 1900, FO 32/720, No. 33; Egerton to Salisbury, Athens, 15 March 1900, FO 32/720, No. 40; Egerton to Salisbury, Athens, 25 March 1900, FO 32/720, No. 51; Dillon, "Constitutional Crises," p. 630.

19. V. Dousmanis, *He stratiotike katastasis kai he politike tou G. N. Theotoki [The Military Situation and the Politics of G. N. Theotokis]* (Athens, 1911), pp. 1-2; Egerton to Salisbury, Athens, 13 November 1899, FO 32/712, No. 96; Egerton to Salisbury, Athens, 26 April 1900, FO 32/720, No. 74; Egerton to Salisbury, Athens, 12 October 1900, FO 32/721, No. 136; Egerton to Lansdowne, Athens, 11 March 1902, FO 32/733, No. 30.

20. Egerton to Lansdowne, Athens, 11 March 1902, FO 32/736, No. 30; Egerton to Lansdowne, Athens, 26 September 1902, FO 32/737. No. 87; Egerton to Lansdowne, Athens, 3 March 1903, FO 32/744, No. 21; Egerton to Lansdowne, Athens, 5 March 1903, FO 32/744, No. 24; Egerton to Lansdowne, Athens, 31 March 1903, FO 32/745, No. 36; Lefkoparidis, ed., [*Danglis*], I, 241-43.

21. Egerton to Lansdowne, Athens, 13 July 1903, FO 32/745, No. 71; Egerton to Lansdowne, Athens, 15 July 1903, FO 32/745, No. 73; Egerton to Lansdowne, Athens, 20 July 1903, FO 32/745, No. 80; Egerton to Lansdowne, Athens, 27 July 1903, FO 32/745, No. 86.

22. "To stratiotikon systema tou 1904" ["The Military Organization of 1904"], *Eleftheron Vema*, 1 August 1928; Greece, General Staff, [Organization of the Greek Army], p. 101; Egerton to Lansdowne, Athens, 4 March 1904, FO 32/751, No. 33; Egerton to Lansdowne, Athens, 14 July 1904, FO 32/751, No. 100; Egerton to Lansdowne, Athens, 27 August 1904, FO 32/751, No. 105.

23. Egerton to Lansdowne, Athens, 4 March 1904, FO 32/751, No. 33; Dousmanis [*Military Situation*], p. 4; "Les projets militaires," *L'Hellenisme*, I (March 1904), 11-12; William Miller, *Greek Life in Town and Country* (London, 1905), p. 250.

24. B. C. Woods, "The Military Upheaval in Greece," *National Defense*, IV (February 1910), 45-48; Kontogiannis [*Our Army*], pp. 181-82; Elliot to Grey, Athens, 25 May 1906, FO 371/81, No. 71; Elliot to Grey, Athens, 10 December 1906, FO 371/81, No. 166; Elliot to Grey, Athens, 21 January 1907, FO 371/264, No. 4, "General Report on Greece for the Year 1906," pp. 5-6 (hereafter referred to as: "FO General Report on Greece, 1906").

25. "FO General Report on Greece, 1906," pp. 5-6; Elliot to Grey, Athens, 9 February 1906, FO 371/81, No. 27; Elliot to Grey, Athens, 14 February 1906, No. 31; Young to Grey, Athens, 13 July 1906, FO 371/81, No. 88; Young to Grey, Athens, 24 July 1906, FO 371/81, No. 94.

26. "FO General Report on Greece, 1906," p. 6; Miller, *Greek Life*, p. 251.

27. Elliot to Grey, Athens, 21 December 1907, FO 371/264, No. 174; Elliot to Grey, Athens, 19 February 1908, FO 371/464, No. 21; Elliot to Grey, Athens, 23 April 1908, FO 371/464, No. 59; La Boulinière to Pichon, Athens, 2 July 1907, XI, No. 60, *Documents diplomatique français* (2e série), pp. 105-06; Douglas Dakin, "The Greek Proposals for the Alliance with France and Great Britain, June-July 1907," *Balkan Studies*, III (1962), 56-59; I. Theophanides, *Historia tou Hellenikou Naftikou: 1909-1913* [*History of the Greek Navy: 1909-1913*] (Athens, 1922), pp. 10-13.

28. "FO General Report on Greece, 1906," p. 5.

29. The following statistics are taken from J. Scott Keltie, ed., *The States-man's Yearbook* (London, 1908). "The peace strength of the Bulgarian army is about 52,500 of all ranks, but the field army . . . will amount when all units are formed, to about 375,000 combatants . . . the army is a very large one for so small a state" (p. 1587). "The peace strength of the Serbian army according to the 1907 Budget amounts to 36,605 officers and men, including non-comba-tants and 1838 gendarmerie" (p. 1487).

30. Paraskevopoulos [*Recollections*], pp. 85-87; Pangalos [*My Memoirs*], pp. 43-45; Dousmanis [*Memoirs*], pp. 29-31; Mazarakis-Ainian [*Memoirs*], pp. 92-94.

31. Foreign Office, 25 January 1923, FO 371/10765, "Memorandum Re-specting the International Finance Commission at Athens," pp. 1-5; A. M. Andreades, "Les Contrôles Financiers Internationaux," *Erga* [*Works*] (Athens, 1939), II, 120-29; Herbert Feis, *Europe the World's Banker, 1870-1910* (New Haven, 1930), p. 286. Regarding the post-1898 loans and the restrictions of the International Finance Commission, Feis states: "Future Greek wars at any rate were not to be fought at the direct expense of her creditors, though the risk had been obvious when the loans were made."

32. Elliot to Grey, Athens, 8 April 1906, FO 371/81, No. 58; Elliot to Grey, Athens, 29 November 1907, FO 371/264, No. 166 (Secret); Elliot to Grey, Athens, 30 April 1909, FO 371/678, No. 60, "Annual Report, 1908," pp. 5-8.

33. A. C. Angelopoulos, "Ai vaseis tou phorologikou systematos tes Hel-lados" ["Foundations of the Taxation System in Greece"], *Epitheoresis Koi-nonikes kai Demosias Oikonomias* [*Review of Social and Political Economy*], January-April 1932, pp. 96-99; Theodore Saloutos, *The Greeks in the United States* (Cambridge, 1964), pp. 6-7, 13; Elliot to Lansdowne, Athens, 7 March 1904, FO 32/751, No. 34.

34. Saloutos, *The Greeks in the United States*, pp. 5-31; N. J. Polyzos, *Essai sur l'émigration Grecque* (Paris, 1947), pp. 33-36; L. S. Stavrianos, *The Balkans since 1453* (New York, 1958), pp. 480-81; V. G. Valaoras, "A Recon-

struction of the Demographic History of Modern Greece," *The Milbank Memorial Fund Quarterly*, XXXVIII, no. 12 (April 1960), pp. 121-32; Emmanuel Repoulis, *Melete meta schediou nomou peri metanastefseos* [*Study with Legislative Plans for Emigration*] (Athens, 1912). This last study, by the minister of interior in Eleftherios Venizelos's cabinet, provides a thorough examination with appropriate statistics of the patterns of emigration and the impact on Greece's economy.

35. "FO General Report on Greece, 1906," pp. 18-20; Korisis, *Die politischen Parteien*, p. 118. In 1870 there were only 166 towns with more than 1,000 inhabitants, but by 1907 the number had jumped to 430. More significantly, urban centers with over 5000 people increased from 16.5 to 24.18 percent of the total population between 1861 and 1907.

36. John Kordatos, *Historia tou Hellenikou ergatikou kinematos* [*History of the Greek Labor Movement*] (Athens, 1956), pp. 7, 31; Basil P. Mathiopoulos, *Die Geschichte der sozialen Frage und des Sozialismus in Griechenland: 1821-1961*, (Hanover, 1961), pp. 53-56; G. D. H. Cole, *A History of Socialist Thought* (London, 1956), III, 586-605; for details on the origins of socialism in southeastern Europe, see W. G. Vettes, "The Balkan Socialist Movement from Its Beginnings to 1917," Diss. Northwestern University, 1958.

37. Kordatos [*Greek Labor Movement*], pp. 57-74.

38. Kordatos [*Greek Labor Movement*], pp. 106-19.

39. A. T. Speliotopoulos, *Te einai Rizospastismos* [*What Is Radicalism?*] (Athens, 1910), pp. 1-19; Gregory Daphnis, *Ta Hellenika politika kommata, 1821-1961* [*Greek Political Parties, 1821-1961*] (Athens, 1961), pp. 89-90; *Rizospastis*, 21 February 1908; Mathiopoulos, *Geschichte der sozialen Frage*, pp. 51, 66.

40. The two best accounts of the Greek press are: Kosta Mayer and I. Mytalis, *Hellenike demosiographia* [*Greek Journalism*] (Athens, 1939); Kosta Mayer, *Historia tou Hellenikou typou* [*History of the Greek Press*] (Athens, 1957-1960), 3 vols.

41. I. Mallosis, *He politike historia tou Demetriou P. Gounari: 1902-1920* [*The Political History of Demetrios P. Gounaris: 1902-1920*] (Athens, 1926), pp. 109-20; S. B. Markezinis, *Politike historia tes neoteras Hellados: 1828-1964* [*Political History of Modern Greece*] (Athens, 1967), III, 42-47; A. Alexandris, *Politikai anamneseis* [*Political Recollections*] (Patras, 1947), pp. 5-17.

42. E. J. Dillon, "Parliamentary Islam and Revolutionary Greece," *The Contemporary Review*, January 1910, pp. 119-22.

43. Doros Alastos, *Venizelos* (London, 1942), pp. 42-55; see for extensive coverage of Venizelos's role on Crete: C. D. Svolopoulos, *Ho Eleftherios Venizelos kai he politike krisis eis ten autonomon Kreten, 1901-1906* [*Eleftherios Venizelos and the Political Crisis in Autonomous Crete, 1901-1906*] (Athens, 1974); see for the role of the great powers on Crete: Jean-Stanislaw Dutkowski, *L'occupation de la Crète (1897-1909): Une expérience d'administration internationale d'un territoire* (Paris, 1952).

44. For a thorough account of Greek policy in Macedonia, refer to Douglas Dakin, *The Greek Struggle in Macedonia, 1899-1912* (Thessaloniki, 1966).

45. "FO General Report on Greece, 1906," pp. 1-5; Elliot to Grey, Athens, 19 February 1908, FO 371/464, No. 21, "Annual Report, 1907," pp. 1-4.

46. Dakin, "Greek Proposals for Alliance," *Balkan Studies*, pp. 51-60.

47. Elliot to Grey, Athens, 8 July 1907, FO 371/264, No. 90 (Very Confidential); Grey to Elliot, Foreign Office, 8 August 1907, FO 371/264, No. 90 (Very Confidential).

48. Grey to Bertie, Foreign Office, 7 November 1907, FO 371/264, No. 622.

Chapter II

1. As quoted in L. S. Stavrianos, *The Balkans since 1453* (New York, 1958), p. 526.

2. Andrian to Aehrenthal, Athens, 7 August 1908, HHS XVI/59, No. 28. Copy of *Patris* front page in Andrian to Aehrenthal, Athens, 13 August 1908, HHS XVI/59, No. 29A-B.

3. Elliot to Grey, Athens, 30 April 1909, FO 371/678, No. 60, "Annual Report, 1908," p. 2 (hereafter referred to as "FO Annual Report, 1908").

4. "FO Annual Report, 1908," pp. 3-4; Britain, Historical Section of the Foreign Office, *Greece* (London, 1920), pp. 57-58; Édouard Driault, *Histoire diplomatique de la Grèce de 1821 à nos jours* (Paris, 1926), V, 22. Eleftherios Venizelos was included in this Executive Committee of five men.

5. "FO Annual Report, 1908," pp. 4-5; Driault, *Histoire diplomatique,* V, 22; E. J. Dillon, "Parliamentary Islam and Revolutionary Greece," *The Contemporary Review,* January 1910, p. 121; Britain, Historical Section of the FO, *Greece,* p. 58.

6. "FO Annual Report, 1908," p. 2; Driault, *Histoire diplomatique,* V, 23.

7. Elliot to Grey, Athens, 31 December 1908, FO 371/677, No. 174; "FO Annual Report, 1908," pp. 5-6.

8. *Akropolis,* 2 and 25 February 1909; 2 April 1909, 6 May 1909, 7 and 24 August 1909.

9. Several editorials among many: *Akropolis,* 2 October 1908, 9 November 1908, 28 February 1909. For more information on the editor of *Akropolis,* see Th. Synadinos, ed., *Vlases Gavrielides* (Athens, 1929).

10. Elliot to Grey, Athens, 31 December 1908, FO 371/677, No. 174; A. Theodorides, *He epanastasis kai to ergon aftes [The Revolution and Its Accomplishments]* (Athens, 1914), p. 18; John Kordatos, *Historia tes neoteras Helladas [History of Modern Greece]* (Athens, 1958), V, 77; *Akropolis,* 17 December 1908. Gavrielides hailed the demonstration.

11. Elliot to Grey, Athens, 6 January 1909, FO 371/677, No. 4. The British minister remarked: "The Chamber has little to boast of in its record 28 sittings during 50 days, except the self-restraint of having abstained from troublesome interpellations upon foreign politics, and notably the Cretan question."

12. Elliot to Grey, Athens, 31 December 1908, FO 371/677, No. 172; Elliot to Grey, Athens, 25 February 1909, FO 371/677, No. 31; Elliot to Grey, Athens, 6 March 1909, FO 371/677, No. 36. Elliot submitted a report of Alban Young, the British representative in the IFC: "From the point of view of the committee [IFC], Gounaris's fall is to be regretted, as the principal rock on which he was shipwrecked was the considerable tax which he proposed to impose on alcohol, and which would incidentally have done something towards retrieving the lamentable position of our petroleum revenues." Alcohol produced from currants was used as fuel in Greece.

13. *Le Messager d'Athènes,* March 13, 1909. "It will be difficult to enumer-

ate the number of Greeks, clubs, associations which animate the noble desire to save the country."

14. *Akropolis,* 18 February 1909; *Rizospastis,* 30 July 1908 and 20 November 1908.

15. *Le Monde Hellènique,* 23 February 1909; *Akropolis,* 25 February 1909; *Neon Asty,* 25 February 1909; Elliot to Grey, Athens, 25 February 1909, FO 371/677, No. 31; Elliot to Grey, Athens, 3 March 1909, FO 371/678, No. 33; Andrian to Aehrenthal, Athens, 3 March 1909, HHS XVI/60, No. 108.

16. X. Lefkoparidis, ed., *Stratigou P. Dangli: Anamneseis—Engrapha— Allelographia [General P. Danglis; Recollections—Personal Papers—Correspondence]*(Athens, 1965), I, 439.

17. *Nea Hemera,* 13 March 1909. This issue listed per capita tax burdens for the Balkan nations: Greece—39 drachmas; Rumania—26 drachmas; Serbia— 25 drachmas; Bulgaria—23 drachmas.

18. Elliot to Grey, Athens, 3 March 1909, FO 371/678, No. 33; Elliot to Grey, Athens, 5 March 1909, FO 371/678, No. 35; *Akropolis,* 4 March 1909; Theodorides [*The Revolution and Its Accomplishments*], pp. 16-22.

19. Elliot to Grey, Athens, 2 April 1909, FO 371/678, No. 48; Elliot to Grey, Athens, 2 April 1909, FO 371/678, No. 48; Riepenhausen to Bülow, Athens, 7 April 1909, AA 41/18, No. 9; *Akropolis,* 1 April 1909.

20. Elliot to Grey, Athens, 2 April 1909, FO 371/678, No. 49; Andrian to Aehrenthal, Athens, 3 April 1909, HHS XVI/60, No. 178.

21. Elliot to Grey, Athens, 2 April 1909, FO 371/678, No. 48. Elliot enclosed a dispatch from Alban Young, the IFC representative, on Theotokis's economic problems.

22. Elliot to Grey, Athens, 4 April 1909, FO 371/678, No. 50.

23. Even attempts such as that of Rallis's son during the early March demonstrations to push public agitation in the direction of his father's party provided no concrete results—this would not have been the case in earlier years.

24. Elliot to Grey, Athens, 24 May 1909, FO 371/678, No. 70; Braun to Aehrenthal, Athens, 16 May 1909, HHS XVI/60, No. 27D; George N. Philaretos, *Semeioseis apo tou 75os ypsomatos [Notes from the 75th Level]* (Athens, 1928), III, 543-44. The bill provided for raising the salary scale of the noncommissioned officers and allowing for their entrance into the civil service after fifteen years with the army time credited towards the civil pension.

25. *Akropolis,* 14 May 1909; *Neon Asty,* 13 May 1909; M. I. Malainos, *He epanastasis tou 1909 [The Revolution of 1909]* (Athens, 1965), p. 23; Theodore Pangalos, *Ta apomnemoneumata mou [My Memoirs]* (Athens, 1950), p. 52; School for Noncommissioned Officers, *Historia Stratiotikes Scholes Ypaxiomatikon [History of the School for Noncommissioned Officers]* (Athens, 1930). This last work includes statistics and laws associated with the school's history and development.

26. Elliot to Grey, Athens, 31 May 1909, FO 371/678, No. 79; Braun to Aehrenthal, Athens, 29 May 1909, HHS XVI/60, No. 30F; Braun to Aehrenthal, Athens, 5 June 1909, HHS XVI/60, No. 31C.

27. Braun to Aehrenthal, Athens, 29 May 1909, HHS XVI/60, No. 30F. Braun remarked: "In a country where everyone feels called upon to criticize and where everyone believes he possesses the stuff of a general or a minister,

it is obvious how difficult it is to properly canalize the completely confused concepts of duty, discipline and respect for the position of the superior."

28. Elliot to Grey, Athens, 24 May 1909, FO 371/678, No. 70; Elliot to Grey, Athens, 13 June 1909, FO 371/678, No. 86.

29. Elliot to Grey, Athens, 13 June 1909, FO 371/678, No. 86; George Aspreas, *Politike historia tes neoteras Hellados* [*Political History of Modern Greece*] (Athens, 1963), II, 102-06; L. I. Paraskevopoulos, *Anamneseis: 1896-1920* [*Recollections: 1896-1920*] (Athens, 1930), p. 86; Braun to Aehrenthal, Athens, 14 July 1909, HHS XVI/60, No. 32 (Very Confidential); Alexander Mazarakis-Ainian, *Apomnemoneumata* [*Memoirs*] (Athens, 1949), pp. 94-95.

30. In the first reports of the Austrian Legation in Athens to Vienna after the military revolt of 28 August, there were references to clandestine activities on the part of certain officers going back to October 1908. Lowenthal to Aehrenthal, Athens, 4 September 1909, HHS XVI/60, No. 50C (Very Confidential); Lowenthal to Aehrenthal, Athens, 18 September 1909, HHS XVI/60, No. 52E. Pangalos [*My Memoirs*], pp. 46-48. Pangalos claimed that eventually 120 signed this document, but there is no further evidence to corroborate this statement. Most of the officers in this early group were in the 7th Infantry Regiment located in Athens.

31. Aspreas [*Political History*], II, 104-05; Pangalos [*My Memoirs*], pp. 52-53; Mazarakis-Ainian [*Memoirs*], pp. 96-97.

32. Pangalos [*My Memoirs*], pp. 52-54.

33. Pangalos [*My Memoirs*], pp. 54-56; Aspreas [*Political History*], II, 106; Nicholas Zorbas, *Apomnemoneumata* [*Memoirs*] (Athens, 1925), p. 10; Mazarakis-Ainian [*Memoirs*], p. 97.

34. Pangalos [*My Memoirs*], pp. 57-58; Kostes Hairopoulos, "Trianta chronia demosiographikes zoës, 1895-1925," ["Thirty Years of a Journalistic Career, 1895-1925"], *Proïa*, 16 February 1926.

35. *Chronos*, 14 July 1909; Pangalos [*My Memoirs*], pp. 57-58; Hairopoulos, ["Thirty Years"], *Proïa*, 15 and 16 February 1926.

36. Zorbas [*Memoirs*], p. 11; Aspreas [*Political History*], II, 108; Pangalos [*My Memoirs*], pp. 60-61; "Constantine Typaldos Statement," Part I, pp. 3-4, Folder G [Gamma] 14 (War Ministries), Stephen Dragoumis Papers. This four-part account details naval Lieutenant Typaldos's activities in the Military League and was apparently written after his arrest for involvement in the mutiny of 28-29 October 1909. Typaldos's signature is at the bottom of each section.

37. Lefkoparidis, ed. [*Danglis: Recollections*], pp. 450-51; Paraskevopoulos [*Recollections*], p. 89; Pangalos [*My Memoirs*], pp. 50-51.

38. Pangalos [*My Memoirs*], pp. 61-62. The new committee had as members: Phikioris, Sarros, Patsogiannis, K. Gouvelis, Mimekos, Parnasides, Hatzekyriakos, Liolios, Zymbrakakis.

39. Hairopoulos ["Thirty Years"], *Proïa*, 17 February 1926. Hairopoulos claimed that the officers asked one politician, Nicholas Demetrakopoulos, to head the Military League, but he refused the offer.

40. Hairopoulos ["Thirty Years"], *Proïa*, 18 February 1926; Aspreas [*Political History*], II, 109.

41. Pangalos [*My Memoirs*], pp. 64-65; Zorbas [*Memoirs*], pp. 11-13; Mazarakis-Ainian [*Memoirs*], p. 93; S. B. Markezinis, *Politike historia tes neoteras Hellados* [*Political History of Modern Greece*] (Athens, 1967), III, 75-76.

42. Spyros Melas, *He epanastasis tou 1909* [*The Revolution of 1909*] (Athens, 1959), p. 198. Melas stated that even the pro-Theotokis newspaper, *Patris,* did not venture to speak out against the movement.

43. *Akropolis,* 27 June and 8 July 1909; 7 July 1909 and succeeding issues for letters on the plebiscite.

44. Hairopoulos ["Thirty Years"], *Proïa,* 14 and 15 February 1926. Hairopoulos revealed that Venizelos wrote from Crete asking that the plebiscite be stopped since his political position on the island might be compromised.

45. Elliot to Grey, Athens, 15 July 1909, FO 371/678, No. 104.

46. "FO Annual Report, 1908," p. 3; Driault, *Histoire diplomatique,* V, 21.

47. Elliot to Grey, Athens, 24 February 1910, FO 371/910, No. 29, "Annual Report, 1909," p. 4 (hereafter referred to as "FO Annual Report, 1909"); Elliot to Grey, Athens, 28 May 1909, FO 286/521, No. 75 (Very Confidential); Elliot to Grey, Athens, 13 June 1909, FO 286/521, No. 87.

48. Britain, FO Historical Section, *Greece,* pp. 58-59; Driault, *Histoire diplomatique,* p. 23; "FO Annual Report, 1909," pp. 4-5.

49. "FO Annual Report, 1909," pp. 4-6.

50. "FO Annual Report, 1909, "pp. 5-6.

51. Elliot to Grey, Athens, 20 July 1909, FO 371/678, No. 106; *Neon Asty,* 20 July 1909.

52. Elliot to Grey, Athens, 26 June 1909, FO 286/521, No. 93. This dispatch included a report by Colonel Surtees, the military attaché, who stated: "It is almost inconceivable that the Greeks can again seriously contemplate provoking hostilities, the result of which can only once more result in economic and military disaster."

53. The demonstration did not take place because of the sudden turn of political events.

54. Elliot to Grey, Athens, 20 July 1909, FO 371/678, No. 106; Britain, FO Historical Section, *Greece,* p. 59.

55. Lowenthal to Aehrenthal, Athens, 24 July 1909, HHS XVI/60, No. 38A; Elliot to Grey, Athens, 20 July 1909, FO 371/678, No. 106; Elliot to Grey, Athens, 21 July 1909, FO 371/678, No. 107. In this last dispatch Elliot stated: "Rallis, it is understood, consented to abate some part of his program, though upon what points is not yet certain." In the new cabinet only Rallis and E. N. Delegiannis, minister of justice, had held office before. The minister of war, Colonel Manoussogiannakis, had been second chief of the general staff. Rear Admiral Athanasios N. Miaoulis became the minister of marine.

56. "FO Annual Report, 1909," pp. 6-7; Britain, FO Historical Section, *Greece,* p. 60; Driault, *Histoire diplomatique,* V, 29-30.

57. "FO Annual Report, 1909," pp. 6-7; Britain, FO Historical Section, *Greece,* pp. 60-61; Driault, *Histoire diplomatique,* V, 31-32.

58. Elliot to Grey, Athens, 2 August 1909, FO 371/677, No. 115. Elliot stated: "Since its accession to office the new Greek government has been principally occupied with the distribution of spoils."

59. Pangalos [*My Memoirs*], pp. 65-67; *Chronos,* 8 August 1909; E. J. Dillon, "Constitutional Crises in Europe," *The Contemporary Review,* November 1909, p. 630; Stylianos Gonatas, *Apomnemoneumata, 1897-1957* [*Memoirs, 1897-1957*] (Athens, 1958), p. 26.

60. *Akropolis,* 21 August 1909, Gavrielides claimed "yellow journalism" was being practiced.

61. *Chronos,* 29 and 31 July 1909; 19 and 20 August 1909.

62. Pangalos [*My Memoirs*], pp. 59-60; *Akropolis,* 10 August 1909; *Chronos,* 11, 16 and 24 August 1909; Lowenthal to Aehrenthal, Athens, 10 August 1909, HHS XVI/60, No. 45; Hairopoulos ["Thirty Years"], *Proïa,* 17 February 1926.

63. "Typaldos Statement," I, 3, Dragoumis Papers.

64. *Chronos,* 20, 22, 24, and 27 August 1909; *Akropolis,* 25 August 1909; Riepenhausen to Bethmann-Hollweg, Athens, 22 August 1909, AA 41/18, No. 67. For greater detail on student activities, see P. K. Tsitsilias, *He epanastasis tou 1909 kai he Panepistemiake Enosis* [*The Revolution of 1909 and the University Union*] (Athens, 1964).

65. Elliot to Grey, Athens, 29 August 1909, FO 371/678, No. 133; *Akropolis,* 23 August 1909; *Esperini,* 22 and 23 August 1909; *Chronos,* 23 August 1909; *Neon Asty,* 27 August 1909; *Le Messager d'Athènes,* 25 August 1909.

66. *Chronos,* 23 August 1909. Elliot to Grey, Athens, 29 August 1909, FO 371/678, No. 133. Elliot commended: "On the arrival of the British Mediterranean Fleet on the 24th instant a rumour was put into circulation that it had come at the request of the King for his protection; and I then regretted (as I afterwards told His Majesty) that owing to a delay in the post, I had not received sufficient notice of the proposed visit of the fleet to be able to ask His Majesty whether it would be agreeble to him in the circumstances of the moment." *Akropolis,* 24 August 1909. There were 3 cruisers and 7 destroyers.

67. *Chronos,* 20, 25 and 26 August 1909; *Akropolis,* 21 and 25 August 1909.

68. *Akropolis,* 24, 25 and 26 August 1909; *Chronos,* 29 August 1909; Elliot to Grey, Athens, 29 August 1909, FO 371/678, No. 133.

69. *Akropolis,* 22 August 1909; *Chronos,* 24 August 1909; Hairopoulos ["Thirty Years"], *Proïa,* 18 February 1926; Pangalos [*My Memoirs*], p. 67; Riepenhausen to Bethmann-Hollweg, Athens, 22 August 1909, AA 41/18, No. 67.

70. Pangalos [*My Memoirs*], p. 67.

71. Pangalos [*My Memoirs*], pp. 68-69; *Akropolis,* 27 August 1909; *Chronos,* 27 August 1909.

72. Hairopoulos ["Thirty Years"], *Proïa,* 20 February 1926. The editor of *Chronos* claimed that Rallis's minister of marine met with members of the League's administrative committee in a room of the "Panhellenic" restaurant on the evening of August 26-27. Rallis then agreed to reconvene the *Boule. Chronos,* 27 August 1907; "Typaldos Statement," I, 5, Dragoumis Papers. Typaldos referred to the intermediary role played by John Rallis, the prime minister's son.

73. Zorbas [*Memoirs*], p. 14; Pangalos [*My Memoirs*], pp. 69-70; Hairopoulos ["Thirty Years"], *Proïa,* 20 February 1909.

74. Zorbas [*Memoirs*], pp. 14-15; Pangalos [*My Memoirs*], p. 81.

75. *Chronos,* 30 August 1909; Zorbas [*Memoirs*], pp. 22-23; Pangalos [*My Memoirs*], pp. 72-73; Elliot to Grey, Athens, 29 August 1909, FO 371/678, No. 133.

76. Zorbas [*Memoirs*], pp. 25-26; Pangalos [*My Memoirs*], pp. 73-74; Elliot to Grey, Athens, 29 August 1909, FO 371/678, No. 133; *Chronos,* 31 August 1909.

77. Elliot to Grey, Athens, 29 August 1909, FO 371/678, No. 133. In the early morning Elliot visited Rallis who stated "the town was at the mercy of the military."

78. Pangalos, [*My Memoirs*], pp. 75, 82; Zorbas [*Memoirs*], pp. 26-27.

79. Elliot to Grey, Athens, 29 August 1909, FO 371/678, No. 133; Riepenhausen to Bethmann-Hollweg, Athens, 21 August 1909, AA 41/18, Tel. No. 125. The German envoy claimed that the Military League had sought the cooperation of Demetrios Gounaris.

80. "Typaldos Statement," I, 9, Dragoumis Papers; Zorbas. [*Memoirs*], p. 27.

81. Zorbas [*Memoirs*], pp. 28-29; Elliot to Grey, Athens, 29 August 1909, FO 371/678, No. 133.

82. Mavromichalis had been minister of interior in 1902 and 1903 under Delegiannis and Rallis, minister of war and marine in 1905 under Delegiannis until his death and then minister of war and interior for a short time after under Rallis.

83. Lowenthal to Aehrenthal, Athens, 4 September 1909, HHS XVI/60, No. 50B; Elliot to Grey, Athens, 29 August 1909, FO 371/678, No. 133; Elliot to Grey, Athens, 2 September 1909, FO 371/678, No. 144; "Typaldos Statement," I, 11, Dragoumis Papers.

84. Zorbas [*Memoirs*], pp. 23-24.

Chapter III

1. The complete Greek text is in Nicholas Zorbas, *Apomnemonevmata* [*Memoirs*] (Athens, 1925), pp. 15-22; a translation from the Greek is in Elliot to Grey, Athens, 29 August 1909, FO 371/678, No. 133.

2. Elliot to Grey, Athens, 31 August 1909, FO 371/678, No. 137 (Very Confidential); Elliot to Grey, Athens, 9 September 1909, FO 371/678, No. 151.

3. Elliot to Grey, Athens, 31 August 1909, FO 371/678, No. 137 (Very Confidential). Elliot paraphrased the king's feelings, mentioning: "How could he allow these mutinous officers to kiss the Queen's hand at the New Year's reception?" Elliot to Grey, Athens, 2 September 1909, FO 371/678, No. 141 (Very Confidential); Lowenthal to Aehrenthal, Athens, 11 September 1909, HHS XVI/60, No. 51D.

4. Elliot to Grey, Athens, 2 September 1909, FO 371/678, No. 141 (Very Confidential). An officer of lower rank than colonel would not claim as a right to be placed *en disponibilité*.

5. Elliot to Grey, Athens, 2 September 1909, FO 371/678, No. 141 (Very Confidential); Elliot to Grey, Athens, 6 September 1909, FO 371/678, No. 149.

6. Cartwright to Grey, Marienbad, 29 August 1909, FO 371/678, Telegram, unnumbered; Elliot to Grey, Athens, 31 August 1909, No. 137 (Very Confidential); Elliot to Grey, Athens, 2 September 1909, FO 371/678, No. 141 (Very Confidential).

7. De Salis to Grey, Berlin, 1 September 1909, FO 371/678, No. 310; Metternich to Bethmann-Hollweg, London, 7 September 1909, AA 41/18, Tel. No. 911.

8. Lowenthal to Aehrenthal, Athens, 18 September 1909, HHS XVI/60, No. 52A; Grey to Elliot, Foreign Office, 6 September 1909, FO 286/524, No. 272. Aehrenthal told the British that George's "abdication . . . would greatly complicate the situation in the Near East and he hoped that everything would be done to persuade the King not to abandon his post of duty at this moment."

9. Pichon to Deville, Paris, 6 September 1909, XII, No. 123, *Documents diplomatique français,* (2e série), pp. 447-48.

10. Bertie to Grey, Paris, 6 September 1909, FO 371/678, No. 360; Zorbas [*Memoirs*], pp. 22-23. *Nea Hemera,* the Greek weekly published in Trieste, provided regular coverage of the reactions of the European press to the Greek situation.

11. Elliot to Grey, Athens, 31 August 1909, FO 371/678, No. 138; Elliot to Grey, Athens, 31 August 1909, FO 371/678, Tel. No. 67; Lowenthal to Aehrenthal, Athens, 2 September 1909, HHS XVI/60, Tel. No. 122.

12. *Chronos,* 31 August 1909. For example: Argos, Nauplion, Patras, Corinth, Lamia.

13. Theodore Pangalos, *Ta apomnemoneumata mou* [*My Memoirs*] (Athens, 1950), pp. 88-89; Zorbas [*Memoirs*], p. 33; Elliot to Grey, Athens, 2 September 1909, FO 371/678, No. 141 (Very Confidential); Lowenthal to Aehrenthal, Athens, 11 September 1909, HHS XVI/60, No. 51C (Very Confidential); Lowenthal to Aehrenthal, Athens, 30 September 1909, HHS XVI/60, No. 55C; L. I. Paraskevopoulos, *Anamneseis: 1896-1920* [*Recollections: 1896-1920*] (Athens, 1930), p. 95; "Constantine Typaldos Statement," Part II, pp. 3, 5, Folder G (Gamma) 14 (War Ministries), Stephen Dragoumis Papers; Riepenhausen to Bethmann-Hollweg, Athens, 5 September 1909, AA 41/18, No. 77.

14. Zorbas [*Memoirs*], p. 33; Theseus Pangalos, ed., *Epanastasis 1909: To archeion tou Stratiotikou Syndesmou* [*1909 Revolution: The Archives of the Military League*] (Athens, 1974). This latter work publishes some of the records of the Military League which had been in the possession of the editor's father, Theodore Pangalos. Membership lists of the Military League are to be found here (pp. 146-92).

15. Lowenthal to Aehrenthal, Athens, 18 September 1909, HHS XVI/60, No. 52E (Very Confidential); Elliot to Grey, Athens, 2 September 1909, FO 371/678, No. 141 (Very Confidential); Elliot to Grey, Athens, 6 September 1909, FO 371/678, No. 149; Elliot to Grey, Athens, 22 September 1909, FO 371/678, No. 159; Riepenhausen to Bethmann-Hollweg, Athens, 20 September 1909, AA 41/18, No. 94. Lowenthal to Aehrenthal, Athens, 4 September 1909, XVI/60, No. 50A (Very Confidential).

16. *Chronos,* 8 and 9 September 1909; Elliot to Grey, Athens, 9 September 1909, FO 371/678, No. 152; Elliot to Grey, Athens, 13 September 1909, FO 371/678, No. 154.

17. Elliot to Grey, Athens, 9 September 1909, FO 371/678, No. 152.

18. *Chronos,* 9 September 1909; *Neon Asty,* 9 September 1909; *Akropolis,* 9 September 1909; *Athenai,* 11 September 1909; *Le Messager d'Athènes,* 18 September 1909; Elliot to Grey, Athens, 13 September 1909, FO 371/678, No. 154; Elliot to Grey, Athens, 14 September 1909, FO 371/678, No. 156; Folder: Military Uprising, Dragoumis Papers. This folder contains clippings of articles critical of the Military League from provincial newspapers.

19. Riepenhausen to Bethmann-Hollweg, Athens, 12 September 1909, AA 41/18, No. 87; Elliot to Grey, Athens, 13 September 1909, FO 371/678, No. 154; *Chronos,* 10 September 1909.

20. Moses to Knox, Athens, 6 September 1909, NA 208/1950/13, No. 26.

21. Elliot to Grey, Athens, 6 September 1909, FO 371/678, No. 149; Elliot to Grey, Athens, 9 September 1909, FO 371/678, No. 151.

22. *Athenai,* 11 September 1909; *Le Messager d'Athènes,* 18 September 1909; Elliot to Grey, Athens, 13 September 1909, FO 371/678, No. 154; Elliot to Grey, Athens, 14 September 1909, FO 371/678, No. 156.

23. Elliot to Grey, Athens, 13 September 1909, FO 371/678, No. 154; Elliot to Grey, Athens, 14 September 1909, FO 371/678, No. 156.

24. *Chronos,* 12 and 15 September 1909; on 14 September 1909 *Chronos* also referred to Theotokis as "the Rigoletto of Athens."

25. Riepenhausen to Bethmann-Hollweg, Athens, 20 September 1909, AA 41/18, No. 92; Elliot to Grey, Athens, 14 September 1909, FO 371/678, No. 156; Elliot to Grey, Athens, 22 September 1909, FO 371/678, No. 159; *Nea Hemera,* 25 September 1909.

26. "Typaldos Statement," II, 3-4, Dragoumis Papers. Typaldos indicated that Zorbas and the administrative committee encouraged the organization of the demonstration. Zorbas [*Memoirs*], pp. 36-37; Riepenhausen to Bethmann-Hollweg, Athens, 28 September 1909, AA 41/18, No. 99.

27. *Chronos,* 28 September 1909, provided a long list of participating groups.

28. *Chronos,* 28 September 1909.

29. Elliot to Grey, Athens, 28 September 1909, FO 371/678, No. 163.

30. *Chronos,* 28 September 1909; Zorbas [*Memoirs*], pp. 36-42; Elliot to Grey, Athens, 30 September 1909, FO 371/677, No. 164; *The Times* of 2 October 1909 stated that along with the demonstration in Athens "others took place in Patras, Larissa, Chalcis, Laurium, and other important towns in Greece with the exception of Corfu, where comparative indifference seems to prevail. . . . Even in some of the gaols the prisoners held meetings and sent addresses to the king."

31. *Chronos,* 29 September 1909.

32. Elliot to Grey, Athens, 28 September 1909, FO 371/678, No. 163A (Very Confidential); Elliot to Grey, Athens, 2 October 1909, FO 371/678, No. 165.

33. Zorbas [*Memoirs*], pp. 52-54; Elliot to Grey, Athens, 3 October 1909, FO 371/678, Tel. No. 82; Elliot to Grey, Athens, 4 October 1909, FO 371/678, No. 166; Elliot to Grey, Athens, 6 October 1909, FO 371/678, No. 167; Elliot to Grey, Athens, 13 October 1909, FO 371/678, Tel. No. 84; Elliot to Grey, Athens, 21 October 1909, FO 371/679, No. 178; *Chronos,* 13 October 1909; *Neon Asty,* 24 October 1909; *Esperini,* 10 and 15 October 1909.

34. Elliot to Grey, Athens, 8 October 1909, FO 371/678, No. 169. This dispatch contains a letter to Elliot from Colonel Surtees, the British military attaché in Athens, which summarizes an interview with King George.

35. Elliot to Grey, Athens, 7 October 1909, FO 371/678, No. 168. This dispatch includes a letter to Elliot from Colonel Surtees which relates the contents of an interview with Prince Nicholas.

36. Particularly *Chronos* and George Philaretos's weekly, *Rizospastis.*

37. *Athenai,* 6 October 1909; Elliot to Grey, Athens, 9 October 1909, FO 371/678, No. 172.

38. Lowenthal to Aehrenthal, Athens, 26 September 1909, HHS XVI/60, No. 54A; Riepenhausen to Bethmann-Hollweg, Athens, 27 September 1909, AA 41/18, unnumbered; Elliot to Grey, Athens, 8 October 1909, FO 371/678, No. 169; Elliot to Grey, Athens, 9 October 1909, FO 371/678, No. 171; Elliot to Grey, Athens, 21 October 1909, FO 371/679, No. 178; Zorbas [*Memoirs*], p. 43.

39. Édouard Driault, *Histoire diplomatique de la Grèce de 1821 a nos jours* (Paris, 1926), V, 33; Braun to Aehrenthal, Athens, 22 October 1909, HHS XVI/60, Tel. No. 148 (Very Confidential); Braun also heard the name of Duke Luitpold of Bavaria mentioned. Riepenhausen to Bethmann-Hollweg, Athens,

4 October, AA 41/18, unnumbered; Elliot to Grey, Athens, 21 October 1909, FO 371/679, No. 178; Elliot to Grey, Athens, 27 October 1909, FO 371/679, No. 185; Johnstone to Grey, Copenhagen, 18 October 1909, FO 371/678, Tel. No. 14; Johnstone stated that the Duke of Teck had been suggested for the governorship of Crete.

40. *Chronos,* 4 October 1909; Riepenhausen to Bethmann-Hollweg Athens, 11 October 1909, AA 41/19, No. 105; Braun to Aehrenthal, Athens, 8 October 1909, HHS XVI/60, No. 57B; Elliot to Grey, Athens, 4 October 1909, FO 371/678, No. 166; Elliot to Grey, Athens, 6 October 1909, FO 371/678, No. 167; Elliot to Grey, Athens, 21 October 1909, FO 371/679, No. 178.

41. Romas gave up the ministry of interior for his new position. Mavromichalis temporarily assumed the responsibilities of this ministry. Elliot to Grey, Athens, 13 October 1909, FO 371/677, No. 174; *Chronos,* 10 October 1909.

42. Elliot to Grey, Athens, 13 October 1909, FO 371/677, No. 174.

43. Article 4 of the 28 May 1887 law was to be abrogated. The princes who had previously held officer rank according to this article would now be promoted to higher ranks by the king but no command or service in the military or naval forces was given to them. Elliot to Grey, Athens, 13 October 1909, FO 371/677, No. 175.

44. *Chronos,* 12 and 14 October 1909; Elliot to Grey, Athens, 13 October 1909, FO 371/677, No. 174; Elliot to Grey, Athens, 14 October 1909, FO 371/677, No. 176; *Le Messager d'Athènes,* 16 October 1909.

45. *Chronos,* 15 October 1909; Elliot to Grey, Athens, 21 October 1909, FO 371/679, No. 178.

46. *Chronos,* 15 and 16 October 1909; Elliot to Grey, Athens, 21 October 1909, FO 371/679, No. 178.

47. *Athenai,* 5 and 6 October 1909; Braun to Aehrenthal, Athens, 8 October 1909, HHS XVI/60, No. 57B; Elliot to Grey, Athens, 21 October 1909, FO 371/679, No. 178.

48. Elliot to Grey, Athens, 21 October 1909, FO 371/679, No. 178; Elliot to Grey, Athens, 25 October 1909, FO 371/679, No. 182.

49. "Typaldos Statement," III, 1-2, Dragoumis Papers; Pangalos [*My Memoirs*], pp. 102-03; *Chronos,* 30 October 1909.

50. "Typaldos Statement," III, 1-14, Dragoumis Papers.

51. "Typaldos Statement," III 15-23, Dragoumis Papers.

52. "Typaldos Statement," III, 23-29, Dragoumis Papers.

53. Pangalos [*My Memoirs*], p. 103; Zorbas [*Memoirs*], p. 155. Zorbas stated that the administrative committee had not wanted violence to break out in the house in which they were meeting.

54. "Typaldos Statement," III, 29-30; Braun to Aehrenthal, Athens, 31 October 1909, HHS XVI/60, No. 62; Elliot to Grey, Athens, 1 November 1909, FO 371/679, No. 187; *Le Messager d'Athenes,* 30 October 1909.

55. Pangalos [*My Memoirs*], p. 104; Elliot to Grey, Athens, 1 November 1909, FO 371/679, No. 187; Braun to Aehrenthal, Athens, 31 October 1909, HHS XVI/60, No. 62.

56. "Typaldos Statement," IV, Dragoumis Papers, for details of the conflict from Typaldos's vantage point; Pangalos [*My Memoirs*], p. 104; Elliot to Grey, Athens, 1 November 1909, FO 371/679, No. 185; Braun to Aehrenthal, Athens, 31 October 1909, HHS XVI/60, No. 62.

57. *Chronos,* 29 October 1909.

58. *Neon Asty,* 1 November 1909; *Embros,* 29 October 1909, as referred to in: Elliot to Grey, Athens, 3 November 1909, FO 371/679, No. 188; Zorbas [*Memoirs*], pp. 54-55; "Typaldos Statement," III, 2-3, Dragoumis Papers; A. Alexandris, *Politikai anamneseis* [*Political Recollections*] (Patras, 1947), pp. 32-33. Alexandris admitted conversations with Typaldos, a distant relative, and other naval officers but denied any involvement with their conspiratorial ventures.

59. Braun to Aehrenthal, Athens, 6 November 1909, HHS XVI/60, No. 63D; Elliot to Grey, Athens, 3 November 1909, FO 371/679, No. 188.

60. Braun to Aehrenthal, Athens, 6 November 1909, HHS XVI/60, No. 63C; Elliot to Grey, Athens, 4 November 1909, FO 371/679, No. 189.

61. Zorbas [*Memoirs*], p. 55; Pangalos [*My Memoirs*], p. 106; Elliot to Grey, Athens, 3 November 1909, FO 371/679, No. 188; Braun to Aehrenthal, Athens, 6 November 1909, HHS XVI/60, No. 63D.

62. Braun to Aehrenthal, Athens, 6 November 1909, HHS XVI/60, No. 63D; Elliot to Grey, Athens, 3 November 1909, FO 371/679, No. 188; Elliot to Grey, Athens, 6 November 1909, FO 371/679, No. 189.

63. *Chronos,* 4 November 1909.

64. *The Times,* 4 November 1909; Elliot to Grey, Athens, 3 November 1909, FO 371/9, No. 188.

65. Wangenheim to Bethmann-Hollweg, Athens, 28 November 1909, AA 41/19, No. 122; Braun to Aehrenthal, Athens, 6 November 1909, HHS XVI/60, No. 63H; Elliot to Grey, Athens, 11 November 1909, FO 371/677, No. 196 (Elliot stated: ". . . I find it impossible to keep pace with the great volume of legislation which is being pushed through with such unexampled rapidity"). *The Times,* 6 November 1909.

66. *The Times,* 10 and 18 November 1909. Trikoupis in 1886 reduced the number and increased the area of the constituencies to diminish the force of local influences, but his rival, Delegiannis, restored the small areas. The number was again reduced by Theotokis in 1906 and the Mavromichalis government sought to reduce further the number of prefectures.

67. Braun to Aehrenthal, Athens, 20 November 1909, HHS XVI/60, No. 65C; Elliot to Grey, Athens, 17 November 1909, FO 371/679, No. 196; *Le Messager d'Athènes,* 20 November 1909.

68. Elliot to Grey, Athens, 17 November 1909, FO 371/679, No. 196; *The Times,* 18 November 1909; *Chronos,* 17 November 1909.

69. *Nea Hemera,* 20 November 1909; Braun to Aehrenthal, Athens, 13 November 1909, XVI/60, No. 64A; Elliot to Grey, Athens, 17 November 1909, FO 371/678, No. 196; Elliot to Grey, Athens, 8 November 1909, FO 371/677, No. 194; Merlin to Elliot, Volos, 21 November 1909, FO 286/527; *The Times,* 17 November 1909; *Chronos* 4 and 15 November and 4 December 1909; *Le Messager d'Athènes,* 6, 17 and 27 November 1909.

70. *Chronos,* 22 and 24 November 1909; *The Times,* 24 and 25 November 1909; Elliot to Grey, Athens, 3 December 1909; FO 371/677, No. 204.

71. Wangenheim to Bethmann-Hollweg, Athens, 28 November 1909, AA 41/19, No. 122; Elliot to Grey, Athens, 24 November 1909, FO 371/679, No. 198; *Chronos,* 23 November 1909; *Le Messager d'Athènes,* 27 November 1909.

72. Braun to Aehrenthal, Athens, 26 November 1909, HHS XVI/60, No. 66B; Elliot to Grey, Athens, 24 November 1909, FO 371/679, No. 198.

73. *Chronos*, 28 November 1909; *The Times*, 28, 29 and 30 November 1909; Merlin to Elliot, Volos, 2 December 1909, FO 286/527; Elliot to Grey, Athens, 28 February 1910, FO 371/909, No. 40; Braun to Aehrenthal, Athens, 26 November 1909, HHS XVI/60, No. 66B.

74. Braun to Aehrenthal, Athens, 4 December 1909, HHS XVI/60, No. 67A; Elliot to Grey, Athens, 3 December 1909, FO 371/677, No. 204; Elliot to Grey, Athens, 24 November 1909, FO 371/679, No. 198; *Chronos*, 3 December 1909; *The Times*, 3 December 1909.

75. *The Times*, 1 December 1909. The correspondent of *The Times* remarked: "The malcontent officers are for the most part those who have risen from the ranks and who, not having passed through the Military School, are regarded as unfit for promotion to the rank of captain."

76. Elliot to Grey, Athens, 3 December 1909, FO 371/677, No. 204. Elliot commented: "A further cause [of dissatisfaction] arose from the action of certain members of the committee in connection with the proposal of the Minister of Finance for the taxation of alcohol in one of the measures on which he principally relies for raising the revenue required for the projects of military reorganization. The members in question were working for a reduction of the proposed tax as a favor to the president of the guild of spirit merchants, to whose efforts the success of the mass meeting of the 27th September was attributed."

77. Zorbas [*Memoirs*], pp. 61-62; Pangalos [*My Memoirs*], p. 107; Elliot to Grey, Athens, 3 December 1909, FO 371/677, No. 204; Braun to Aehrenthal, Athens, 4 December 1909, HHS XVI/60, No. 67A; Wangenheim to Bethmann-Hollweg, Athens, 8 December 1909, AA 41/19, No. 124.

78. Pangalos [*My Memoirs*], pp. 107-08; Zorbas [*Memoirs*], p. 62; Wangenheim to Bethmann-Hollweg, Athens, 11 January 1910, AA 41/19, No. 3.

79. "Typaldos Statement," II, 3-9; III, 14, Dragoumis Papers; Elliot to Grey, Athens, 26 November 1909, FO 371/679, No. 200; Zorbas [*Memoirs*], pp. 134-42; *Chronos*, 19 November 1909.

80. Elliot to Grey, Athens, 3 December 1909, FO 371/677, No. 202; Elliot to Grey, Athens, 15 December 1909, FO 371/677, No. 221.

81. Elliot to Grey, Athens, 3 December 1909, FO 371/677, No. 202. Elliot included the report from Alban Young who stated pessimistically: ". . . the government acts under the orders of a committee of military officers sincere but ignorant; that the legislature is voting at the point of the bayonet the crudest measures of taxation and reorganization to meet the blind outcry for military rehabilitation; in short, that the country is drifting towards an impasse from which civil anarchy or foreign war may easily prove the only issue."

82. Elliot to Grey, Athens, 9 December 1909, FO 371/677, No. 208. This dispatch includes a report from Alban Young. Grey's comment was on the folder for this communication from Athens.

83. Elliot to Grey, Athens, 3 December 1909, FO 371/677, No. 202; Elliot to Grey, Athens, 9 December 1909, FO 371/677, No. 208.

84. Elliot to Grey, Athens, 3 December 1909, FO 371/677, No. 204; Elliot to Grey, Athens, 9 December 1909, FO 371/677, No. 209.

85. *Chronos,* 8 December 1909; Elliot to Grey, Athens, 8 December 1909, FO 371/677, No. 209.

86. These funds were usually directed for propaganda in Macedonia, the maintenance for three years of 30,000 refugees from Bulgaria, and above all the system of advances to communes for primary education.

87. Elliot to Grey, Athens, 14 February 1910, FO 371/910, No. 29, "Annual Report, 1909," pp. 11-12 (hereafter referred to as "FO Annual Report, 1909").

88. *Chronos,* 17 December 1909; *The Times,* 17 and 18 December 1909; "FO Annual Report, 1909," pp. 11-12.

89. Elliot to Grey, Athens, 6 November 1909, FO 371/679, No. 190; Elliot to Grey, Athens, 11 November 1909, FO 371/677, No. 195; Elliot to Grey, Athens, 11 December 1909, FO 371/679, No. 210; Elliot to Grey, Athens, 5 March 1910, FO 371/910, No. 45. The last dispatch includes a report from the military attaché which lists and details the army laws. *The Times,* 27 November 1909.

90. *Chronos,* 21 December 1909; Elliot to Grey, Athens, 22 December 1909, FO 371/679, No. 215.

91. Elliot to Grey, Athens, 22 December 1909, FO 371/679, No. 215; Zorbas [*Memoirs*], p. 121. The Military League leader wrote that Mavromichalis at the height of this crisis suggested the formation of a dictatorship. Zorbas replied that it would be better for him to resign immediately.

92. *Chronos,* 21 December 1909; Zorbas [*Memoirs*], pp. 128-29; Elliot to Grey, Athens, 22 December 1909, FO 371/679, No. 215.

93. Wangenheim to Bethmann-Hollweg, Athens, 26 December 1909, AA 41/19, No. 131; Elliot to Grey, Athens, 22 December 1909, FO 371/679, No. 215; Elliot to Grey, Athens, 25 December 1909, FO 371/679, No. 217.

94. Elliot to Grey, Athens, 22 December 1909, FO 371/679, No. 216.

95. *Chronos,* 22, 23 and 24 December 1909; Elliot to Grey, Athens, 25 December 1909, FO 371/679, No. 217.

96. Zorbas [*Memoirs*], pp. 108-09; Braun to Aehrenthal, Athens, 25 December 1909, HHS XVI/60, No. 70A; Braun to Aehrenthal, Athens, 5 January 1910, HHS XVI/61, No. 28; Elliot to Grey, Athens, 25 December 1909, FO 371/679, No. 217. Elliot states; "On leaving the King, Colonel Zorbas saw His Majesty's private secretary (from whom I have obtained this information), and told him that the extreme spirits in the League were advocating a military dictatorship. . . ."

97. Merlin to Elliot, Volos, 24 December 1909, FO 286/527; Wangenheim to Bethmann-Hollweg, Athens, 24 December 1909, AA 41/19, Tel. No. 204.

98. There were to be promotions of six to lieutenant general, four to colonel and 178 advancements to other ranks. Elliot to Grey, Athens, 25 December 1909, FO 371/679, No. 217; Braun to Aehrenthal, Athens, 25 December 1909, HHS XVI/60, No. 70A; *Chronos,* 25 December 1909; Zorbas [*Memoirs*], pp. 128-32. Mavromichalis gave up the ministry of justice which was taken over by Panagiotis Zaïmis, the minister of education.

99. Pangalos [*My Memoirs*], pp. 93-94; Paraskevopoulos [*Recollections*], pp. 97-100.

100. The letter was published in most Athenian newspapers. This translation is based on that found in Elliot to Grey, Athens, 2 January 1910, FO 371/908, No. 2.

214

101. *Chronos*, 2 January 1910; Elliot to Grey, Athens, 2 January 1910, FO 371/908, No. 2.

102. *Chronos*, 2 and 5 January 1910. Among the fifteen laws were included those doing away with the commander-in-chief position in the army, the inheritance tax, Sunday closings of business, age limits on officers, buying of the armored cruiser and police supervision over indirect taxation.

103. *Chronos*, 1 January 1910; Zorbas [*Memoirs*], p. 126, Elliot to Grey, Athens, 2 January 1910, FO 371/908, No. 20.

104. Braun to Aehrenthal, Athens, 5 January 1910, HHS XVI/61, No. 2A; Elliot to Grey, Athens, 2 January 1910, FO 371/908, No. 2; *Chronos*, 3 January 1910.

105. Elliot to Grey, Athens, 2 January 1910, FO 371/908, No. 2.

106. *Chronos*, 7 January 1910; Elliot to Grey, Athens, 7 January 1910, FO 371/908, No. 3.

107. Elliot to Grey, Athens, 7 January 1910, FO 371/908, No. 3.

108. *Chronos*, 7 January 1910; Elliot to Grey, Athens, 7 January 1910, FO 371/908, No. 3; Elliot to Grey, Athens, 8 January 1910, FO 371/908, No. 4.

109. Elliot to Grey, Athens, 8 January 1910, FO 371/908, No. 4; Braun to Aehrenthal, Athens, 8 January 1910, HHS XVI/61, No. 4.

110. Elliot to Grey, Athens, 11 January 1910, FO 371/908, No. 6. *Esperini* on 9 January 1910 concluded an editorial very critical of the English with: "P.S. The translator of the English Legation is requested to translate these few lines to His Excellency the English minister."

111. Elliot to Grey, Athens, 11 January 1910, FO 371/908, No. 6. This is a translated editorial from *Kavion*, 9 January 1910.

112. Elliot to Grey, Athens, 11 January 1910, FO 371/908, No. 6.

113. Elliot to Grey, Athens, 11 January 1910, FO 371/908, No. 6; Wangenheim to Bethmann-Hollweg, Athens, 20 November 1909, AA 50/15, No. 120 (Secret). The German minister related the important role of the British ships in curbing anti-dynastic elements in the League. He also referred to a statement attributed to George—that the English had proved to be his only friends in time of need.

114. Elliot to Grey, Athens, 11 December 1909, FO 371/679, Tel. No. 95.

115. Foreign Office to Admiralty, 14 December 1909, FO 371/679; Elliot to Grey, Athens, 11 January 1910, FO 371/908, No. 6.

Chapter IV

1. *Keryx*, 31 August 1909, 8 and 15 September 1909.

2. *Keryx*, 8 September 1909.

3. *Neos Kosmos*, 25 December 1933. This pro-Venizelist newspaper serialized "He politike historia tou kommatos ton Phileleftheron" [*The Political History of the Liberal Party*] which treated certain phases of the 1909-10 period in a thorough fashion, particularly Venizelos's role. This letter was from the personal papers of John Phikioris, held by a lawyer-nephew in Sparta. George Papantonakis, *He politike stadiodromia tou Eleftheriou Venizelou* [*The Political Career of Eleftherios Venizelos*] (Athens, 1928), p. 244. The author refers to a letter sent by Venizelos to G. Moatsos, a friend, in Athens on 22 October 1909, stating that he would not go to the capital mainly because of

the commotion it would stir up, something he wished to avoid. Elliot to Grey, Athens, 4 October 1909, FO 371/678, No. 166. Since there are no other sources which refer to Venizelos's presence in Greece during October, the validity of Sir Francis Elliot's dispatch must be dismissed: "The arrival of M. Venizelos from Crete is thought by some to be ominous of the intention of the officers to place him at the head of a 'Cabinet d'Affaires,' should M. Mavromichalis's government not do what is expected of them."

4. *Neos Kosmos,* 3 December 1933.

5. Nicholas K. Zorbas, *Apomnemoneumata* [*Memoirs*] (Athens, 1925), pp. 63-64; Theodore Pangalos, *Ta apomnemoneumata mou* [*My Memoirs*] (Athens, 1950), pp. 107-08; George Aspreas, *Politike historia tes neoteras Hellados* [*Political History of Modern Greece*] (Athens, 1963), II, 126. Aspreas states that in the final balloting only Captain Constantine Gouvelis voted against the proposal.

6. Zorbas [*Memoirs*], p. 64; Pangalos [*My Memoirs*], p. 108. Both Zorbas and Pangalos claimed their inability to find a copy of this letter.

7. Zorbas [*Memoirs*], pp. 64-65.

8. *Chronos,* 9 January 1910. Venizelos had first departed from Crete on 8 January with the steamer *Goudhi* but rough seas forced the boat to return to port. From there he left on the *Singapore.*

9. Kostes Hairopoulos, "Trianta chronia demosiographikes zoës, 1895-1925," ["Thirty Years of a Journalistic Career, 1895-1925"], *Proïa,* 7 March 1926. Despite Zorbas's generally favorable coverage in his memoirs of Venizelos's role, Hairopoulos wrote that upon asking the League head after the first meeting what he thought of Venizelos, the disparaging reply was: "A Delegiannis, third class."

10. Zorbas [*Memoirs*], pp. 65-66; Pangalos [*My Memoirs*], pp. 109-10.

11. Zorbas [*Memoirs*], pp. 66-67; Pangalos [*My Memoirs*], p. 110.

12. Zorbas [*Memoirs*], pp. 67-68; Pangalos [*My Memoirs*], pp. 112-13.

13. Zorbas [*Memoirs*], p. 68; Pangalos [*My Memoirs*], p. 113; for an excellent summary of Venizelos's positions, see an interview with him: *Nea Hemera,* 5 February 1910.

14. For example: *Neon Asty,* 11 and 13 January 1910; *Esperini,* 13 January 1910; *Chronos* was relatively silent. Wratislaw to Grey, Chanea, 21 January 1910, FO 371/908, No. 8.

15. *The Times,* 13 January 1910.

16. *Chronos,* 14 January 1910.

17. Zorbas [*Memoirs*], p. 68.

18. Hairopoulos ["Thirty Years"] *Proïa,* 8 March 1926; Pangalos [*My Memoirs*], pp. 115 and 117. Pangalos conjectured that Loidorikis's action might have been the result of his close ties with Mavromichalis. After this incident Loidorikis was replaced in his position by Pangalos.

19. Venizelos to Zorbas in Zorbas [*Memoirs*], p. 69.

20. Venizelos to Theotokis in Zorbas [*Memoirs*], pp. 69-70.

21. Theotokis to Venizelos in Zorbas [*Memoirs*], pp. 70-71.

22. Venizelos to Military League in Zorbas [*Memoirs*], p. 71.

23. Zorbas [*Memoirs*], pp. 71-72.

24. Zorbas [*Memoirs*], p. 73.

25. Zorbas [*Memoirs*], pp. 69 and 73; *The Times,* 29 January 1910. Bourchier

wrote: "After much deliberation this condition was accepted by the . . . League."

26. Zorbas [*Memoirs*], p. 73.

27. Braun to Aehrenthal, Athens, 22 January 1910, HHS XVI/60, No. 7; Elliot to Grey, Athens, 27 January 1910, FO 371/908, No. 14; *Chronos,* 27 January 1910; *The Times,* 28 January 1910.

28. Braun to Aehrenthal, Athens, 5 February 1910, HHS XVI/61, No. 98 (Secret); Elliot to Grey, Athens, 27 January 1910, FO 371/908, No. 14; Elliot to Grey, Athens, 31 January 1910, FO 371/908, No. 17. Elliot reported in this last dispatch: "I heard yesterday from Captain Philemore of His Majesty's ship *Aboukir* that he had been told by a Greek naval officer that the yacht could not be moved, being short of officers and men, and her engines being out of order." Elliot to Grey, Athens, 28 January 1910, FO 371/908, Tel. No. 8 (Very Confidential); Elliot to Grey, Athens, 31 January 1910, FO 371/908, No. 17; Wangenheim to Bethmann-Hollweg, Athens, 29 January 1910, AA 41/19, Tel. No. 17.

29. Elliot to Grey, Athens, 31 January 1910, FO 371/908, No. 17; George also expressed similar thoughts to the Belgian minister who, in turn, relayed them to the German envoy: Wangenheim to Bethmann-Hollweg, Athens, 30 January 1910, AA 41/19, Tel. No. 18.

30. Moses to Knox, Athens, 31 January 1910, NA 868.00/1950/27, No. 74; Elliot to Grey, Athens, 31 January 1910, FO 371/908, No. 17; *The Times,* 31 January 1910.

31. *Chronos,* 30 January 1910; Elliot to Grey, Athens, 31 January 1910, FO 371/908, No. 17; "Minutes of 29 January meeting," *Epanastasis 1909: To archeion tou Stratiotikou Syndesmou* [*1909 Revolution: The Archives of the Military League*], ed. Theseus Pangalos (Athens, 1974), pp. 13-14 (hereafter referred to as [*Military League Archives*]).

32. Elliot to Grey, Athens, 31 January 1910, FO 371/908, No. 17.

33. "Minutes of 29 January 1910 meeting," [*Military League Archives*], pp. 13-14; Wangenheim to Bethmann-Hollweg, Athens, 2 February 1910, AA 50/15, No. 12; Elliot to Grey, Athens, 31 January 1910, FO 371/908, No. 17; *The Times,* 15 February 1910; Braun to Aehrenthal, Athens, 30 January 1910, HHS XVI/61, Tel. No. 23; Zorbas [*Memoirs*], p. 73.

34. "Minutes of 30 January 1910 meeting," [*Military League Archives*], p. 17; Braun to Aehrenthal, Athens, 5 February 1910, HHS XVI/61, No. 9B (Secret); Elliot to Grey, Athens, 31 January 1910, FO 371/908, No. 17.

35. George Philaretos, *Semeioseis apo tou 75os ypsomatos* [*Notes from the 75th Level*] (Athens, 1928), III, 574-75; Tasos Michalakeas, ed., *Vivlos tou Eleftheriou Venizelou* [*The Bible of Eleftherios Venizelos*] (Athens, 1964), pp. 283-85; Zorbas [*Memoirs*], pp. 75-76; Elliot to Grey, Athens, 8 February 1911, FO 371/1130, No. 20, "Annual Report, Greece," p. 7 (hereafter referred to as "FO Annual Report, 1910").

36. "Minutes of 30 January 1910 meeting," [*Military League Archives*], p. 17; Zorbas [*Memoirs*], pp. 75-76.

37. "Minutes of 30 January 1910 meeting," Military League Archives, p. 17; *Chronos,* 1 February 1910; Elliot to Grey, Athens, 1 February 1910, FO 371/908, No. 21; Zorbas [*Memoirs*], p. 78.

38. Braun to Aehrenthal, Athens, 5 February 1910, HHS XVI/61, No. 9A.

39. Elliot to Grey, Athens, 3 February 1910, FO 371/908, No. 24; Zorbas [*Memoirs*], pp. 81-83.

40. Elliot to Grey, Athens, 31 January 1910, FO 371/908, No. 20; Elliot to Grey, Athens, 4 February 1910, FO 371/908, No. 24.

41. Elliot to Grey, Athens, 31 January 1910, FO 371/908, No. 20. Elliot reported that the telegram was given to the press but that its publication was stopped by threats from the Military League.

42. Wratislaw to Grey, Chanea, 4 February 1910, FO 371/909, No. 13; *The Times,* 5 February 1910.

43. Édouard Driault, *Histoire diplomatique de la Grèce de 1821 à nos jours* (Paris, 1926), V, 32-34; Elliot to Grey, Athens, 14 February 1910, FO 371/910, No. 29, "Annual Report, 1909," p. 9 (hereafter referred to as "FO Annual Report, 1909").

44. The question of Venizelos's citizenship would be the subject of ongoing debate. Lowther to Grey, Constantinople, 27 January 1910, FO 371/908, Tel. No. 7; *The Times,* 4 February 1910; "FO Annual Report, 1910," p. 5. "The Grand Vizier said that Turkey was prepared to incur the cost of war with Greece, perhaps 7,000,000 [pounds] and 30,000 men, with no material advantage to be gained, rather than submit to the idea of Cretan deputies sitting in Athens."

45. Rodd to Grey, Rome, 1 February 1910, FO 371/909, No. 16; Nicolson to Grey, St. Petersburg, 2 February 1910, FO 371/909, No. 65; Grey to Nicolson, Foreign Office, 10 February 1910, FO 371/909, No. 45.

46. Grey to Elliot, Foreign Office, 5 February 1910, FO 371/908, No. 11, *Chronos,* 5 February 1910; *The Times,* 4 and 5 February 1910.

47. Wratislaw to Grey, Chanea, 18 February 1910, FO 371/909, No. 19.

48. *The Times,* 16 February 1910; Elliot to Grey, Athens, 17 February 1910, FO 371/910, No. 32; Elliot to Grey, Athens, 23 February 1910, FO 371/909, No. 37. Theotokis referred to the French using Crete in their dispute with the Turks over Tripolis, and the English, "though no doubt not openly," in their dispute over the Euphrates steamers. Grey to Nicolson, Foreign Office, 10 February 1910, FO 371/909, No. 45. In this dispatch Grey highlighted the secondary concern about Greek interests in his comments to Count Beckendorff, the Russian ambassador to London: "I told him that we must be careful to avoid giving umbrage to the Turks by acting at Constantinople and Athens simultaneously and in the same form, and so giving the impression that Greece and Turkey were on an equal footing, and had equal rights with regard to Crete. It was essential to make the communication formally at Constantinople, but, if we said anything at Athens, it must in any case be said unofficially."

49. *Chronos,* 4 February 1910; *The Times,* 15 February 1910; Elliot to Grey, Athens, 3 February 1910, FO 371/908, No. 24.

50. Braun to Aehrenthal, Athens, 7 January 1910, HHS XVI/61, No. 3D; Elliot to Grey, Athens, 1 January 1910, FO 371/909, No. 1; Elliot to Grey, Athens, 17 January 1910, FO 371/908, No. 12 (Very Confidential); *The Times,* 11 January 1910; Elliot to Grey, Athens, 9 February 1910, FO 371/909, No. 27; *The Times,* 9 February 1910; "Minutes of 3 February and 4 February 1910 Meetings," [*Military League Archives*], pp. 24-26; Zorbas [*Memoirs*], pp. 56-58; King George to Stephen Dragoumis, 7 February, Folder G [Gamma] 14

(War Ministries), Dragoumis Papers. The monarch in this note stipulated the terms of amnesty and the necessity that Typaldos travel abroad.

51. On 21 February the four cavalry officers who had supported Colonel Metaxas and Captain Kalinskis in trying to keep their cavalry regiment loyal to the government on the morning of 28 August were dismissed from the army by a Royal decree. The king unwillingly yielded on this issue, also.

52. Braun to Aehrenthal, Athens, 19 February 1910, XVI/61, No. 12E; Elliot to Grey, Athens, 3 February 1910, FO 371/909, No. 26; Elliot to Grey, Athens, 28 February 1910, FO 371/909, No. 40; *The Times,* 5 and 10 February 1910.

53. "Minutes of 4, 7, 12 and 14 February 1910 Meetings," [*Military League Archives*], pp. 26, 27-29, 31, 32.

54. "Minutes of 12 and 14 February 1910 Meeting," [*Military League Archives*], pp. 31, 33.

55. *Le Messager d'Athènes,* 21 February 1910; *The Times,* 15 February 1910; Wangenheim to Bethmann-Hollweg, Athens, 15 February 1910, AA 41/19, Tel. No. 26; Elliot to Grey, Athens, 17 February 1910, FO 371/909, No. 33; Braun to Aehrenthal, Athens, 19 February 1910, HHS XVI/61, Tel. 42. Braun heard reports that Mavromichalis planned to subsidize five newspapers for the purpose of writing against the proposed National Assembly.

56. For the list of names, see *Chronos,* 13 February 1910.

57. *Esperini,* 14 February 1910; *Chronos,* 16 February 1910; Zorbas [*Memoirs*], pp. 83-84; *The Times,* 15 and 17 February 1910; Braun to Aehrenthal, Athens, 19 February 1910, HHS XVI/61, No. 12B; Elliot to Grey, Athens, 19 February 1910, FO 371/909, No. 34.

58. "Minutes of the 3, 7 and 23 February 1910 Meetings," [*Military League Archives*], pp. 24-25, 27-28, 41-42; Wangenheim to Bethmann-Hollweg, Athens, 22 February 1910, AA 41/20, No. 23; *The Times,* 17 February 1910.

59. *Chronos,* 24 February 1910; *The Times,* 25 February 1910; Wangenheim to Bethmann-Hollweg, Athens, 23 February 1910, AA 41/20, Tel. No. 36; Braun to Aehrenthal, Athens, 26 February 1910, HHS XVI/61, No. 13B; Elliot to Grey, Athens, 26 February 1910, FO 371/909, No. 38.

60. Venizelos's presence in Athens from February 14 to 28 did not attract the publicity of his earlier visit. He spoke several times with the various politicians but no significant decisions were made on this trip. *Chronos,* 25 February 1910; *The Times,* 26 February 1910; Elliot to Grey, Athens, 26 February 1910, FO 371/909, No. 38.

61. Elliot to Grey, Athens, 19 February 1910, FO 371/909, No. 34; Elliot to Grey, Athens, 28 February 1910, FO 371/909, No. 40.

62. *Chronos,* 19 February 1910; *The Times,* 19 February 1910; Elliot to Grey, Athens, 19 February 1910, FO 371/909, No. 34.

63. Moses to Knox, Athens, 23 February 1910, NA 868.00/1950/30, No. 89; Wangenheim to Bethmann-Hollweg, 22 February 1910, AA 41/20, No. 23; Elliot to Grey, Athens, 19 February 1910, FO 371/909, No. 34. George informed Elliot that he had consented, on the advice of Theotokis and Rallis, to depart from the strict letter of the constitution in summoning a revisionist National Assembly after a vote of the present Chamber only, but the revisionist National Assembly would be bound by the program prepared for it, and if the Assembly attempted to go beyond it, the king would have the power to dissolve. But an Assembly summoned by Royal decree would be absolutely

unconstitutional and therefore unrestricted, and if it chose to declare itself constituent, nothing could stop it.

64. *Chronos,* 17 and 18 February 1910; *Athenai,* 18 February 1910; Braun to Aehrenthal, Athens, 20 February 1910, HHS XVI/61, Tel. No. 45 (Very Secret); Elliot to Grey, Athens, 22 February 1910, FO 371/909, No. 36; *The Times,* 21 February 1910; Zorbas to Dragoumis, Folder G [Gamma] 4 (*Boule*-Palace), Dragoumis Papers. In polite but emphatic terms Zorbas stated he learned from the newspapers of plans for the crown prince to return and that he hoped this information was untrue.

65. *Chronos,* 27 February 1910; *The Times,* 28 February 1910; Elliot to Grey, Athens, 1 March 1910, FO 371/909, No. 41. Elliot summarized the attitude of the king from an interview: "His Majesty . . . doubted the authenticity of the interview with the Crown Prince, as his Royal Highness's brother, Prince Andrew, who had met him last week at Brindisi had found him animated by less conciliatory sentiments."

66. Elliot to Grey, Athens, 28 February 1910, FO 371/909, No. 40.

67. "Minutes of the 21 February 1910 Meeting," [*Military League Archives*], pp. 39-40.

68. *Chronos,* 26 February 1910; *Le Messager d'Athènes,* 3 March 1910; *The Times,* 26 February 1910.

69. Elliot to Grey, Athens, 1 March 1910, FO 371/909, No. 41; *Chronos,* 27 February 1910; *The Times,* 28 February 1910.

70. *Chronos,* 1, 2 and 3 March 1910; *The Times,* 4 and 5 March 1910; Pangalos [*My Memoirs*], p. 125.

71. Rallis and Mavromichalis exchanged insults. Also, Colonel Lymbritis, an archenemy of the League, declared that while the officers embroiled themselves in politics, they neglected military exercises.

72. Moses to Knox, Athens, 4 March 1910, NA 868.00/1950/33, No. 96; Elliot to Grey, Athens, 8 March 1909, FO 371/909, No. 47; *Chronos,* 4 March 1910; *Le Messager d'Athènes,* 8 March 1910; *The Times,* 4 March 1910.

73. Elliot to Grey, Athens, 8 March 1910, FO 371/909, No. 47; *Chronos,* 4 and 5 March 1910; *Le Messager d'Athènes,* 8 March 1910; *The Times,* 4 and 5 March 1910.

74. Elliot to Grey, Athens, 31 January 1910, FO 371/908, No. 19; Elliot to Grey, Athens, 8 March 1910, FO 371/909, No. 46; Elliot to Grey, Athens, 1 March 1910, FO 371/909, No. 41. According to Elliot, the king eventually said that "if it was desired that the ships should leave, he would raise no objection, although their presence was very reassuring to the Queen and Princes, and had been very useful on several occasions." Moses to Knox, Athens, 8 March 1910, NA 868.00/1950/35, No. 98. Moses stated that "Elliot has never concealed from his colleagues that the ships were here to offer asylum to the Royal Family in case the King should abdicate or be dethroned."

75. *Chronos,* 9 and 10 March 1910; *The Times,* 10 March 1910; Braun to Aehrenthal, Athens, 12 March 1910, HHS XVI/61, No. 15B; Elliot to Grey, Athens, 17 March 1910, FO 371/910, No. 48.

76. *The Times,* 12 April 1910 (Bourchier provided an excellent summary of events and issues in this long article); X. Zolotas, *Agrotike politike* [*Agrarian Politics*] (Athens, 1934), pp. 75-80; A. D. Sideris, *He georgike politike tes Hellados kata ten lexasan ekatontaetias: 1833-1933* [*The Agrarian Politics of*

220

Greece during the Past Century: 1833-1933] (Athens, 1934), pp. 101-03, 141-47; Demetrios Pournaras, *Historia tou agrotikou kinematos en Helladi* [*History of the Agrarian Movement in Greece*] (Athens, 1931), pp. 48-50; Wangenheim to Bethmann-Hollweg, Athens, 13 March 1910, AA 41/20, No. 28. Wangenheim stated that of 303 *chifliks* 249 belonged to Greeks and 54 to Turks.

77. Zolotas [*Agrarian Politics*], pp. 79-80; Elliot to Grey, Athens, 17 March 1910, FO 371/910, No. 48; *The Times,* 18 March 1910.

78. Elliot to Grey, Athens, 17 March 1910, FO 371/910, No. 48; Braun to Aehrenthal, Athens, 19 March 1910, HHS XVI/61, No. 16B; *The Times,* 12 April 1910.

79. *Chronos,* 17 March 1910; *The Times,* 18 and 21 March 1910; Sideris [*Agrarian Politics of Greece*], pp. 144-46; Elliot to Grey, Athens, 17 March 1910, FO 371/910, No. 48; Braun to Aehrenthal, Athens, 26 March 1910, HHS XVI/61, No. 17B.

80. John Kordatos, *Historia tou agrotikou kinematos sten Hellada* [*History of the Agrarian Movement in Greece*], 2nd ed. (Athens, 1973), pp. 47-57; *Chronos,* 20 and 21 March 1910; *The Times,* 21 March 1910; Elliot to Grey, Athens, 24 March 1910. Elliot's report included dispatches from the British consul, Merlin, in Volos. In his report of 21 March Merlin commented: "All damage done to the train was caused by stones, and it is certain that most, if not all, of the countrymen were unarmed."

81. *Chronos,* 22-25 March 1910; *The Times,* 22, 24 and 25 March 1910; Elliot to Grey, Athens, 28 March 1910, FO 371/910, No. 56.

82. General Petmezas resigned as minister of interior on 5 March, ostensibly for health reasons, but really over a difference of opinion with Dragoumis on policy towards the gendarmerie. Two days later, Epaminondas Mavromatis, a friend of Dragoumis, took over the position.

83. Elliot to Grey, Athens, 18 February 1910, FO 371/909, Tel. No. 23; Elliot to Grey, Athens, 19 February 1910, FO 371/909, No. 34; Braun to Aehrenthal, Athens, 12 March 1910, HHS XVI/61, No. 15B; *The Times,* 12 March 1910; *Chronos,* 11 March 1910. Though not mentioning any names, the *Chronos* editorial accused Zorbas of having forgotten his associates in the League.

84. *Chronos,* 11 March 1910.

85. *Chronos,* 20-27 March 1910; *Le Messager d'Athènes,* 26 March and 2 April 1910; *Nea Hemera,* 2 April 1910; *The Times,* 21 March 1910. Many of the university chairs had become virtual hereditary fiefs.

86. *Chronos,* 19 March 1910.

87. *Chronos,* 20-23 March 1910; *The Times,* 22 and 23 March 1910; Braun to Aehrenthal, Athens, 26 March 1910, XVI/61, No. 17A; Pangalos [*My Memoirs*], pp. 121-23. Pangalos mentioned three examples of officers dismissed —all for theft.

88. *Nea Hemera,* 2 April 1910; *Chronos,* 20 and 21 March 1910; *The Times,* 21 March 1910; Elliot to Grey, Athens, 24 March 1910, FO 371/910, No. 55.

89. *Nea Hemera,* 2 April 1910; *Chronos,* 22-24 March 1910; *The Times,* 24 March 1910.

90. *Chronos,* 20 March 1910; *The Times,* 8 March 1910; Elliot to Grey, Athens, 17 March 1910, FO 371/909, No. 50; Elliot to Grey, Athens, 20 April 1910, FO 371/910, No. 64; Young to Grey, Athens, 18 July 1910, FO 371/910, Tel. No. 76.

91. *Chronos,* 27 March 1910; *Le Messager d'Athènes,* 2 April 1910; *The Times,* 28 March 1910; Elliot to Grey, Athens, 30 March 1910, FO 371/910, No. 58; Elliot to Grey, Athens, 26 July 1910, FO 371/912, No. 101. Comparative statistics for the two budgets are:

1909: Army 18,082,430 drs.	1910: Army 23,150,238 drs.
Navy 8,506,347 drs.	Navy 11,984,076 drs.

92. Elliot to Grey, Athens, 30 March 1910, FO 371/910, No. 58; *Chronos,* 28-30 March 1910; Pangalos [*My Memoirs*], p. 129; Zorbas [*Memoirs*], p. 129; Zorbas [*Memoirs*], pp. 88-89. Zorbas and Pangalos placed the date of the protocol as 15/28 March, but the newspapers and diplomatic dispatches indicated that the administrative committee meeting was held and the protocol released on 16/29 March.

93. [*Military League Archives*], p. 48.

94. Wangenheim had consistently shown opposition to the sequence of events in Greece after the League's revolt, particularly as they affected the prestige and position of the crown prince and his Prussian wife.

95. *Chronos,* 31 March 1910; *The Times,* 31 March 1910; Braun to Aehrenthal, Athens, 2 April 1910, HHS XVI/61, No. 18; Elliot to Grey, Athens, 30 March 1910, FO 371/909, No. 58.

96. *Chronos,* 31 March 1910; *The Times,* 31 March 1910.

97. *Chronos,* 31 March 1910.

98. This definition is from David Sills, ed., *International Encyclopedia of the Social Sciences* (New York, 1968), XIII, 561.

99. For example: Spyros Melas, *He epanastasis tou 1909* [*The Revolution of 1909*] (Athens, 1957); M. I. Malainos, *He epanastasis tou 1909* [*The Revolution of 1909*] (Athens, 1965); A. Theodorides, *He epanastasis kai to ergon aftes* [*The Revolution and Its Accomplishments*] (Athens, 1914); John Kordatos, the Marxist historian, referred to the events as "the military revolution of 1909" in his *Historia tes neoteras Helladas* [*History of Modern Greece*] (Athens, 1958), V, 113.

100. For example: Tasos Vournas, *Goudhi: To kinema tou 1909 Goudhi:* [*The Uprising of 1909*] (Athens, 1957); Victor Dousmanis, pro-Constantine and pro-Theotokis, referred to the events as a pronunciamento in his *Apomnemonevmata* [*Memoirs*] (Athens, 1946), pp. 32-33.

101. For details on the early supporters of a republic, see George Aspreas, "Hoi protoi demokratai eis ten neoteran Hellada" ["The First Republicans in Modern Greece"], *Neos Kosmos,* 25, 26 and 27 March 1934.

102. "FO Annual Report, 1909," p. 9.

103. The most convenient listings of the many laws are to be found in "FO Annual Report, 1909," pp. 16-17; "FO Annual Report, 1910," pp. 19-20.

104. "FO Annual Report, 1909," pp. 9-11; "FO Annual Report, 1910," pp. 10-13. For more details on the military and naval legislation passed during this period, see Zorbas [*Memoirs*], pp. 96-106.

Chapter V

1. Nicholas Zorbas, *Apomnemonevmata* [*Memoirs*] (Athens, 1925), p. 85; Theodore Pangalos, *Ta apomnemonevmata mou* [*My Memoirs*] (Athens, 1950), p. 122.

2. Elliot to Grey, Athens, 18 May 1910, FO 371/911, No. 80; Elliot to Grey, Athens, 2 July 1910, FO 371/909, No. 103.

3. Elliot to Grey, Athens, 8 February 1911, FO 371/1130, No. 20, "Annual Report, 1910," p. 13 (hereafter referred to as "FO Annual Report, 1910").

4. "FO Annual Report, 1910," pp. 2-3.

5. Moses to Knox, Athens, 18 July 1910, NA 868.00/1950/40, No. 160. Regarding the lists of new candidates, Moses wrote: ". . . Greece at last has a political party formed for some other purpose than to gain the offices, and is of much promise for the future of political life here, regardless of the outcome of the National Assembly."

6. Young to Grey, Athens, 7 August 1910, FO 371/912, No. 120. Young commented on the controversy surrounding Venizelos's citizenship: "He appears to have more birthplaces than Homer."

7. For statistics on this election, see Gregory Daphnis, *Ta Hellenika politika kommata, 1821-1961* [*Greek Political Parties, 1821-1961*] (Athens, 1961), pp. 104-09.

8. Constantine arrived in Athens three weeks earlier for the first time in eleven months.

9. As referred to in Elliot to Grey, Athens, 4 November 1910, FO 371/913, No. 169.

10. *Chronos*, 28 November 1910; Elliot to Grey, Athens, 29 November 1910, FO 371/913, No. 186.

11. Daphnis [*Greek Political Parties*], pp. 121-26.

12. Elliot to Grey, Athens, 12 February 1912, FO 371/1380, No. 15, "Annual Report, 1911," pp. 15-16 (hereafter referred to as "FO Annual Report, 1911"); E. G. Kyriakopoulos, *Ta syntagmata tes Hellados* [*The Constitutions of Greece*] (Athens, 1960), pp. 202-19.

13. "FO Annual Report, 1911," pp. 16-19.

14. "FO Annual Report, 1911," pp. 13-14; Elliot to Grey, Athens, 3 April 1912, FO 371/1380, No. 44.

15. "FO Annual Report, 1911," pp. 10-12.

16. "FO Annual Report, 1911," pp. 12-13; Elliot to Grey, Athens, 25 March 1912, FO 371/1380, No. 37.

17. Elliot to Grey, Athens, 29 June 1911, FO 371/1131, No. 86.

18. For relevant statistics, see Daphnis [*Greek Political Parties*], p. 124.

19. Figures for emigration rates are available in E. Repoulis, *Melete meta schediou nomou peri metanastefseos* [*Study with Legislative Plans for Emigration*] (Athens, 1912), p. 10. A valuable study of agrarian problems and politics is to be found in Nicos Mouzelis, "Greek and Bulgarian Peasants: Aspects of Their Sociopolitical Situation during the Interwar Period," *Comparative Studies in Society and History*, 18, No. 1 (January 1976), pp. 85-105.

20. The most thorough treatment of patronage-clientage relationships in twentieth-century Greece is found in Keith R. Legg, *Politics in Modern Greece* (Stanford, 1969).

21. Wangenheim to Schoen, Athens, 6 May 1910, AA 41/20, unnumbered. This dispatch included the copy of a letter to Wangenheim by Crown Princess Sophie from Frankfurt (dated 29 April 1910) which thanked the German minister for his many detailed letters on conditions in Greece. Wangenheim to Bethmann-Hollweg, Athens, 25 April 1910, AA 41/20, No. 41; Wangenheim to Bethmann-Hollweg, Athens, 31 October 1910, AA 50/16, No. 98 (Very

223

Confidential); "FO Annual Report, 1910," p. 9. Elliot remarked on Wangenheim's activities: "The Baron, I fear, confirms Her Royal Highness the Crown Princess in her irreconcilable attitude towards the party of reform, whom she identifies with the leaders of the military movement of 1909, which she cannot forgive. Neither she nor apparently her Imperial Brother [Kaiser Wilhelm], realize the necessity for the reigning dynasty here of passing the sponge over the distasteful events of that year."

22. Zorbas [*Memoirs*], p. 113; "FO Annual Report, 1910," p. 9; "FO Annual Report, 1910," p. 10; Wangenheim to Bethmann-Hollweg, 25 April 1910, AA 47/16, No. 42; C. Christedes, ed., *I. Metaxas: To prosopiko tou hemerologhio* [*Metaxas: His Personal Diary*] (Athens, 1952), II, 41 (hereafter referred to as [*Metaxas Diary*]).

23. Wangenheim to Bethmann-Hollweg, Athens, 11 December 1909, AA 47/15, No. 130; Braun to Aehrenthal, Athens, 30 April 1910, HHS XVI/61, No. 22D; "FO Annual Report, 1910," p. 9.

24. Braun to Aehrenthal, Athens, 30 April 1910, HHS XVI/61, No. 22D; Braun to Aehrenthal, Athens, 6 May 1910, HHS XVI/61, Tel. No. 68; Wangenheim to Bethmann-Hollweg, Athens, 7 June 1910, AA 47/16, No. 66.

25. [*Metaxas Diary*], pp. 39-40; Wangenheim to Bethmann-Hollweg, Athens, 18 November 1910, AA 47/16, No. 104; Wangenheim to Bethmann-Hollweg, Athens, 19 November 1910, AA 47/16, No. 105 (Very Confidential); Wangenheim to Bethmann-Hollweg, Athens, 24 November 1910, AA 47/16, No. 107.

26. Zorbas [*Memoirs*], pp. 113-14.

27. Wangenheim to Bethmann-Hollweg, Athens, 19 November 1910, AA 47/16, No. 105 (Very Confidential); Wangenheim to Bethmann-Hollweg, Athens, 18 January 1911, AA 47/16, No. 6; [*Metaxas Diary*], pp. 32, 29, 49; Young to Grey, Athens, 29 July 1910, FO 371/910, Tel. No. 80. The British representative on the IFC provided the following information on the loan: "As a condition of underwriting the quotation of the loan the French government has an understanding with the Greek government that the latter should not modify unfavorably at the approaching revision of tariffs, taxes on French produce and that when Government orders are given French industry should be favorably considered."

28. Braun to Aehrenthal, Athens, 2 April 1910, HHS XVI/61, Tel. No. 62; Wangenheim to Bethmann-Hollweg, Athens, 18 November 1910, AA 47/16, No. 104; [*Metaxas Diary*], p. 40.

29. Wangenheim to Bethmann-Hollweg, Athens, 19 November 1910, AA 47/16, No. 105 (Very Confidential); Wangenheim to Bethmann-Hollweg, Athens, 29 December 1910, AA 50/16, No. 120 (Secret); [*Metaxas Diary*], pp. 49-50.

30. Riepenhausen to Bethmann-Hollweg, Athens, 29 July 1909, AA 47/14, unnumbered.

31. Elliot to Grey, Athens, 2 August 1911, FO 371/1131, No. 102; Elliot to Grey, Athens, 6 December 1911, FO 371/1131, No. 142. Elliot to Grey, Athens, 20 July 1912, FO 371/1181, No. 102; Elliot to Grey, Athens, 11 August 1913, FO 371/1656, No. 188; Elliot to Grey, Athens, 20 May 1914, FO 371/1999, No. 128, "Annual Report, 1913," p. 9.

Epilogue

A major part of this Epilogue appears as "The Military in Greek Politics: A Historical Survey" in *Greece in Transition: Essays in the History of Modern Greece, 1821-1974,* ed. John T. A. Koumilides (London: Zeno Booksellers and Publishers, 1977), pp. 173-89.

1. This opinion on the political breakdown of the officer corps is expressed by the following authors, whose political leanings range from right to left: G. Th. Phessopoulos, *Ai dichonoiai ton axiomatikon mas kai he dialysis tou stratou mas en M. Asia* [*The Dissension of Our Officers and the Dissolution of Our Army in Asia Minor*] (Athens, 1934), pp. 118-19; A. Mazarakis-Ainian, *Apomnemoneumata* [*Memoirs*] (Athens, 1949), p. 227; S. Saraphis, *Historikes Anamneseis* [*Historical Recollections*] (Athens, 1952), p. 148.

2. The clearest account of the October 1923 events and Metaxas's involvement appears in Gregory Daphnis, *He Hellas metaxy duo polemon, 1923-1940* [*Greece between Two Wars, 1923-1940*] (Athens, 1955), I, 110-60.

3. No attempt will be made to recount the minor military revolts of the 1924-35 period.

4. Reacting to political pressures and seeking to eliminate their praetorian potential, Kondylis ordered the Athenian garrisons to crush the Republican Guard units on 9 September 1926 in a bloody confrontation on the streets of the capital.

225

Selected Bibliography

I. Unpublished Sources

Greece

The investigation of archival material and personal papers in Greece provided limited results. The files of the Ministry of Foreign Affairs are, in general, incomplete and offered no substantive information for the subject under study. Efforts to peruse the Ministry of War archives also proved futile since all relevant holdings for the period prior to 1940 were destroyed in the 1950s under government orders. In 1972 Philippos Dragoumis, son of Prime Minister Stephen Dragoumis, graciously granted permission for me to examine some of his father's papers which are stored in the Gennadius Library (Athens). Mr. Dragoumis, however, has established a policy whereby the family's personal papers will not be completely opened to scholars until 2000. In 1968 Theseus Pangalos, son of the Military League's secretary, gave me access to his late father's limited collection of the League's meeting minutes. Subsequently, in 1972 Mr. Pangalos published these and other relevant documents. The Eleftherios Venizelos Papers in the Benaki Museum (Athens) furnished no significant insights for the years 1909-11—apparently many of Venizelos's papers were destroyed or lost in the political turmoil which began in 1916.

Austria-Hungary

The diplomatic dispatches of the Austro-Hungarian Legation in Athens are available on microfilm. The material on 1908 was investigated at the Academy of Athens; the dispatches for 1909-10 were ordered from Vienna.

227

Haus-, Hof- und Staatsarchiv, Vienna
1908—Griechenland, Politisches Archiv, XVI/59
1909—Griechenland, Politisches Archiv, XVI/60
1910—Griechenland, Politisches Archiv, XVI/61

Germany

The German diplomatic correspondence is of particular importance for detailing the sentiments of Crown Prince Constantine and his Prussian wife, Sophie. The dispatches of Baron Hans von Wangenheim were highly opinionated and rarely articulated detached sentiments for the sequence of events in Greece. The victorious Allies after World War II undertook an extensive microfilming of German archival holdings and the documents from the *Auswärtiges Amt* on Greece were read at the London School of Economics.

Auswärtiges Amt
1909-12— Griechenland, Allgemeine Angelegenheiten
41/17-21 (LSE 29/271-683)
1909-12—Griechenland, Militär- und Marine-
Angelegenheiten, 47/14-17 (LSE 35/446-636)
1909-12—Griechenland, Die Königlich Griechische
Familie, 50/14-16 (LSE 36/338-525)

Great Britain

The resources of the Foreign Office, housed in the Public Record Office, London, supplied the best single source of information for this period. British diplomats regularly compiled detailed dispatches on political events which frequently recorded the confidential attitudes of King George. The coverage of Greece's economic problems was also very thorough and in many respects more reliable than the data of Greek governments. This attention to Greek matters reflected London's decades-old concern for British influence in this country specifically and in the Mediterranean generally. Since certain dispatches, including military attaché reports, were either lost or transferred to other departments, the drafts of these documents, stored in the Embassy and Consular Archives, were also consulted to fill in certain gaps in information for the 1909-1910 period.

Public Record Office, London
Greece, Foreign Office, Political Correspondence

1898—32/702-703	1907—371/264
1899—32/712	1908—371/464-465
1900—32/719-724	1909—371/677-679
1901—32/728-729	1910—371/908-913
1902—32/736-737	1911—371/1130-1131
1903—32/744-745	1912—371/1380-1381
1904—32/751	1913—371/1654-1656
1905—32/754	1914—371/1994-1999
1906—371/81	

Greece, Embassy and Consular Archives
1909—286/521-524, 527
1910—286/531-534, 537-538

United States

American interest in Greek affairs was peripheral for these pre-World War I years. George Moses, nevertheless, composed insightful communications which accurately assessed Greek politics and took into consideration the rivalries of the European powers. Department of State documents for 1909 are under the Numerical File in the National Archives, Washington, D.C. The dispatches for 1910-12, classified under the Decimal File, are available on microfilm: Department of State, Internal Affairs of Greece, 1910-12, 868.00/—182 (Political Affairs), Roll 4.

II. Published Documents and Official Publications

France, Ministère des affaires étrangères. *Documents diplomatiques français (1871-1914)* 2e série (1901-1914). Vols. 10-12. Paris, 1947, 1950, 1954.

Great Britain, Naval Intelligence Division. *Greece.* 3 vols. London, 1944.

Great Britain, Historical Section of the Foreign Office. *Greece.* London, 1920.

Greece, General Staff to the Army, Historical Division. *Historia tes organoseos tou Hellenikou stratou: 1821-1954* [His-

tory of the Organization of the Greek Army: 1821-1954]. Athens, 1957.

Greece, Military School for Noncommissioned Officers. *Historia Stratiotikes Scholes Ypaxiomatikon [History of the Military School for Noncommissioned Officers].* Athens, 1930.

Pangalos, Theseus, ed. *Epanastasis 1909: To archeion tou Stratiotikou Syndesmou [1909 Revolution: The Archives of the Military League].* Athens, 1974.

III. Newspapers

A. In Greek

Akropolis. Athens. 1908-10.
Athenai. Athens. 1909-10.
Chronos. Athens. 1909-10.
Eleftheron Vema. Athens. 1928.
Esperini. Athens. 1909-10.
Keryx. Chanea. 1909-10.
Nea Hemera. Trieste. 1908-10.
Neon Asty. Athens. 1909-10.
Neos Kosmos. Athens. 1933-34
Rizospastis. Athens. 1908-10.

B. In other languages

Le Messager d'Athènes. Athens. 1908-10.
Le Monde Hellénique. Athens. 1909-10.
The Times. London. 1843, 1862, 1909-10.

IV. Memoirs, Diaries, Published Letters

A. In Greek

Alexandris, Apostolos. *Politikai anamneseis [Political Recollections].* Patras, 1947.

Argyropoulos, P. A. *Apomnemonevmata [Memoirs].* 2 vols. Athens, 1970

Christedes, C., ed. *I. Metaxas: To prosopiko tou hemerologhio [I. Metaxas: His Personal Diary].* Vol. 2. Athens, 1952.

Dousmanis, Victor. *Apomnemonevmata [Memoirs].* Athens, 1946.

Gonatas, Stylianos. *Apomnemonevmata: 1897-1957* [*Memoirs: 1897-1957*]. Athens, 1958.

Hairopoulos, Kostes. "Trianta Chronia demosiographikes zoës, 1895-1925" ["Thirty Years of a Journalistic Career, 1895-1925"]. *Proïa,* 14 February to 18 March 1926.

Kostis, C. N. *Anamneseis ek tes avles Georgiou tou A'* [*Recollections from the Court of George I*]. Athens, 1949.

Lefkoparidis, X., ed. *Stratigou P. Dangli: Anamneseis—Engrapha—Allelographia* [*General P. Danglis: Recollections—Papers—Correspondence*]. 2 Vols. Athens, 1965.

———, ed. *Alexandrou Papanastasiou: Meletes, Logoi, Arthra* [*Alexander Papanastasiou: Studies, Speeches, Articles*]. Athens, 1957.

Maria, Princess of Greece. *Anamneseis tes Vasilopaidos Marias* [*Recollections of Princess Maria*]. Athens, 1951.

Mazarakis-Ainian, Alexander. *Apomnemonevmata* [*Memoirs*]. Athens, 1949.

Pangalos, Theodore. *Ta apomnemonevmata mou* [*My Memoirs*]. Athens, 1950.

Paraskevopoulos, Leonidas I. *Anamneseis: 1896-1920* [*Recollections: 1896-1920*]. Athens, 1930.

Philaretos, George N. *Semeioseis apo tou 75os ypsomatos* [*Notes from the 75th Level*]. Vol. 3, Athens, 1928.

Romanos, A., ed. *Epistolai tes A. M. tou Vasileos Georgiou tou A', 1903-1913* [*Letters of H. M. King George I, 1908-1913*]. Athens, 1935.

Saraphis, Stephen. *Historikes anamneseis* [*Historical Recollections*]. Athens, 1952.

Spais, L. *Penenta chronia stratiotes* [*Fifty Years as a Soldier*]. Athens, 1970.

Zavitzianos, Constantine. *Ai anamneseis tou* [*His Recollections*]. 2 vols. Athens, 1946.

Zorbas, Nicholas. *Apomnemonevmata* [*Memoirs*]. Athens, 1925.

B. In other languages

Christopher, Prince of Greece. *Memoirs of H.R.H. Prince Christopher of Greece.* London, 1938.

Nicholas, Prince of Greece. *My Fifty Years.* London, 1926.

V. Biographies

A. In Greek

Daphnis, Gregory, *Sophokles Venizelos* [*Sophocles Venizelos*]. Athens, 1970.

Gatopoulos, D. *Georgios A': Ho demokrates Vasileos (1863-1913)* [*George I: The Democratic King (1863-1913)*]. Athens, 1950.

Gyparis, P. *Eleftherios Venizelos: O megas demiourgos* [*Eleftherios Venizelos: The Great Creator*]. Athens, 1955.

Mallosis, I. *He politike historia tou Demetriou P. Gounari: 1902-1920* [*The Political History of Demetrios P. Gounaris: 1902-1920*]. Athens, 1926.

Merkouris, S. *Georgios Kondylis: 1879-1936* [*George Kondylis: 1879-1936*]. Athens, 1954.

Papantonakis, G. E. *He politike stadiodromia tou Eleftheriou Venizelou* [*The Political Career of Eleftherios Venizelos*]. Vol. I. Athens, 1928.

Peponis, I. A. *Nikolaos Plastiras* [*Nicholas Plastiras*]. Athens, 1947.

Pipinelis, P. *Georgios B'* [*George II*]. Athens, 1951.

Plastiras, I. A. *Nikolaos Plastiras sta gegonota 1909-1945* [*Nicholas Plastiras in the Events of 1909-1945*]. Athens, 1947.

Pournaras, Demetrios. *Eleftherios Venizelos: He zoë kai to ergon tou* [*Eleftherios Venizelos: His Life and Work*]. Vol. I. Athens, 1959.

Skandamis, Andreas. *Pringips Georgios* [*Prince George*]. Athens, 1955.

_____. *He Vasilissa Sophia* [*Queen Sophie*]. Athens, 1947.

Synadinos, Th., ed. *Vlases Gavrielides* [*Vlases Gavrielides*]. Athens, 1929.

Vaïdis, T. A. *Eleftherios Venizelos* [*Eleftherios Venizelos*]. Athens, 1934.

Vakas, D. *Eleftherios Venizelos* [*Eleftherios Venizelos*]. Athens, 1949.

B. In other languages

Alastos, Doros. *Venizelos*. London, 1942.

Chester, S. B. *Life of Venizelos*. London, 1921.

Christmas, Walter. *King George of Greece*. New York, 1914.

Gibbons, Herbert Adams, *Venizelos*. London, 1921.

Kerofilas, C. *Eleftherios Venizelos: His Life and Work*. London, 1915.

VI. Monographs, Dissertations, General Studies

A. *In Greek*

Anastasopoulos, George, *Historia tes Hellenikes viomehaneas: 1840-1940* [*A History of Greek Industry: 1840-1940*]. 3 vols. Athens, 1947.

Andreadis, Andreas. *Erga* [*Collected Works*]. 3 vols. Athens, 1938-40.

Aspreas, George. *Politike historia tes neoteras Hellados* [*History of Modern Greece*]. 2 vols. Athens, 1963.

Boulalas, K. *He Hellas kai hoi synchronoi polemoi* [*Greece and the Recent Wars*]. Athens, 1965.

Danielides, Demosthenes. *He neohellenike koinonia kai oikonomia* [*Modern Greek Society and Economy*]. Athens, 1934.

Daphnis, Gregory. *He Hellas metaxy duo polemon, 1923-1940* [*Greece between Two Wars, 1923-1940*]. 2 vols. Athens, 1955.

_____. *Ta Hellenika politika kommata, 1821-1961* [*Greek Political Parties, 1821-1961*]. Athens, 1961.

Daskalakis, George D. *Hellenike syntagmatike historia: 1821-1935* [*Greek Constitutional History: 1821-1935*]. Athens, 1952.

_____. *Politika kommata kai demokratia* [*Political Parties and Democracy*]. Athens, 1958.

Dousmanis, Victor. *He stratiotike katastasis kai he politike tou G. N. Theotoki* [*The Military Situation and the Politics of G. N. Theotokis*]. Athens, 1911.

Enepekides, P. *He doxa kai dichasmos: Apo ta mystika archeia tes Viennes, 1908-1916* [*Glory and Division: From the Secret Archives of Vienna, 1908-1916*]. Athens, 1962.

Evelpides, C. *He georgia tes Hellados* [*The Agriculture of Greece*]. Athens, 1944.

_____. *Oikonomike kai koinonike historia tes Hellados* [*Economic and Social History of Greece*]. Athens, 1950.

Georgiades, G. A. *He pali ton taxeon en Helladi* [*The Class Struggle in Greece*]. Athens, 1921.

Gounaris, Tasos. *He Naupliake epanastasis* [*The Nauplion Revolution*]. Athens, 1963.

Gyalistras, Sergios. *Ethnikoi agones: 1909-1959* [*National Struggles: 1909-1959*]. Athens, 1963.

Haritakis, G. *He Hellenike viomehania* [*Greek Industry*]. Athens, 1927.

Harkner, Eric, and Demetrios Kalitsounakis. *To ergatikon zetema* [*The Labor Problem*]. 2 vols. Athens, 1919-1920.

Karolides, Paul. *Historia tou Hellenikou ethnous* [*History of the Greek Nation*]. Athens, 1932.

Kontogiannes, P. *Ho stratos mas kai hoi teleftaioi polemoi* [*Our Army and the Recent Wars*]. Athens, 1924.

Kordatos, John. *Hoi epemvaseis ton Anglon sten Hellada* [*The Intervention of the English in Greece*]. Athens, 1946.

————. *Historia tou agrotikou kinematos sten Hellada* [*History of the Agrarian Movement in Greece*]. 2nd ed. Athens, 1973.

————. *Historia tou Hellenikou ergatikou kinematos* [*History of the Greek Labor Movement*]. Athens, 1956.

————. *Historia tes neoteras Helladas* [*History of Modern Greece*]. Vol. 5. Athens, 1958.

Koronis, Sp. B. *He ergatike politike ton eton 1909-1918* [*Labor Politics for the Years 1909-1918*]. Athens, 1944.

Ktenaveas, S. *Ai Hellenikai kyverneseis—Ai ethnikai synelevseis kai ta demopsifismata apo to 1821 mechri semeron* [*Greek Governments—National Assemblies and Plebiscites from 1821 to the Present*]. Athens, 1947.

Kyriakopoulos, E. *Ta syntagmata tes Hellados* [*The Constitutions of Greece*]. Athens, 1960.

Kyriakopoulos, K. A. *Selides apo ten neoteran Helleniken historian* [*Pages from Modern Greek History*]. Athens, 1965.

Kyriakos, A. N. *He nea Hellas* [*The New Greece*]. Athens, 1910.

Lamprinou, G. *He monarchia sten Hellada* [*The Monarchy in Greece*]. Athens, 1945.

Laskaris, S. Th. *Diplomatike historia tes Hellados: 1821-1914* [*A Diplomatic History of Greece: 1821-1914*]. Athens, 1947.

Logothetis, Th. *He epanastasi tou 1909 kai hoi k. k. S. Melas, St. Stephanou, kai D. Pournaras* [*The Revolution of 1909 and Messrs. S. Melas, St. Stephanou, and D. Pournaras*]. Athens, 1960.

Malainos, E. I. *Historia ton xenikon epemvaseon* [*History of Foreign Intervention*]. Vol. 2. Athens, 1957.

Malainos, M. I. *He epanastasis tou 1909* [*The Revolution of 1909*]. Athens, 1965.

————. *Selides Hellenikes historias* [*Pages from Greek History*]. Athens, 1964.

234

Manesis, A., and E. Kyriakopoulos. *Ekatontaeteris tou syntagmatos: 1864-1964* [*One Hundred Years of the Constitution: 1864-1964*]. Thessaloniki, 1966.

Markezinis, Sp. B. *Politike Historia tes neoteras Hellados: 1828-1964* [*A Political History of Modern Greece: 1828-1964*]. 4 vols. Athens, 1966-68.

Mayer, Kosta. *Historia tou Hellenikou typou* [*History of the Greek Press*]. 3 vols. Athens, 1957-60.

Melas, Spyros. *He epanastasis tou 1909* [*The Revolution of 1909*]. Athens, 1959.

Michalakeas, Tasos, ed. *Vivlos Eleftheriou Venizelou* [*The Bible of Eleftherios Venizelos*]. Vol. I. Athens, 1964.

Moskof, Kostes. *He ethnike kai koinonike syneidese sten Hellada, 1820-1909* [*National and Social Conscience in Greece, 1830-1909*]. Thessaloniki, 1972.

Mylonas, A. *Eklogika systemata* [*Electoral Systems*]. Athens, 1946.

Mytalis, I., and K. Mayer. *Hellenike demosiographia* [*Greek Journalism*]. Athens, 1939.

Papandreou, George. *Politika themata* [*Political Topics*]. Vol. I. Athens, 1941.

Petrakakos, Demetrios. *Koinovouleftike historia tes Hellados* [*Parliamentary History of Greece*]. Vol. 7. Athens, 1944.

Phessopoulos, G. Th. *Ai dichonoiai ton axiomatikon mas kai he dialysis tou stratou mas en M. Asia* [*The Dissension of Our Officers and the Dissolution of Our Army in Asia Minor*]. Athens, 1934.

Pournaras, Demetrios. *Historia tou agrotikou kinematos en Helladi* [*History of the Agrarian Movement in Greece*]. Athens, 1931.

_____. *Sosialismos, Kommounismos, kai Agrotismos: To koinonikon zetema eis ten Hellada* [*Socialism, Communism, and Agrarianism: The Social Question in Greece*]. Athens, 1937.

Repoulis, Emmanuel. *Melete meta schediou nomou peri metanastefseos* [*Study with Legislative Plans for Emigration*]. Athens, 1912.

Sgouritsas, C. *Epanastasis, politeia, kai dikaion* [*Revolution, State and Law*]. Athens, 1925.

Sideris, A. D. *He georgike politike tes Hellados kata ten lexasan ekatontaetias: 1833-1933* [*The Agrarian Politics of Greece during the Past Century: 1833-1933*]. Athens, 1934.

Skleros, George. *To koinoniko mas zetema* [*Our Social Question*]. Athens, 1922.

———. *To synchrona provlemata tou Hellenismou* [*The Contemporary Problems of Hellenism*]. Alexandria, 1919.

Stasinopoulos, E. K. *He historia tes Scholes ton Evelpidon: 1828-1953* [*History of the School of Evelpidon: 1828-1953*]. Athens, 1954.

———. *Ho stratos tes protes ekatontaetias* [*The First Hundred Years of the Army*]. Athens, 1935.

Svolopoulos, Constantine. *Ho Eleftherios Venizelos kai he politike krises eis ten autonomon Kreten, 1901-1906* [*Eleftherios Venizelos and the Political Crisis on Autonomous Crete, 1901-1906*]. Athens, 1974.

Tasolampros, L. *Politika saranta chronon: 1909-1949* [*The Politics of Forty Years: 1909-1949*]. Athens, 1949.

Theodorides, A. *He epanastasis kai to ergon aftes* [*The Revolution and Its Accomplishments*]. Athens, 1914.

Theophanides, I. *Historia tou Hellenikou naftikou: 1909-1913* [*History of the Greek Navy: 1909-1913*]. Athens, 1923.

Tsakonas, Demetrios. *Dokimia epanastaseos: Ap' to Goudhi sto paron* [*Essays on Revolution: From Goudhi to the Present*]. Athens, 1962.

Tsitsilias, P. K. *He epanastasis tou 1909 kai he Panepistemiake Enosis* [*The Revolution of 1909 and the University Union*]. Athens, 1964.

Venteres, George. *He Hellas tou 1910-1920* [*Greece: 1910-1920*]. Vol. I. Athens, 1931.

Vlachos, Nicholas. *Historia ton kraton tes Chersonisou tou Aimou: 1908-1914* [*History of the States of the Balkan Peninsula: 1908-1914*]. Athens, 1954.

Vournas, Tasos. *Goudhi: To kinema tou 1909* [*Goudhi: The Uprising of 1909*]. Athens, 1957.

Vratsanos, D. *He historia ton en Helladi epanastaseon: 1824-1935* [*The History of Revolutions in Greece: 1824-1935*]. Athens, 1936.

Zakythinos, D. A. *He politike historia tes neoteras Hellados* [*A Political History of Modern Greece*]. Athens, 1965.

Zevgos, John. *Syntome melete tes neohellenikes historias* [*A Short Study of Modern Greek History*]. 2 vols. Athens, 1945.

Zolotas, X. E. *Agrotike politike* [*Agrarian Politics*]. Athens, 1934.

_____. *He Hellas eis to stadion tes ekviomehanias* [*Greece on Its Path to Industrialization*]. Athens, 1964.

B. *In other languages*

Abbott, G. F., ed. *Greece in Evolution*. London, 1909.

_____. *Turkey in Transition*. London, 1909.

Ahmad, Feroz. *The Young Turks*. Oxford, 1969.

Anderson, M. S. *The Eastern Question*. New York, 1966.

Bacopoulos, George T. *Outline of the Greek Constitution: Political Systems since the Greek Revolution of 1821*. Athens, 1950.

Bickford-Smith, R. A. H. *Greece under King George*. London, 1893.

Black, C. E. *The Dynamics of Modernization: A Study in Comparative History*. New York, 1966.

Campbell, John, and Philip Sherrard. *Modern Greece*. London, 1968.

Cole, G. D. H. *A History of Socialist Thought,* Part II, Vols. III, IV. London, 1956.

Couclelis, Alexander P. *Les Régimes gouvernementaux de la Grèce de 1821 à nos jours*. Paris, 1921.

Couloumbis, T. A., J. A. Petropulos, and H. J. Psomiades. *Foreign Interference in Greek Politics: An Historical Perspective*. New York, 1976.

Dakin, Douglas. *The Greek Struggle in Macedonia: 1899-1913*. Thessaloniki, 1966.

_____. *The Unification of Greece, 1770-1923*. London, 1972.

Daskalakis, Ap. B. *La Presse néo-hellénique: La Journalisme et la Renaissance Hellénique Journaux et Journalistes*. Paris, 1930.

Djiras, A. C. *L'organization politique de la Grèce*. Paris, 1927.

Dontas, Donna. *Greece and the Great Powers: 1863-1875*. Thessaloniki, 1966.

Driault, Édouard. *La Grande Idée: La Renaissance de l'Hellénisme*. Paris, 1920.

_____. *La Grèce d'aujourd'hui et la Grèce èternelle*. Paris, 1934.

_____. *Histoire diplomatique de la Grèce de 1821 à nos jours,* Vol. 5. Paris, 1926.

Dutkowski, Jean-Stanislaw. *L'Occupation de la Crète (1897-1909): Une expérience d'administration internationale d'un territoire.* Paris, 1952.

Feis, Herbert. *Europe, the World's Banker, 1870-1914.* New Haven, 1930.

Ferriman, Z. Duckett. *Home Life in Hellas: Greece and the Greeks.* London, 1910.

Finer, S. E. *The Man on Horseback: The Role of the Military in Politics.* London, 1962.

Finlay, George. *A History of Greece.* Rev. and ed. H. F. Tozer. Vol. VII. Oxford, 1877.

Forbes, Nevill, and Arnold J. Toynbee, D. Mitrany, D. G. Hogarth. *The Balkans.* Oxford, 1915.

Garnett, Lucy M. J. *Greece of the Hellenes.* London, 1914.

Gershenkron, Alexander. *Economic Backwardness in Historical Perspective: A Book of Essays.* Cambridge, Mass., 1962.

Gewehr, Wesley M. *The Rise of Nationalism in the Balkans, 1800-1930.* New York, 1931.

Goodspeed, D. J. *The Conspirators: A Study of the Coup d'État.* New York, 1961.

Hallman, Hans. *Neugriechenlands Geschichte, 1820-1948.* Bonn, 1949.

Halpern, Paul G. *The Mediterranean Naval Situation, 1908-1914.* Cambridge, Mass., 1971.

Huntington, Samuel P., ed. *Changing Patterns of Military Politics.* New York, 1962.

———. *Political Order in Changing Societies.* New Haven, 1968.

———. *The Soldier and the State: The Theory and Politics of Civil-Military Relations.* New York, 1957.

Jecchinis, Chris. *Trade Unionism in Greece: A Study in Political Paternalism.* Chicago, 1967.

Jelavich, Barbara. *Russia and the Greek Revolution of 1843.* Munich, 1966.

Johnson, John J., ed. *The Role of the Military in Underdeveloped Countries.* Princeton, 1962.

Kalopothakes, D. *A Short History of the Greek Press.* Athens, 1928.

Kaltchas, Nicholas. *Introduction to the Constitutional History of Modern Greece.* New York, 1940.

Keltie, J. Scott, ed. *The Statesman's Year-Book: 1908.* London, 1908.

Korisis, Hariton. *Die politischen Parteien Griechenlands: Ein neuer Staat auf dem Weg zur Demokratie: 1821- 1910.* Hersbruck/Nürnberg, 1966.

Lee, Arthur S. Gould. *The Royal House of Greece.* London, 1948.

Lefeuvre-Méaulle, H. *La Grèce économique et financière en 1915.* Paris, 1916.

Legg, Keith R. *Politics in Modern Greece.* Stanford, 1969.

Leon, George B. *Greece and the Great Powers, 1914-1917.* Thessaloniki, 1974.

———. *The Greek Socialist Movement and the First World War: The Road to Unity.* Boulder, 1976.

Levandis, John A. *The Greek Foreign Debt and the Great Powers: 1821-1898.* New York, 1944.

Lewis, Bernard. *The Emergence of Modern Turkey.* Oxford, 1968.

Lhéritier, Michael. *La Grèce.* Paris, 1921.

Manousakis, Gregor. *Hellas—Wohin? Das Verhältnis von Militär und Politik in Griechenland seit 1900.* Godesberg, 1967.

Markesinis, B. S. *The Theory and Practice of Dissolution of Parliament.* Cambridge, 1972.

Martin, Percy F. *Greece of the Twentieth Century.* London, 1913.

Mathiopoulos, Basil P. *Die Geschichte der Sozialen Frage und des Sozialismus in Griechenland: 1821-1961.* Hannover, 1961.

Mavrogordato, John. *Modern Greece: A Chronicle and a Survey: 1800-1931.* London, 1931.

Mavromichalis, Kyriakoulis. *Affairs d'Orient.* Paris, 1911.

Meynaud, Jean. *Les forces politiques en Grèce.* Paris, 1965.

Miller, William. *Greece.* London, 1928.

———. *Greek Life in Town and Country.* London, 1905.

———. *The Ottoman Empire and Its Successors: 1801-1927.* Cambridge, 1936.

———. *Travels and Politics in the Near East.* London, 1898.

Pallis, A. A. *Greece's Anatolian Venture—and After.* London, 1937.

Passades, Augustin. *La Question d'Orient et la Grèce.* Paris, 1929.

Peristiany, J. G., ed. *Contributions to Mediterranean Sociology.* Paris, 1968.

Petropulos, John. *Politics and Statecraft in the Kingdom of Greece: 1833-1843.* Princeton, 1968.

Polyzos, N. J. *Essai sur l'émigration grecque.* Paris, 1947.

Prevelakis, Eleftherios. *British Policy towards the Change of Dynasty in Greece, 1862-1863.* Athens, 1953.

Ramsaur, Ernest E. *The Young Turks: Prelude to the Revolution of 1908.* Princeton, 1957.

Saloutos, Theodore. *The Greeks in the United States.* Cambridge, Mass., 1964.

Saripolos, N. N. *Das Staatsrecht des Königreichs Griechenland.* Tübingen, 1909.

Sentupery, Leon. *L'Europe Politique: La Grèce—L'Italie.* Paris, 1895.

Sergeant, Lewis. *Greece in the Nineteenth Century.* London, 1897.

Seton-Watson, R. W. *The Rise of Nationality in Balkans.* New York, 1918.

Smith, Michael L. *Ionian Vision: Greece in Asia Minor, 1919-1922.* London, 1973.

Stavrianos, L. S. *Balkan Federation: A History of the Movement toward Balkan Unity in Modern Times.* Northampton, Mass., 1944; rpt. Hamden, Conn., 1964.

———. *The Balkans since 1453.* New York, 1958.

Steiner, Zara S. *The Foreign Office and Foreign Policy, 1898-1914.* Cambridge, 1969.

Struck, Adolf. *Zur Landeskunde von Griechenland: Kulturgeschichtliches und Wirtschaftliches.* Frankfurt a. M., 1912.

Strupp, Karl. *Die Beziehungen zwischen Griechenland und der Turkei von 1820-1930.* Breslau, 1932.

Svoronos, Nicolas. *Histoire de la Grèce moderne.* Paris, 1953.

Theodoulou, Christos. *Greece and the Entente* (August 1, 1914-September 25, 1916). Thessaloniki, 1971.

Thery, Edmund. *La Grèce actuelle, au point de vue économique et financier.* Paris, 1905.

Thompson, W. R. "Explanations of the Military Coup." Ph.D. dissertation, University of Washington, 1972.

Toynbee, Arnold J., and Kenneth P. Kirkwood, *Turkey.* London, 1926.

Tsakonas, D. *Geist und Gesellschaft in Griechenland.* Bonn, 1965.

Tsoucalas, Constantine. *The Greek Tragedy.* Baltimore, 1964.

Tsouderos, E.-J. *Le Relevement economique de la Grèce.* Paris, 1920.

Vettes, William G. "The Balkan Socialist Movement from Its Beginnings to 1917." Ph.D. dissertation, Northwestern University, 1958.

Wogasli, D. D. K. *La solution de la question agraire en Grèce*. Athens, 1919.

Woodhouse, C. M. *A Short History of Modern Greece*. New York, 1968.

Young, Kenneth. *The Greek Passion*. London, 1969.

Zakynthinos, D. A. *La Grèce et les Balkans*. Athens, 1947.

VII. Articles

A. *In Greek*

Angelopoulos, A. C. "Ai vaseis tou phorologhikou systematos tes Hellados" ["The Bases of the Taxation System in Greece"]. *Epitheoresis Koinonikes kai Demosias Oikonomias* [*Review of Social and Political Economy*], January-April 1932, pp. 45-109.

Aspreas, George. "He stratiotike epanastasis tou etous 1909 kai he metaklesis tou Eleft. Venizelou" ["The Military Revolt of 1909 and the Summoning of Eleftherios Venizelos"]. *Hestia*, 22-30, December 1927.

Kalitsounakis, D. "He koinonike politike kai nomothesia tes Hellados" ["The Social Politics and Legislation of Greece"]. *Hellas Jahrbuch*, 1929, pp. 30-38.

Laïou, George. "Erevna en tois Archeiois tes Viennes pros mikrophotographesin e graphon aphoronton eis neoteran Helleniken historian" ["Research into the Archives of Vienna for the Microfilming of Documents Relating to Greek History"]. *Praktika tes Akademias Athenon* [*Proceedings of the Academy of Athens*], XL (1965), 660-69.

Maccas, Leon. "Na panegyristhe he 50eteris tes epanastaseos tou 1909" ["In Celebration of the 50th Anniversary of the Revolution of 1909"]. *He koine gnome* [*Social Thought*], 15 April 1959, pp. 8-9.

Melas, Spyros. "He nykta tes 14es Aughoustou" ["The Night of August 14th"]. *Hestoria kai Zoë* [*History and Life*], III, 15 August 1957, 182-87.

Papanastasiou, Alexander. "He Tourkike epanastasis" ["The Turkish Revolution"]. *Epitheoresis Koinonikon kai Nomik-*

on *Epistemon* [*Review of Social and Legal Sciences*]. I (1908), 232-43.

Poulemenos, A. "He Hellas kai ho koinonismos" ["Greece and Socialism"]. *Ho Noumas,* 28 September 1908, pp. 5-7.

B. *In other languages*

Adossides, A. "Une ère nouvelle en Grèce." *Revue des Français,* January 25, 1911, pp. 47-57.

Britsch, A. "Une démocratie en orient—La nation grecque." *Le Correspondent,* 25 April 1909, pp. 330-47.

Bushkoff, Leonard, "Marxism, Communism and the Revolutionary Tradition in the Balkans, 1878-1924: An Analysis and an Interpretation." *East European Quarterly,* I, No. 4 (Jan. 1968), pp. 371-400.

Campbell, Spencer. "Greece—Renaissance or Revolution?" *The Fortnightly Review,* February 1910, pp. 274-85.

Dakin, Douglas. "The Greek Proposals for the Alliance with France and Great Britain: June-July 1907." *Balkan Studies,* III, No. 1(1962), 43-60.

Dertilis, P. B. "L'Endettement de la Grèce." *Les Balkans,* VI (Oct.-Nov. 1934), pp. 563-98.

Dillon, E. J. "Constitutional Crises in Europe." *The Contemporary Review,* November 1909, pp. 618-40.

_____. "The Cretan Danger." *The Contemporary Review,* February 1910, pp. 245-52.

_____. "Parliamentary Islam and Revolutionary Greece." *The Contemporary Review,* January 1910, pp. 110-28.

Drakoulis, P. E. "Le Socialisme en Grèce." *Le mouvement socialist,* No. 233 (July-August 1911), pp. 101-04.

Evelpidis, C. "L'Agriculture en Grèce." *Les Balkans,* V (January-February 1934), 28-71.

Garvin, J. "The Pronunciamento at Athens." *The Fortnightly Review.* October 1909, pp. 569-76.

Grimanelli, P. "Le Hellénisme et la Jeune-Turquie." *L'Hellénisme,* January 1909, pp. 3-17.

Jelavich, Barbara. "Russia, Bavaria, and the Greek Revolution of 1862/63." *Balkan Studies,* II (1961), pp. 125-50.

Leune, Jean. "L'Effort militaire de la Grèce." *De la Nouvelle Revue,* 15 April 1912, pp. 5-29.

Luckham, A. R. "A Comparative Typology of Civil-Military Relations." *Government and Opposition,* Vol. 6, No. 1(Winter 1971), pp. 5-35.

Markesinis, B. S. "The Greek Crown and Its Ministers." *Parliamentary Affairs,* XXVI, No. 1(Winter 1972/73), 56-68.

Martel, Charles. "The Greek Army." *The Army and Navy Magazine,* 82 (August 1887), pp. 331-43.

Mathiopoulos, Basil P. "Die politischen Parteien Griechenlands." *Internationales Jahrbuch der Politik,* October 1955, pp. 308-14.

Mouzelis, Nicos. "Greek and Bulgarian Peasants: Aspects of Their Sociopolitical Situation during the Interwar Period." *Comparative Studies in Society and History,* Vol. 18, No. 1 (January 1976), 85-105.

Pantel, Hans-Henning. "Die Geschichte der griechischen Presse von Ihren Anfängen bis 1940." *Leipziger Vierteljahrschrift für Südosteuropa,* VII (1943), 1-22.

Papanastasiou, E. "The Greek Labor Movement." *Near and Far East,* February 1923, Part I, pp. 59-65; March 1923, Part II, pp. 57-62.

Pepelasis, A. A. "The Legal System and Economic Development of Greece." *The Journal of Economic History,* XIX, No. 2 (June 1959), pp. 173-98.

Psomiades, Harry J. "The Economic and Social Transformation of Modern Greece." *Journal of International Affairs,* XIX, No. 1 (1965), 194-205.

Rudolph, Felix. "Socialism in Greece." *The Socialist Review,* February 1911, pp. 463-68.

Swenson, Victor R. "The Military Rising in Istanbul, 1909." *The Journal of Contemporary History,* Vol. 5, No. 4 (1970), 171-84.

Veremis, T. "The Officer Corps in Greece, 1912-1936." *Byzantine and Modern Greek Studies,* II (1976), 113-33.

Woods, H. C. "The Military Upheaval in Greece." *National Defense,* IV (February 1910), 37-52.

VIII. Periodicals and Newspapers Consulted

Bulletin d'Orient. Athens. 1904-08.
Dynamis. Athens. 1909-10.
The Hellenic Herald. London. 1904-10.
Hellenike Epitheoresis. Athens. 1909-10.
Hellenismos. Athens. 1904-10.

INDEX

ment as leader of Military League, 53; and Typaldos mutiny, 91-95; and expression of support from officers, 100; meeting with King George, 107; and promotion contro-

versy, 109; on National Assembly question, 122; appointment as minister of war, 176

Zymbrakakis, Epaminondas, 50, 51, 53, 92